COMMERCIAL BANK BEHAVIOR AND ECONOMIC ACTIVITY

CONTRIBUTIONS TO ECONOMIC ANALYSIS

43

Edited by

J. JOHNSTON

J. SANDEE

R. H. STROTZ

J. TINBERGEN

P. J. VERDOORN

1966

NORTH-HOLLAND PUBLISHING COMPANY

AMSTERDAM

COMMERCIAL BANK BEHAVIOR AND ECONOMIC ACTIVITY

A STRUCTURAL STUDY OF MONETARY POLICY IN THE POSTWAR UNITED STATES

by

STEPHEN M. GOLDFELD

Assistant Professor, Department of Economics, Princeton University

1966

NORTH-HOLLAND PUBLISHING COMPANY

AMSTERDAM

INTRODUCTION TO THE SERIES

This series consists of a number of hitherto unpublished studies, which are introduced by the editors in the belief that they represent fresh contributions to economic science.

The term *economic analysis* as used in the title of the series has been adopted because it covers both the activities of the theoretical economist and the research worker.

Although the analytical methods used by the various contributors are not the same, they are nevertheless conditioned by the common origin of their studies, namely theoretical problems encountered in practical research. Since for this reason, business cycle research and national accounting, research work on behalf of economic policy, and problems of planning are the main sources of the subjects dealt with, they necessarily determine the manner of approach adopted by the authors. Their methods tend to be "practical" in the sense of not being too far remote from application to actual economic conditions. In addition they are quantitative rather than qualitative.

It is the hope of the editors that the publication of these studies will help to stimulate the exchange of scientific information and to reinforce international cooperation in the field of economics.

THE EDITORS

To K, L and M

PREFACE

The research underlying this study began as a doctoral dissertation at the Massachusetts Institute of Technology. I am especially indebted to Albert Ando who served as chairman of my dissertation committee and who, beginning with that phase and extending to the present, proffered valuable assistance and encouragement. I am similarly indebted to the other members of my dissertation committee, Edwin Kuh and Franco Modigliani, and to the Ford Foundation for a grant supporting the writing of the dissertation.

The research was completed at Princeton University and its final form owes much to the counsel and support of my colleagues in the Department of Economics. In particular, Edward Kane read the entire manuscript and significantly improved the presentation, Richard Quandt helped clarify several basic issues, and Oskar Morgenstern, Director of the Econometric Research Program, provided constant encouragement and generous financial support. I am also grateful to Procter and Gamble for a Faculty Fellowship and to the National Science Foundation for their support of the Princeton computer facilities.

I also wish to thank Frank de Leeuw for some extremely helpful comments and James Tobin for permission to use material from an unpublished manuscript. Two drafts of this book were cheerfully and efficiently typed by Mrs. Helen Peek.

My greatest debt of gratitude is to my wife, Laura, who contributed patience, good humor and a sympathetic ear throughout the vigil.

February, 1966

STEPHEN M. GOLDFELD

CONTENTS

CHAPTER 1

INTRODUCTORY REMARKS

1.1. Introduction

This study presents an aggregate quarterly model of the postwar United States economy. The primary aims in constructing the model are (1) to examine commercial bank portfolio behavior, (2) to relate investment and consumption expenditures directly to financial variables, and (3) to investigate the impact of monetary policy on both financial and non-financial variables.

Extended effort is devoted to the commercial-banking sector for several reasons. For one, we wish to increase current empirical knowledge of bank behavior. While much has been written about bank portfolio management, little of this has been quantitative in nature. This study, by disaggregating bank assets and by further disaggregating data by bank classes, seeks to shed light on many of the quantitative issues surrounding the management of bank funds.

Second, variations in the size and composition of bank assets play a large part in transmitting the influence of monetary policy to the economy. For example, the market for bank loans to commercial and industrial customers has long been deemed a key element in the process of income determination. As for the money supply itself, banks' ability to vary the level of excess and borrowed reserves they wish to hold provides an important reason for treating the supply of money as an endogenous variable. The interest responsiveness (revealed below) of excess and borrowed reserves implies a money-supply function which is similarly responsive. To allow for this dependence, Teigen [110], has estimated a relationship in which the money supply is made a function of certain Federal Reserve parameters and of interest rates. While ours is a slightly higher-order approach in that we derive the money supply from bank behavior, a function of the Teigen-type is implicit in our model.[1] By removing the assumption of money-supply exogeneity, we discard the standard reserve-multiplier approach with its fixed expansion multipliers and currency-drain ratios.

Third, the estimation of detailed bank equations provides a way in which to assess the impact of monetary policy on the composition of bank portfolios. Even if two different policies produce the same short-run effect on income, interest rates, or the money stock, they may have different impacts on bank portfolios. While we shall not pursue this, such equations might provide a basis for choosing between two otherwise equivalent policies. For example, such policies might have different implications for bank profits. In the longer-run planning of the monetary authorities, bank profits must receive careful consideration.

To implement the second aim of the study, both the theoretical and empirical aspects of the effect of financial variables on investment and consumption expenditures are considered. By including financial variables in equations for fixed investment, inventory investment, and durable consumption, we open broad avenues for the operation of monetary policy. Specifying the demand side of financial-asset markets closes the model and permits us to carry out our third aim. Only in the context of this kind of model, can we realistically evaluate the effects of such instruments as open-market operations and reserve-requirement changes.

1.2. Organization of the Study

The study is divided into four main chapters. The first of these presents a detailed analysis of bank portfolio decisions. For each bank class, we investigate portfolio decisions with respect to excess and borrowed reserves, short- and long-term securities, and municipal securities. In this chapter, we also examine the supply of commercial loans. However, data considerations make it necessary to do so at an aggregate level. In chapter 3

---

[1] It is easy to see, in a somewhat formal way, that the supply of money (or at least the demand-deposit component) is a function of bank decisions with respect to excess and borrowed reserves. Imagine a stylized banking system with no time deposits and a uniform reserve requirement k on demand deposits. Denoting total, required, unborrowed, free, excess, and borrowed reserves by R^T, R^R, R^u, R^F, E and B respectively we can write: $R^T - B = R^u$; $E - B = R^F$; $R^T - R^R = E$; $R^R = kD$. These can be manipulated to yield $D = (R^u - R^F)/k$. Hence, demand deposits supplied depend on the bank portfolio variable, free reserves. A more general version of this equation which allows for both currency and time deposits is developed in section 5.4.2.

we proceed to the demand side of such financial assets as currency, demand deposits, time deposits, and commercial loans. In addition, that chapter provides the beginnings of an endogenous explanation of the term-structure of interest rates. Following this, chapter 4 treats investment and consumption decisions. In each of these three chapters, preliminary specifications of behavioral relationships are made and estimations performed by ordinary least-squares.

In chapter 5, we pull these various elements together in the specification of what turns out to be a thirty-two-equation model. Because of its many simultaneous relationships, the model is estimated by structural methods. In the choice of the final form of the model, considerable attention is paid to alternative specifications of the individual relationships.

Following this, the predictive performance of the model is examined. In addition, some evidence on the importance of structural estimation is gleaned from a comparison of our two-stage and ordinary least-squares estimates. Finally, in the context of the parameters of the reduced form, we assess the quantitative impact of various monetary- and fiscal-policy instruments. The study itself concludes with a summary of our findings and some indications of directions for further research.

CHAPTER 2

BANK PORTFOLIO BEHAVIOR
THE BASIS FOR A MONEY SUPPLY FORMULATION

2.1. Introduction

In the previous chapter we suggested that the supply of money can in part
be regarded as a product of certain bank liquidity decisions. This chapter
examines the nature of these decisions in some detail, leaving to a later
chapter the task of integrating these results into a complete determination
of the money supply. We argue that a successful explanation of bank
liquidity decisions can best be achieved by examining the entire spectrum
of bank portfolio behavior. Only in this expanded context is it possible to
understand the many interactions which account for bank holdings of
various assets.

Aside from serving as a basis for a formulation of money-supply
theory, a study of bank portfolio behavior is interesting in its own right.
As an example of financial behavior under uncertainty, such a study
should offer further evidence on the suitability of explaining this behavior
by relatively modest models.

Furthermore, a detailed analysis of commercial bank behavior will
aid immensely in translating hypothetical actions of the monetary
authorities into their effects on the non-monetary sectors. The bank
commercial loan market, for example, is one of the major linkages
between the monetary and real sectors. Traditionally, central bankers
have held that it is through this market that the effects of monetary policy
are transmitted to the expenditure stream. By manipulating aggregate
reserves, discount rates, or reserve requirements, the Fed can affect the
supply of credit in this and (via spillover effects) other markets, and
consequently its price and volume. If one is interested in policy questions
it is clearly relevant to examine bank behavior since the strength of

monetary policy is mediated, in part, by the investment decisions of the commercial banks.

The chapter begins with a discussion of the various sources of uncertainty facing a bank and examines how these sources create a need for a bank to have sources of liquid assets. We then turn briefly to an examination of one conventional measure of bank liquidity: the level of free reserves. Following this, we present a rather general analysis of portfolio considerations, concentrating on behavioral assumptions necessary for the specification of the model. Prior to the actual specification we advocate disaggregation of portfolio data in the following three respects: (1) separation of the bank data into homogeneous bank class categories; (2) disaggregation of bank holdings of U.S. Government securities into a short-term and a long-term category; and (3) decomposition of free reserves into its proximate components, i.e., excess reserves and borrowed reserves. The chapter culminates in the specification and estimation of equations explaining bank holdings of excess reserves, borrowed reserves, short-term government, long-term government and municipal securities, and the supply of commercial loans.

2.2. Uncertainty and Bank Liquidity

2.2.1. *Sources of Uncertainty*

A commercial bank faces many sources of uncertainty. The complicated nature of this phenomenon is suggested by a how-to-measure-liquidity-needs section of a recent study of the commercial banking system [4, pp. 275–277]. In particular, the headings of this section indicate the various aspects of the general problem: what is the share of time deposits? how many deposit accounts does the bank have? who are the large depositors? how stable are their accounts? what other unstable accounts does the bank have? and is the bank retaining its proportionate share of the business in its trade area?

Broadly speaking, we can distinguish three types of uncertainty. First, there is uncertainty with respect to the future level of deposit liabilities. Second, there is a set of problems concerned with the proper evaluation of the loan component of the bank's portfolio. Third, there is uncertainty with respect to the direction and magnitude of shifts in the current interest rate structure and hence with regard to the market value of the non-matured securities in the bank's portfolio.

There are several different types of deposit variability, and they may have different consequences for the bank. The first is variation in the aggregate level of deposits, maintaining the same relative distribution of deposits between banks. This, for example, might be caused by a cyclical decline in the aggregate demand for bank loans. The second is a systematic redistribution of demand deposits among banks with the total level of deposits remaining the same. This, for example, could reflect competitive pressures within a region or perhaps inter-regional shifts occasioned by firm relocation. Thirdly, there are random influences of a purely temporary nature. In practice, of course, banks experience two or more of these sources of variation at one time and may not be able to separate out the transitory and permanent variability. For example, it is often argued that if a bank is "in step" with general expansion it can expect its share of deposit growth, but if it overexpands loans relative to the banking system, it can expect greater deposit variation [100]. The difficulty, of course, in applying this rule is to determine the quantitative meaning of "in step".

In any event, an unfavorable change in a member bank's deposit liabilities can, in the absence of prior excess reserves, create a shortage of reserves, and in these circumstances it will have need of assets convertible into reserves at its Federal Reserve Bank.

Let us now briefly examine the nature of the uncertainties associated with the loan component of a bank's portfolio. In this regard perhaps the major source of uncertainty is connected with the future level of new loan demand. As we shall see later, since there are strong reasons for granting customer loan requests, loan demand uncertainties mean that a bank must be prepared to provide large amounts of funds on relatively short notice. In addition to uncertainty with respect to new demand, there are other types of uncertainties associated with the loan portfolio.

Survey studies at various times have established that business firms who borrow from commercial banks are often of less than average profitability and also tend to be repeat customers [100, p. 96]. In addition, these firms are often in the initial phase of establishment. These characteristics point up two sources of uncertainty with respect to the loan portfolio, namely, the proportion of borrowers who will default and, as Porter has phrased it, the extent of "frozenness" of the loan portfolio [97]. The latter refers to the percentage of renewal requests which may precede a loan's maturation. They are an indication of the fact that the nominal maturity distribution of a loan portfolio may have very little to do with the actual maturity of the portfolio. For the same reasons that a bank will cater to its customer loan demand at the initiation of a loan, it will presumably be motivated to renew the loan. However, in the case of renewals, something in addition to customer goodwill may be at stake. That is, the borrower may be unable to repay the loan and the bank is consequently faced with the alternatives of renewal or default. Thus, the degree of frozenness depends both on the willingness and the ability of the customers to accept the refusal of loan renewals.

A final uncertainty associated with the loan portfolio concerns the interrelationship between the volume of loans and deposit variability. As the Appendix to this chapter shows, increasing loans serves to increase deposit variability and heightens the chance of failing to meet the reserve test.

The remaining source of uncertainty, i.e., the nature of future shifts in the interest rate structure, has important consequences for bank portfolio behavior but we shall reserve discussion of this until a later point.

2.2.2. *Consequences of Uncertainty: Bank Liquidity*

This discussion has indicated some of the sources of uncertainty which face a bank. These uncertainties mean that a bank must be prepared to convert rapidly a part of its assets either to deposits at its Federal Reserve Bank so as to meet the reserve test or into funds available for making loans to customers. With respect to the latter, one author has stated ". . . the greatest source of liquidity to meet new credit requests should, of course, come from the loan portfolio itself, through the turnover of loans." [78, p. 16]. However, this author goes on to admit that, in the face of pronounced seasonal variation for loans, this maxim may not prove very helpful. In addition, he recognizes the need for additional liquidity if a bank's loans are growing steadily. Thus, this "principle" may offer little solace to a bank concerned with providing for growing or variable customer loan demands. Such a bank will presumably be forced to forecast its loan demand and in general to provide funds beyond those obtainable from maturing loans.

In view of these established bank needs for funds on short notice, it seems reasonable to inquire about how, in practice, banks provide for these contingencies. A bank in need of funds has a variety of alternatives open to it including: (1) drawing down excess reserves, (2) calling outstanding loans, (3) borrowing from the Federal Reserve Bank or in the Federal Funds market, or (4) selling some securities. Loosely speaking, these alternatives involve either:

(a) the transformation of one asset (e.g. a security) into a reserve-eligible asset (e.g. Federal Reserve deposits) or

(b) the simultaneous creation of an asset (e.g. reserves) and a liability (e.g. borrowings at the Fed).

When, as is the case with borrowing from the Fed, the liability created is of a short-run nature, then the bank may simply have postponed its funds problem. It is, of course, possible that the need for funds is only short-run as well (such as might be the case with random deposit flows). In such circumstances a short-run solution is all that is needed. This principle of matching short-run needs and solutions appears to be at the heart of the New York Federal Reserve Bank's description of borrowing from the Fed:

> "The source of funds to which a member bank turns when it finds itself in need of reserves will depend on the expected duration of the need for reserves, the availability of liquid short-term investment assets in portfolio, and the money management practices of the bank. Reserve shortages that are expected to be of some duration may be covered by liquidating Treasury bills or other secondary reserve assets, if they are available in sufficient amount in the bank's portfolio . . . When the reserve need is expected to be of only a few days or, at most a very few weeks duration, a member bank may properly borrow from its Federal Reserve Bank." [39, p. 138].

We shall have occasion to examine bank-borrowing decisions in greater detail later, but for the time being we shall restrict our attention to alternative (a) above. Even within this alternative, a bank must choose which of its assets to convert into the funds needed.

Of all available assets, excess reserves, cash, and deposits at other banks are most easily transferable into needed funds. Since each of these assets provides no income, banks may not hold sufficiently large quantities of these in their portfolios to supply the needed funds. While theoretically possible, the calling of loans is, in general, not considered sound banking practice. As we have already remarked, there is a high priority associated with the making of customer loans. No bank is likely to do anything which will damage the potentialities of a commercial account. On the other hand, there are certain classes of loans which are exempt from this consideration. By common consent, loans to security brokers and dealers may be called by a bank.

The final asset shift available to a bank in need of funds is the sale of open-market securities. The major source of differentiation among securities is their maturity. While it is generally true that a longer-term security, if held to maturity, will yield more than a shorter one, it is also generally true that there is a greater degree of uncertainty associated with the price of a longer-term security if sold before it matures.[1] These offsetting factors suggest that there is in some sense an optimum between the two extremes of holding zero-yield, perfectly liquid cash, and relatively high-yielding long-term securities. As a result of this economic tradeoff, which we examine in greater detail later, commercial banks have tended to rely on short-term U.S. securities (bills, certificates, notes and bonds nearing maturity) as the major source of assets to convert into needed funds. In conjunction with the cash assets mentioned earlier, it is the stock of these assets which comprise a bank's liquid portfolio. Briefly and somewhat loosely speaking, the liquidity of a credit instrument refers to the property of being easily transferable between creditors. Among the numerous aspects inherent in the liquidity concept are negotiability, reversibility, and marketability. Negotiability is a self-explanatory legal concept. Reversibility refers to the ability of the asset (representing future sums) to be converted into present sums in a short period of time and without appreciable money loss. Marketability refers to the existence of a regular transactions market for a particular type of credit instrument and clearly influences the immediate cash value of an asset.[2]

Short-term governments provide a natural choice for secondary reserves or for bank liquidity. They are assets of highly-predictable money value, constituting a large homogeneous stock traded in a broad market. In addition, they are free from the risk of default and can be used at par to secure advances from the Federal Reserve Banks. There is no definite maturity separating short- from long-term, and bankers vary in their opinions on the matter. However, one year appears to be a widely-accepted rule of thumb. In fact, the Federal Reserve in its monthly statistics on bank liquidity appearing in the Federal Reserve Bulletin, employs the sum of free reserves and U.S. Government securities within one year as its measure of liquidity.

---

[1] It should be noted that transactions costs and dealer spreads decline with maturity. These considerations further complicate the comparison between short- and long-term securities.

[2] One might define portfolio liquidity in terms of a probability distribution of cash recoverable from the sale of assets of a portfolio on short-term notice and hence one can give formal meaning to the cash equivalent of an asset. For a discussion of this point and a related liquidity discussion see [71, pp. 16–17].

It should be mentioned that, to the extent banks choose alternative (b) above, i.e., simultaneously create an asset and a liability to obtain reserves (say), they are tapping a source of what we might term *latent* liquidity. In other words, the existence of a stock of liquid assets is not strictly necessary in order for a bank to be able to provide against unforeseen contingencies. In recent years, the emergence of the certificate-of-deposit, whereby a bank can in effect actively seek out time deposits, has been associated with (at least for large city banks) a decline in bank holdings of government securities. In view of the fact that we will be largely concerned with the period prior to 1962 during which such instruments were relatively unimportant, this will not prove to be a terribly important consideration.

To conclude this section, let us summarize where we stand. Banks face many sources of uncertainty and are often called upon suddenly to raise cash assets within brief intervals of time. In view of this banks have chosen to hold a buffer stock of liquid assets to allow for these contingencies. This buffer stock has consisted primarily of short-term securities and of excess reserves net of borrowings (i.e. free reserves). In what follows, our interest will be to build up an explanation of bank decisions with respect to these liquid assets. As will become clear, a satisfactory explanation of these decisions requires an examination of the entire complex of bank portfolio decisions. In the first instance, however, we shall proceed slowly and discuss briefly two partial-equilibrium solutions which have been offered to explain the components of bank liquidity.[3]

2.3. Bank Liquidity and Free Reserves: A First Approximation

Traditional analysis of the relationship between central-bank action and commercial-bank response ties fluctuations in bank demand deposits to prior changes in the available supply of reserves. The standard reserve-multiplier approach, even in its most sophisticated variants (e.g., which

---

[3] It should be noted that the liquidity position of a bank is in many ways analogous to the transactions balances of an individual. It is well established that the inventory theoretic approach yields fruitful results in the latter instance (e.g., see the demand-for-money discussion appearing below). Hence, it is not surprising to find various writers discussing bank liquidity in terminology appropriate to an inventory framework. For example, PORTER [97], has observed, "Cash and other assets readily convertible into cash represent 'inventories', the carrying cost of these 'inventories' is the surrender of earning power and various penalties are incurred for insufficient 'inventories'." A similar observation has been applied, in a limited context, by ORR and MELLON [92].

allow for various types of reserve drains) has at least two glaring deficiencies. First, it ignores the behavior (and *a fortiori*, the logic behind such behavior) of commercial bankers. Second, since it uses a constant reserve-multiplier, it implicitly assumes that bank demand for free reserves is constant over time. This constancy assumption has come under increasing attack in recent years and various writers have argued for the use of a more realistic theory which recognized that the demand for free reserves results from economic calculations by the banks. For example, Tobin has argued:

> "There is more to the determination of the volume of bank deposits than the arithmetic of reserve supplies and reserve ratios . . . The thirties exemplify in extreme form a phenomenon which is always in some degree present: the use to which commercial banks put the reserves made available to the system is an economic variable depending on lending opportunities and interest rates."[4]

The remainder of this section will be devoted to presenting a summary of two ways in which the constancy of free reserves may be relaxed. The first is due to Tobin [114] and the second to Meigs [83].

According to Tobin

> "If the Federal Reserve maintains the discount rate unchanged, there is a tendency for net free reserves to rise by some fraction of a dollar whenever the Federal Reserve augments the supply of primary reserves by one dollar." [114, chapter 9, pp. 18ab].

The mechanism by which this occurs can be described as follows. If we start from an equilibrium level of free reserves (R^F), then Federal Reserve open-market purchases (conducted in bills, say) will raise R^F above its former equilibrium level. These open-market operations lower the bill rate and decrease the incentive of the banks to economize cash and to borrow from the Fed and consequently raise the equilibrium level of free reserves. It should be noted that in attempting to reduce their free reserve position, the banks by purchasing short-term securities will further depress the bill rate.

Under the hypothesis which keeps R^F constant, a dollar change in the supply of reserves is necessary and sufficient to cause an equal change in the volume of required reserves. The Tobin approach, however, loosens the causal link between the volume of bank assets (and deposits) and the reserve base. Thus, banks may change their equilibrium level of R^F even if

---

[4] TOBIN [112]. Also MEIGS [83, chapter 2] has a historical discussion of this point.

the supply of primary reserves remains constant. This can result from one or more of the following consequences: (1) the discount rate may change; (2) the banks' cash preferences and expectations of future economic magnitudes may change; and (3) the various money-market rates may change as a result of the asset choices of the non-bank public.

As an examination of U.S. banking data will reveal, the variability of the banking system's holdings of free reserves is more than a theoretical possibility. For example, R^F varied from -5% to 5% of required reserves during 1951–1959. A more explicit determination of the demand for free reserves can be given as follows. Let us, following Tobin, define the defensive position P' of a bank or a set of banks as the sum of its (their) free and secondary reserves.[5] Tobin's solution, in terms of this construct, is a sequential one in which he considers two questions: (1) what determines P'? (2) given P', what determines its division into its two components? The magnitude of P' or perhaps the ratio of P' to total assets is simply taken to depend on the differential between the loan rate and the Treasury bill rate, $r_e - r_s$. This differential is the opportunity cost of maintaining the defensive position since a bank could earn r_e by investing a dollar of P' in loans but would sacrifice r_s dollars in doing so. With regard to the determination of R^F/P' Tobin has noted that

> "Other things equal, banks will wish to hold a larger share in secondary reserves the higher the rate of return they can earn on these assets, i.e., the higher the Treasury bill rate, and the lower the rate on net free reserves, represented by the Federal Reserve discount rate." [114, chapter 9, p. 22].

With a fixed discount rate (r_d) $0D$, figure 2.1 represents the variation of the average cash-reserve position as a function of the bill rate. When r_s is high relative to r_d a bank short of reserves will be motivated to borrow rather than sell bills and to buy bills rather than repay indebtedness if it has a temporary clearings surplus. There is, of course, an essential difference between $R^F < 0$ and $R^F > 0$. A bank earns nothing on excess reserves but can earn r_d on temporary surplus funds by repaying debt. Thus, for r_s in the neighborhood of r_d a bank might reduce debt rather

---

[5] With respect to the use of aggregate measures it should be noted that the Fed has stated, "Appraisal of bank liquidity must take into account not only aggregate measures but also shifts in the composition of bank liabilities and assets." For example, the recent greater importance of time deposits of "business and large individual investors in the growth of total time and savings deposits increases the potential volatility of such deposits." [41, July 1962, p. 795].

than purchase bills, but would buy bills rather than increase idle excess reserves. The lower r_s is relative to r_d the less frequent will be the use of the discount window, although even with $r_s < r_d$ banks may prefer on occasion to borrow rather than sell bills to meet a reserve shortage (e.g., based on considerations of transaction costs). However, if r_d is well above zero and

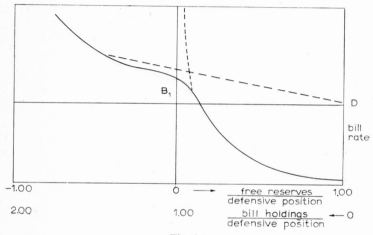

Fig. 2.1

r_s sufficiently below r_d to discourage borrowing, r_s can still be high enough to encourage cash economy. Thus, a high bill rate would yield an incentive to let fluctuations in deposits and loans be reflected in a varying free reserve position. On balance, as figure 2.1 demonstrates, a bank's cash demand is composed of two components. When there is no incentive to borrow, cash demand depends simply on r_s, but when the borrowing incentive is present, it depends on r_s relative to r_d.[6]

---

[6] It should be noted that the borrowing behavior implied by the above is quite consistent with Federal Reserve discount-window policy. For a discussion of this point see below. Tobin also performs a similar analysis after explicitly recognizing the existence of the Federal Funds market. The conclusions, however, remain unchanged. The only effect of that market is to shift the bank's aggregate cash preference curve to the left. This, of course, has operational significance for monetary policy, but if a new preference curve can be determined, will not necessarily reduce the effectiveness of monetary policy. See [114, chapter 9, pp. 30–41].

We thus see that Tobin's free-reserve formulation makes explicit the nature of some of the economic calculations made by a bank in determining the composition of its portfolio. In terms of actual empirical results on this point, the most extensive study of free reserves to date is that of A. J. Meigs. Meigs posits that each bank attempts to maintain a desired free-reserve position which is a function of total deposits, market interest rates, and the discount rate. Actual free reserves are determined by desired free reserves via a partial-stock-adjustment mechanism and by the rate at which Federal Reserve authorities inject or withdraw reserves. Some of the equations we present below are similar in spirit to those presented by Meigs. We shall note some of these similarities at that time. For the present it suffices to note that the extensive empirical evidence offered by Meigs tends overwhelmingly to support the Tobin analysis. Whereas Meigs concerns himself only with free reserves, Tobin's and our own formulations try to explain both the composition and the size of the defensive position.

It will be recalled that the size of the banks' defensive position depended in part on the bank loan rate. It is precisely because of this interdependence that one cannot satisfactorily examine bank liquidity holdings in a partial-equilibrium setting. Even in Tobin's stylized framework, the natural question then becomes: what determines the bank loan rate? It seems reasonable at first glance to suppose that the rate is set via some sort of supply-demand mechanism in which the banks play an integral role. Once we recognize the endogenous nature of the loan market, it becomes important, in order to understand bank loan decisions, to examine how the banks allocate their funds into assets which compete with loans. Unfortunately, as is probably clear by now, carrying this interaction to its logical conclusion requires tremendous resources. Because of this, partial-equilibrium analysis clearly has its place. The problem is essentially one of where to draw the line. The next section examines some general considerations of bank portfolio behavior and indicates exactly where we draw our lines in the work that follows.

2.4. General Portfolio Considerations

2.4.1. *Introduction*

As conservative profit-maximizing entities, banks are faced habitually with the need to reconcile considerations of risk and yield. The nature of the demand-deposit mechanism peculiar to banks means that uncertainty is of paramount importance. This heavy element of uncertainty has, partly for legal reasons and partly via experience, resulted in bank portfolios which include built-in safeguards. In fact, a standard bank-management textbook establishes the following priorities for a bank portfolio: (1) primary reserves (2) secondary reserves (3) customer credit demands (4) open-market investments for income [100, chapter 1]. This section will examine how a bank allocates its funds among these various categories.

We first consider the loan component and customer credit demands. In this regard a not uncommon view is:

"Although there is no legal responsibility to make loans, any bank which wants to enjoy good profits, to perform its expected function in the community, and to attract customers must be prepared to meet all legitimate loan demands." [100, p. 2].

The American Bankers Association in a strongly chauvinistic passage offers some non-profit motive reasons for the same type of behavior. In particular, they state:

"Banks, of course, have a clear obligation to their customers, and to their communities to make, within the limits of their lending ability, such sound loans as are needed to finance the growth and development of their trade areas. This loan demand cannot be turned away arbitrarily when the bank finds itself in a tight position. Legitimate customer demand for credit must be met if the community is to maintain its position in the economy and if the bank is to fulfil its proper function." [4, p. 277].

Since loans provide a high rate of return to a bank, these pronouncements could easily be justified on other grounds. Furthermore, these loans are an integral element of what has now come to be known as the "customer relationship". More particularly, the making of business loans is quite essential to the attracting and maintaining of commercial accounts and, in particular, the availability of bank loans in times of credit stringency is an important banking service necessary to insure retention of these profitable customers. The long-run profits of a bank probably depend to a greater extent on the bank's ability to retain customers who use the essential banking services (e.g., safekeeping and transfer of funds, accurate financial recording, trusteeships, registrarships and loans) than upon skillful short-run choices by the portfolio managers among alternative types of earning assets.[7] Thus, in view of the fact that prospective borrowers tend to be among the best long-term customers of commercial banks, it has been observed: "The primary tenet of commercial bank asset strategy is to reserve sufficient lending capacity to meet anticipated loan requests of larger and more durable deposit customers." [20, p. 2].[8]

None of this, of course, is to say that loans do not also have some distinctive, and undesirable properties. Among all assets from which a bank may choose, loans are the least liquid and possess the greatest default risk. Their lack of liquidity results mainly from the fact that, once acquired, there exists no organized market for the sale of loans. The importance of this particular feature will be elaborated shortly. Both considerations suggest that loans vary considerably in attractiveness over the business cycle.[9] It is to an examination of this point that we now turn.

2.4.2. *Bank Loans: Cyclical Behavior*

At any point of time, banks are presumed to have a desired level of loans which depends on the current and expected yields of both loans and competing assets, on total asset size, and on other elements we shall examine later. The price and nonprice aspects of a loan, which have been called a set of loan terms [95], evolve from negotiation between the bank and the borrower and hence within any time period are subject to some amount of bank control. The institutional setting of customer relation-

---

[7] The notion of a "customer relationship" is somewhat akin to the recent medical approach of treating the "whole patient". The notion of a customer can, of course, be specified formally in terms of various depositor characteristics. Kane and Malkiel specify such items as the account's current size, its future growth prospects, its expected pattern of variability, the length of its attachment to the bank, the apparent cohesion of the attachment, the customer's expected mean indebtedness over the cycle and the correlation between his loans outstanding and aggregate excess demand for loans at that bank. They argue that "the regularity with which the customer has been afforded past loan accommodation, especially during periods of credit restraint, would importantly increase the cohesion of deposit relationships." [67, pp. 122–123].

[8] Although we shall think of it mainly in terms of commercial and industrial loans, the "customer" concept mentioned above applies to a wide variety of types of loans. For example, a large volume of automobile and appliance loans is written directly for the banks by dealers. Attempts to reduce dealer commitments may entail the loss of a profitable account and business relationship. Thus, as in the case of commercial loans, one must consider the long-run account potential. Furthermore, for banks in rural regions relationships with the farm sector may also be of considerable importance.

[9] KANE and MALKIEL [67], have emphasized this point.

ships presumably imparts rigidities to some or all elements of the set of loan terms. Consequently in any given period, a bank cannot adjust the price and nonprice mix to assure that desired loans will equal the loans forthcoming at the prevailing set of terms. To see the problem in more detail it is helpful to consider the bank's loan portfolio in a cyclical setting.

In the initial stages of a cyclical upswing when income is rising and bond prices falling (bond yields rising) bank expectations of future earnings from their loan portfolio are high. This follows from the implicit assumption that loan demand increases with income and hence extrapolating the upswing banks expect a future increase in loan demand. However, the absence of an organized loan market means that banks cannot capitalize on this future expected increase. In particular, as the loan rate changes, the banks can only gain on new loans, not on outstanding ones. This, of course, is to be contrasted with a bank's security portfolio which varies in value as bond prices change. As the expansion continues, loans become more attractive and the set of loan terms becomes more favorable to the bank. Assuming insufficient deposit growth, banks finance the increase in loans by selling securities. Assuming they first deplete their short-term securities (an assumption discussed below) banks contemplating further security sales (of longer maturities) will be faced with declining bond prices and the prospect of capital losses. This increase in the cost of obtaining funds may further drive up the loan rate and/or make the other loan terms more favorable to the banks. In the late stages of the boom, bond prices are near their trough and the risk component of the banks' portfolios is high. At this point in the cycle, the presence of strong loan demand offers a natural opportunity to upgrade standards of credit worthiness [56, p. 85]. Furthermore, there may be strong incentive to do so since banks will have considerably depleted their secondary reserves. In addition, at this juncture banks are becoming increasingly reluctant to bear additional risk.[10] They may be also faced with rising administrative costs of lending which further diminish the attractiveness of loans. At the cyclical peak, bank loans become considerably less attractive vis-a-vis government securities than before. For one thing, the banks' liquidity reserves may be run down. In addition, in the face of increased monetary

---

[10] It has been suggested that the bank's willingness to supply loans is a nonlinear function of the set of loan terms. That is, a bank's limited capital account makes it require ever-increasing stringency of loan terms for a constant increment. See PIERCE [95, p. 50].

tightness and depressed security prices, there are high expectations of future capital gains from securities purchased now. These are especially attractive in view of the special treatment to bank capital gains. In order to purchase securities the bank must transfer funds from some other asset category. Since short-term securities may also be depleted, the obvious candidate is loans. However, funds only become available from loans as they are repaid. Hence the bank may not be able to adjust its security holdings as rapidly as it would like.

In view of the bank's desire to shift funds from loans to securities, even though loan demand may be declining, the bank has an incentive not to increase the attractiveness of loans to borrowers. Hence, in the early stages of the decline, loan rates may not fall at all. The intermediate stages may witness a decline in the loan rate but the exact consequences depend on the duration of the decline and the extent of oligopolistic unwillingness to vary rates and other terms. In the trough, banks will most likely face a dearth of good loan demand. That is, the loans forthcoming may be essentially unattractive at any reasonable set of loan terms.

We earlier stated that loans were the most important earning asset of the banks and that the customer relationship was a very significant consideration in the long-run management of the bank. We have now argued that banks' preferences for loans may vary considerably over the cycle. These two points suggest that there is a basic conflict in a bank's objectives. On the one hand, lack of funds and risk considerations may suggest curtailing or limiting certain loan requests. On the other hand, no bank wishes to damage a potentially-profitable account relationship.[11] The problem, then, takes on a vaguely game-theoretic tone: how can the bank make it look like it is giving in without completely doing so. Here, the negotiation of loan terms may take on a new character. Banks may raise their stated loan rate even though they are reluctant to do so for fear of antagonizing customers. More likely, they will make efforts to scale down loan requests or shorten proposed maturities while continuing to meet

---

[11] Kane and Malkiel, argue quite strongly in favor of this view. Reasoning in a utility analysis framework, they suggest a bank may grant a customer loan even though "compared with its prerequest optimum, it entails a definite sacrifice of utility." [67, p. 121]. A bank will do this because to refuse the request will decrease utility even more. In other words the mere receipt of a customer request disturbs a bank's portfolio optimum.

urgent needs for funds.[12] They might also enforce more strictly agreements with respect to compensating balances. In this way banks can diminish the risks associated with their loan portfolios and still maintain the customer relationship.[13]

2.4.3. *Open-Market Securities*

Having discussed the loan component of the banks portfolio we now turn to the security component. Our discussion above has suggested two considerations that will be important in explaining the banks' security holdings. First, we have noted that the funds to satisfy loan demand will typically be made available via sales of securities. Second, we noted that at the top of the boom and in the early part of the downswing, securities, because of expected capital gains, become increasingly attractive relative to loans. This suggests that, if we are going to explain bank security holdings in part by interest rate considerations, we should use a rate variable which captures these expected capital gains. Finally, it should be reiterated that the banks' actual ability to increase their security holdings will necessarily be limited by the rate of loan repayment and the inflow of new funds (perhaps made available from monetary policy operations).

Since we shall be concerned with explaining disaggregated (by maturity) bank holdings of securities, it is of some interest to examine exactly how loan demand interacts with security holdings. Three plausible hypotheses are as follows: (1) cyclical variation in loan demand will primarily affect bank holdings of short-term issues and only when these have been reduced to a minimum will liquidation affect other maturities; (2) banks may liquidate securities so as to maintain a "balanced" maturity distribution; (3) banks may sell intermediate and longer-term securities in the early stages of an expansion to avoid possible capital losses which may follow if security prices are expected to decline.

With respect to this last point Luckett has maintained that banks, when faced with a funds problem, do in fact liquidate longer-term securities even

---

[12] To the extent that "noncustomer" demand is creating credit pressures on a bank's portfolio it will feel less constrained to honor these loan requests. For example, a bank will be less willing to meet the needs of dealers, brokers, or sales finance companies if it is short of funds.

[13] The more banks rely on nonprice means of adjusting their loan portfolios the less reliable is the loan rate as an indicator of the set of loan terms. This suggests there may be some difficulty in working with the loan rate as a supply variable. We return to this in our specification of the supply-of-commercial-loans function below.

in the intermediate stages of the boom when capital losses are sustained [76]. His justification for this runs something as follows. A bank's short-term securities are its most liquid earning asset and its loans are the least liquid. A bank which substitutes loans for short-term securities, therefore, suffers the maximum possible decline in its liquidity position. Although its liquidity will still be diminished, the deterioration of its position would be lessened if the bank were to sell longer-term Governments instead. In fact, even in the face of loan expansion, a bank can maintain its liquidity position simply by selling more longs than the loan demand it wishes to meet, purchasing short-term securities with the additional funds. Offsetting these liquidity considerations is the greater capital loss that banks must sustain if they sell long-terms during a tight money period, but Luckett dismisses this effect as being relatively weak.

This argument seems to overstate bank preoccupation with liquidity and the extent to which they actually sell longer-term securities. Thus, since part of the liquidity portfolio is held precisely for the purpose of meeting loan demand, it certainly seems appropriate to sell securities one had planned on selling when things got tight. To pursue the inventory analogy somewhat further, the above argument is like saying that a firm will try to maintain its inventory position in the face of sales variations. Of course, the problem is more complicated than we have made it out to be. In order for a bank to feel protected with a diminished liquidity position, the bank must feel confident about its ability to predict when the top of the boom will occur.

In view of these various considerations, it is of interest to examine briefly how banks have actually managed their security holdings over two

TABLE 2.1*

Marketable Treasury securities maturing in	Total publically owned			Held by commercial banks		
	Dec. 54	Mar. 56	Jun. 57	Dec. 54	Mar. 56	Jun. 57
less than 1 year	43.3	37.3	49.6	17.8	6.9	14.6
1–5 years	26.4	35.5	37.3	20.6	23.6	26.0
5–10 years	32.2	29.9	13.7	22.7	20.6	9.4
more than 10 years	27.5	28.5	26.7	5.5	4.9	4.4
Totals	129.4	131.3	127.2	66.6	56.0	54.5

* Data are for end of month and are in billions of dollars. The information contained in this table is originally from Treasury and Federal Reserve sources and is reproduced in GRAMLEY [55, p. 72].

of the postwar cycles. As table 2.1 reveals, commercial banks reduced their holdings of marketable Treasury obligations between December 1954 and June 1957 by about $12 billion. This period was one marked by strong loan demand and restrictive monetary policy. In the first part of this period, bank holdings of under-one-year maturities were reduced by about $11 billion, roughly $5 billion more than the reduction in the supply of these securities, and the banks' share of this category of outstanding debt dropped from over 40% to under 20%. Variations in bank ownership of other maturities are difficult to discern from table 2.1 because the passage of time caused securities to change age brackets. Thus, for example, while bank holdings of 5–10 year maturities decreased by about $13 billion and their holdings of 1–5 year maturities increased over $5 billion, the evidence from Treasury Bulletin data suggests that the bulk of the sales occurred in the 1–5 year category and that the passage of time shortened securities in excess of five years into this category. This pattern of selling intermediate-term maturities also repeated itself in 1959 and early 1960.[14]

Table 2.2 reveals that in the recessions of 1953–54 and 1957–58 banks, in the face of reduced loan demand and expansionary monetary policies, greatly increased their holdings of government securities with a maturity of over five years. In the category of 5–10 years, bank holdings increased by $14 billion from June 1957 to June 1958. In both instances the supply outstanding in this category rose substantially as well, but in spite of this, the banks' share of this category rose from 54% to 70% in the first period and from 69% to 72% in the second. The less vigorous acquisition of long-term securities in the second period may reflect the less liquid position which prevailed at the start of the downswing in June 1957 or less expansionary Federal Reserve action.

In any event, this casual examination of bank security holdings would appear to provide tentative support for the description of loan and security management offered above. In particular, banks appear to sell

---

[14] The failure to distinguish between actual sales and the passage-of-time effect was partly responsible for Luckett's argument. See the comment on his article by SILVERBERG [105]. The evidence, however, does not negate Luckett's position since the passage of time did provide for needed liquidity. With respect to capital losses, data on member-bank earnings show they realized net security losses of $326 million in 1956, $211 million in 1957 and $792 million in 1959. These losses may in part be attributable to the special provisions of the capital gains tax as applied to banks. For a discussion of this point, see MALKIEL and KANE [82].

TABLE 2.2*

Marketable Treasury securities maturing in	Total publically owned		Held by commercial banks		Total publically owned		Held by commercial banks	
	Jun. 53	Dec. 54	Jun. 53	Dec. 54	Jun. 57	Jun. 58	Jun. 57	Jun. 58
less than 1 year	48.9	43.3	22.2	17.8	49.6	43.9	14.6	15.4
1–5 years	25.7	26.4	20.2	20.6	37.3	38.5	26.0	26.9
5–10 years	16.9	32.2	9.1	22.7	13.7	22.0	9.4	15.9
more than 10 years	27.6	27.5	4.7	5.5	26.6	30.2	4.4	5.4
Totals	119.1	129.4	56.2	66.6	127.2	134.6	54.5	63.5

* See table 2.1.

TABLE 2.3*

Assets

	October 1950	June 1962
Reserves, cash, bank balances	30.11	42.85
(1) Reserves at Fed	16.54	16.84
(2) Cash items in process of collection	6.03	16.26
(3) Demand balances	5.69	7.09
Securities – Total	62.77	74.28
(1) U.S. Gov't, 0–5 yrs.	40.10	43.40
(2) U.S. Gov't, over 5 yrs.	11.13	8.52
(3) Municipals	4.56	19.32
Loans – Total (gross)	41.61	111.53
(1) Commercial	18.34	41.44
(2) Real estate	9.36	25.36
(3) Other loans to individuals	2.19	24.01
Other Assets	1.69	3.70
Total	136.18	232.36

Liabilities

	Oct. 1950	Jun. 1962
Demand deposits	95.01	130.34
Time deposits	29.47	75.51
Other liabilities	1.99	7.13
Total liabilities	126.47	213.18
Capital accounts	9.71	19.18
Total	136.18	232.36

* Data are in billions of dollars.
SOURCE: Federal Reserve Call Reports.

largely short and intermediate-term securities when they are in need of funds to make loans and they appear in recessions to lengthen the maturity of their security holdings by acquiring longer-term securities. This qualitative examination, however, is suggestive at best. In order to establish the determinants of bank portfolio behavior in quantitative terms, we have to introduce a more systematic and elaborate specification of bank behavior. It is to this task that we now turn.

2.4.4. *Basic Behavioral Assumptions*

Table 2.3 presents actual balance sheets of the banking system on two distinct dates. The first one relates to the initial quarter of our empirical study; the second one to the end quarter. In order to explain the various items in the balance sheet, we have to make a series of behavioral assumptions. First, banks are assumed to have a desired composition of their asset portfolios which depends on the entire constellation of yields (interest rates) on all financial assets the banks are legally allowed to hold. This desired composition is to be viewed as a set of long-run preferences which, because of time and uncertainty, must depend on expected as well as on current yields. These preferences for individual assets are assumed to be consistent with rational maximizing behavior by the banks. Thus, for example, the desired volume of loans will depend positively on its own yield (the loan rate) and negatively on all other yields. In adopting this view we are slurring over two difficulties: (1) we have not delineated the explicit uncertainties about yields and transaction costs which actually produce portfolio diversification; and (2) we are, throughout this discussion, passing loosely back and forth between the banking system and an individual bank. There is, however, ample precedent for abstracting from these problems.[15]

The next set of assumptions involve the translation of unobservable desired levels into actual portfolio composition. Reminiscent of a capital-stock adjustment model, we posit that quarterly flows of each of the assets (other than required reserves) depend on the discrepancy between current and desired levels.[16] Furthermore, we posit that quarterly flows attempt to adjust only partially for this discrepancy. If we designate the

---

[15] See, for example, MEIGS [83] and DE LEEUW [29].

[16] The capital-stock model is presented below in our discussion of fixed investment. We exclude required reserves from consideration since by law they are functionally related to the two deposit variables and as we shall see shortly, these will be assumed as given by the banks.

beginning-of-the-period value as the current value and replace the desired level by some function of interest rates, then we end up with an equation in which the actual flow depends on interest rates and the lagged stock. The lags which arise out of the partial-adjustment assumption are presumed to reflect uncertainties, and the lags inherent in the decision process.[17]

In addition to these influences, we further assume that other items impinge on the quarterly flows. In particular, we view the banks as taking as given a set of short-run constraints which together influence decidedly the path from actual to desired stocks. This device also has precedent. Meigs, for example, in his study (cited above) makes changes in actual free reserves depend on desired and current free reserves, on interest rates and on the rate-of-change of unborrowed reserves. This last factor, by injecting or withdrawing aggregate reserves, alters the path to desired equilibrium.[18] It seems quite plausible to assume that banks' quarterly adjustments depend on the amount of funds which become newly available. We are, of course, still assuming that in the absence of these flows (e.g. of reserves) banks will proceed each quarter to move part of the way towards their desired portfolio balance. However, the force of the constraint assumption is that banks, taking these flows as given, will necessarily make different quarterly adjustments in their portfolios. In addition to reserves we assume there are three types of flows which banks take as given. More explicitly, we assume that banks accommodate the public's wishes with respect to changes in demand deposits, time deposits and certain types of loans. The critical assumption is, of course, that banks take all three of these items as given. We examine each of these in turn.

The assumption about demand deposits seems relatively straightforward. It implies nothing more than the "willingness of banks to accept deposits and honor checks drawn against them." [29, p. 45]. For time deposits, the situation is somewhat more complicated. Banks can alter the yield they pay on these deposits. In a perfectly-competitive, time-

---

[17] The sources of uncertainty were described above, pp. 5–7. In this context uncertainties with respect to future interest rates would seem to be especially relevant. In the application of the capital stock model to fixed investment, partial adjustment can also be explained by cost considerations (e.g., decreasing returns in the capital-good sector). Here, if anything, there would seem to be increasing returns due to the nature of transactions costs. There are, however, other problems such as the imperfect nature of some of the bank asset markets which will lead to a partial adjustment solution.

[18] See MEIGS [83]. DE LEEUW [29] also contains a discussion of this point.

deposit market with a unique yield, it would make sense to think of each bank determining what volume of deposits it wished to offer at the prevailing yield. For virtually all of the period we consider, institutional considerations make it more reasonable to imagine individual banks as determining a yield and as accepting deposits at the set rate. In recent years, however, the growth of the certificate-of-deposit market means that large banks at least might properly be viewed as demanding part of their time deposits. We shall continue to ignore this complication.

Clearly, the assumption about taking part of the loan demand as given is a more ambiguous one. The part we have in mind is, of course, "customer" loan demand, which we approximate by the category of commercial and industrial loans. Our discussion of the loan market indicated that banks are likely to accommodate customer demand and to attempt to moderate the nature of the loan portfolio by changing the set of loan terms. Certainly, the existence of open credit lines means that part of the volume of loans must be taken as given in the short run. The appropriateness of making this assumption for all commercial loans clearly depends on the time unit underlying the analysis. For a very short period, it is sensible to assume that virtually all loans are prenegotiated, i.e., contracted one period and actually granted the next.[19] Under this view, the variable under bank control would be the interest rate it charged on loans. This would seem to be an appropriate assumption for a weekly analysis. On the other hand, for annual data perhaps one should view changes-in-loans as a variable fully under bank control. Within a quarter, probably part of loan demand is given and part not. Since there appears to be no simple way of disaggregating these components, we shall continue to assume that banks take commercial and industrial loans as a flow constraint and that the relevant supply variable is the set of loan terms.[20]

---

[19] This distinction between loan authorizations and actual loans granted can be implemented by the use of Canadian banking data. H. SHAPIRO [104], by identifying authorized loans as the supply of commercial loans and then estimating a supply function which makes authorizations depend on the prime rate, rate expectations, bank reserves and a loan capacity variable, has made an interesting start in this direction. Under this approach it is appropriate to assume that banks, given their authorizations, react passively to actual loan demand.

[20] See DE LEEUW [29, pp. 45–47] for a similar discussion. He, however, assumes that total loans and investments (including municipals, real estate and consumer loans) are given. This category, as de Leeuw recognizes, is somewhat too broad to justify the constraint assumption.

The net effect of this discussion is to add four flow variables to our specification of the various bank asset equations, i.e., flows of demand deposits, time deposits, commercial loans and reserves.[21] It should be noted that while the banks are viewed as taking the loan and deposit constraint variables as given, these variables are endogenous in the context of the entire model. In a later chapter, we shall have occasion to specify and estimate equations explaining the public's demand for time deposits, demand deposits and for commercial loans. Finally, the reserve constraint will actually be introduced in a form which reflects both reserve requirement changes and open-market operations. The relevant variables will be defined when they are used.

In addition to the current values of the constraint variables, lagged values are assumed to be relevant as well. Since in the face of various flows asset decisions are likely to be based on average or expected inflows, it is appropriate to include both current and lagged values of the constraints to account for this averaging notion. Finally, in addition to the flow constraints, we experiment with the introduction of certain lagged-stock constraints. For example, decisions about securities may depend on the bank's current liquidity position. Hence, stocks of excess reserves and short-term securities may influence bank management of the longer-term securities.

Taking all these considerations into account let us now write out a representative equation. Let A be an asset item whose holdings we wish to explain, let r's be various interest rates and let C represent the various constraints. Then we can write[22]

$$\Delta A_t = b_0 + b_1 A_{t-1} + b_2 r'_t + b_3 r''_t + \ldots + b_{n-1} C_t + b_n C_{t-1}.$$

We shall only be interested in a subset of all bank asset and liability items. In particular, we shall restrict our attention to free reserves, U.S. Government securities, municipals and commercial and industrial loans. We will not explicitly introduce equations explaining bank holdings of

---

[21] DE LEEUW [29] actually consolidates all these flows into one aggregate constraint variable. This implies that the same weight is attached to time deposit flows, demand deposit flows, and loan flows. It would seem, however, that the composition of the aggregate flow would also be an important consideration in bank behavior. For example, one would expect banks to react differently to inflows of time and demand deposits. For this reason we have introduced our constraints individually.

[22] Strictly speaking, the equation should also contain lagged stocks of all the portfolio items. This would not prove feasible on econometric grounds. Hence, we restrict ourselves to those selected lagged stocks contained in the constraint variables.

mortgages and of individual loans. Adequate treatment of these two categories would involve a supply-demand specification well beyond the scope of the model.

It must be remembered, of course, that a balance-sheet identity also connects the various items in table 2.3. This can be treated in either of two ways. One could aggregate all of the items not explicitly treated into a net "other" variable, viewing this as determined, given the other endogenous variables, by the balance sheet identity. We could also decompose this into "other" variables by separating out the loan component. If we regarded the residual as exogenous, we could then view other loans as an endogenous variable. Regardless of which view we adopt we can eliminate the balance sheet identity and the constructed "other" endogenous variable without changing our model. In the interest of simplicity we shall follow this course.

2.4.5. *Disaggregation*

We have indicated which items of the balance sheet we shall be concerned with and have specified the general form of each of these equations. Before estimating these relationships, we have one further issue to settle: the level of aggregation of each of these items. More explicitly, we must answer the following three questions: (1) is free reserves an appropriate behavioral concept?; (2) into what maturity breakdown should we separate bank security holdings?; (3) are aggregate banking data appropriate or should one decompose the data into more homogeneous groups? We take up each of these questions in turn.

It is one of the contentions of this study that the aggregate level of free reserves is not an appropriate behavioral variable in an empirical study of the postwar U.S. economy. In particular, we advocate separation of the free reserve variable into its two components: excess reserves and borrowings. There exist at least two cogent reasons for separating free reserves into its proximate components. United States banking data typically show significant levels of both excess reserves and borrowings existing contemporaneously. In part, this is because the tradition against borrowing from the Fed is distributed quite unevenly among individual banks. While some banks never borrow, others use their discount privilege extensively. As a result, the movement of free reserves may reflect the aggregation of behaviorally diverse bank philosophies. It seems desirable to separate out these effects. Second, separation is desirable because there appear to be factors that influence only excess reserves and others that affect only borrowing. Such effects are inevitably obscured by aggregation. Thus, for example, in the Tobin free-reserve formulation we saw that a bank's cash-demand schedule had two components depending on whether or not there was an incentive to borrow. Thus *a priori* reasoning would suggest that disaggregation of free reserves might be desirable. Of course, ultimately the issue is an empirical one and we return to it below.

As for the second question, we have already established that some maturity breakdown of bank holdings of government securities would be desirable. Moreover, we have suggested that short (0–1 year), intermediate (1–5 years) and long (over 5 years) categories might be useful. Unfortunately, a breakdown of this type, covering the entire sample period, is not available in market-value terms. The primary source of banking data for this study, namely the quarterly Federal Reserve Call Reports, contains for most of the period information on banks holdings of bills, certificates of indebtedness, notes, bonds of maturity five years or less, five to ten years and over ten years. Beginning only in April 1961 is there a breakdown of notes and bonds into an under-one-year category. As there appeared to be no reasonable way to obtain comparable data for the earlier period[23] it was decided to form just two categories as follows:

(1) bills, certificates, notes, bonds under 5 years
(2) other bonds.

Category (1) will be called the short-term category and category (2) the long-term one.

The final question, that of disaggregating banking data into more homogeneous groupings, is suggested by the simple fact that there is considerable (and somewhat predictable) variation in the way commercial banks manage their portfolios. For example, with respect to reserve management, one Federal Reserve Bank has noted:

"The unique characteristic of large banks compared with smaller institutions is that while the day-to-day fluctuations are relatively small in percentage terms, the amount is large enough to justify special action to gain earnings on these transitory balances." [37, p. 1].

---

[23] Treasury Survey data provide a breakdown available monthly (published semiannually) on security holdings by maturity by class of bank which include an under-one-year category. The data, however, are on a par basis and are not for 100% of member banks. (Although they provide 100% coverage for New York, Chicago and after 1956 for Other Reserve City). The relationship between par value and book value presumably varies by both class of bank for a given security and by type of security as well as over the cycle. These and other problems precluded use of the Treasury data.

With respect to the same issue Tobin has observed:

> "Active reserve management earns interest, at the cost of numerous money market and discount window transactions. Differences among banks and bankers in circumstances and temperament are to be expected; the costs of active reserve management loom much larger for small country banks than for big New York or Chicago banks" [114, chapter 9, p. 23].

Despite these and other similar observations, until quite recently there have been only infrequent attempts to disaggregate in the application of econometrics to the study of the banking system.[24]

The Federal Reserve, in the past, separated member banks into three categories: central reserve city (New York and Chicago available separately); reserve city; and country. Although the data for the first two categories are still available, we shall restrict our attention to the two-fold classification of country and noncountry (or "city"). Examination of table 2.4 provides a rough indication of the differences between the country and city classes of banks. For example, country banks have a much higher proportion of their deposits in time deposits and have larger fractions of their assets in securities. Furthermore, the composition of the loan portfolios differ considerably between the two classes. City banks have the bulk of their loans in commercial and industrial loans while country banks are fairly evenly balanced between real estate loans, commercial loans, and other loans to individuals, with commercial loans having the smallest share. Another aspect of the differences between these two classes relates to the striking contrast in the average asset size of bank in each class. As of June 1962 there were 5842 country banks and only 228 city banks. The average bank size (total assets) for the city class was over $620 million while for the country class it was only about $15.5 million.

The basic data appear equally heterogeneous if we examine the components of the banks' portfolios over time. This can be seen by examining excess reserves and borrowings of the two classes. Let us denote by B^N, E^N, D^N and B^C, E^C, D^C the levels of city and country borrowing, excess reserves, and net demand deposits respectively. Figures 2.2 and 2.3 compare borrowing and excess reserves at each class of bank.

As is immediately apparent, there is a pronounced difference in the levels of excess reserves and borrowings which these two categories of banks have held in the postwar period. There is a secularly increasing

---

[24] See CURRIE [25], TINBERGEN [111], and TURNER [115].

TABLE 2.4

Balance sheet as of June 1962

	Country	City		Country	City
Reserves and cash items	13.81	29.04	Demand deposits	46.73	83.81
	(15.3%)	(20.5%)		(51.6%)	(59.1%)
Securities – total	33.53	40.75	Time deposits	34.85	40.66
	(37.0%)	(28.7%)			
(1) U.S. Gov't (0–5 years)	19.06	24.34		(38.5%)	(28.7%)
	(56.8%)	(59.7%)			
(2) U.S. Gov't (over 5 years)	4.74	3.78	Other liabilities	1.65	5.48
	(14.1%)	(9.3%)			
(3) Municipals	8.15	11.17	Total liabilities	83.23	129.95
	(24.3%)	(27.4%)			
Loans – total (gross)	42.31	69.22	Capital accounts	7.32	11.86
	(46.7%)	(48.8%)			
(1) Commercial	10.72	30.72			
	(25.3%)	(44.4%)			
(2) Real estate	13.73	11.63			
	(32.5%)	(16.8%)			
(3) Other loans to individuals	11.79	12.22			
	(27.8%)	(17.7%)			
Other assets	.91	2.80			
Total	90.56	141.81	Total	90.56	141.81

SOURCE: Federal Reserve Quarterly Call Report. The data are in billions of dollars. For the major categories the percentage figures below the data indicate the fraction of total assets. For the subheadings the percentage figures are as a percent of the major category total.

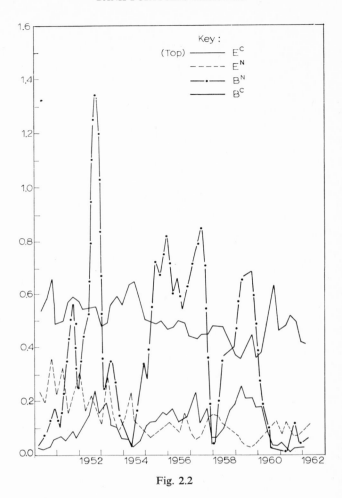

Fig. 2.2

trend in the ratio D^C/D^N, but the average value for the period is only approximately one-half. Thus, differences with respect to excess reserves and borrowing are even more pronounced when one takes into account that country banks have a smaller share of the deposits. This can be seen in figure 2.3 where we have graphed E^N/D^N, E^C/D^C, B^N/D^N, B^C/D^C.

A final factor also points towards the disaggregation of the banking data into country and city classes. Since these two types of banks are likely to experience different seasonal patterns in the demand for funds, they are likely to have seasonally different liquidity needs. Because we

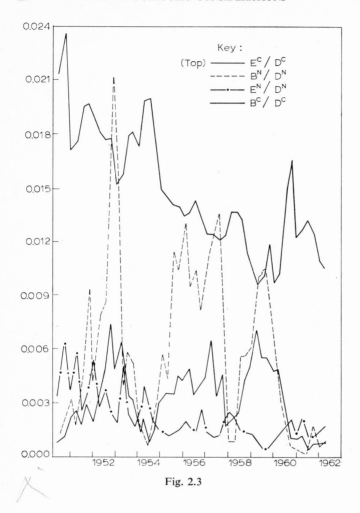

Fig. 2.3

have chosen to work with seasonally-unadjusted data and to account for the seasonal variation by use of dummy variables, these differing seasonal patterns are likely to be obscured by aggregation.

The general overall pattern of business activity consists of a relatively mild first two quarters (except for Easter) with a gradual increase in the third quarter and a pronounced seasonal peak in the fourth quarter (around Thanksgiving-Christmas). This type of seasonal pattern should influence the reserve position of banks in several ways. To the extent that it affects banks via an increase in the use of the check payment mechanism and increased cash drains, it means that banks in all locations will be subject to an increased probability of having adverse clearing balances (*ceteris paribus*). This pattern will affect banks further through a seasonal expansion of loans, to both consumers and business, which will put banks in a less liquid position.

These types of seasonal activity will presumably be the dominant seasonal influences on the reserve positions of banks located in industrial centers. Thus, we should expect a corresponding seasonal pattern to manifest itself in the liquidity portfolio of our noncountry bank classification. However, commercial banks located in principally agricultural areas, resort areas, or regions in which a single type of business predominates will not only be subject to large seasonal variations (relative to their deposit liabilities) but also may find themselves facing a local seasonal pattern superimposed on the national one. A bank located in an agricultural area (presumably a country bank by our classification) will find that its customers receive most of their cash income in the fall (harvest time). Consequently, its deposits will rise significantly at that time. In the spring when the time comes to plant and cultivate crops, the bank will have to furnish credit to cover the purchase of seed, fertilizer, labor and other costs. Hence, prior to the harvest, its deposits should reach a seasonal trough. Differing seasonal patterns suggest that, with unadjusted data, disaggregation of the two classes of banks may be desirable.

There thus appear to be several reasons favoring disaggregation of the banking data. On this score, several points should be noted before we proceed. First, while it represents an improvement, there is nothing to suggest that the classification we have chosen is the most appropriate one. The choise was dictated primarily by data availability. Furthermore, in order to keep the size of the model within manageable proportions, we decided to aggregate even more than we had to, recognizing only two classes. Second, the qualitative investigation conducted above only suggests bank class differences; it is not sufficient to establish these differences. Strictly speaking, only through a careful examination of our parameter estimates, can we gauge the importance of disaggregation. Finally, it should be emphasized that each bank class can not be regarded as an independent one. As we shall see later, monetary policy measures are not determined for classes of banks but rather for the banking system as a whole. In view of this, basic interrelationships preclude attempts to isolate each class.

From this general discussion of bank portfolio behavior, we turn now to the focal section of this chapter which specifies and estimates relationships explaining the various components of bank portfolios.

2.5. Specification and Estimation of Bank Equations

2.5.1. *Introduction*

In this section we specify and estimate equations relating to each bank class' holdings of excess reserves, borrowings, short-term government securities, long-term government securities, municipal securities, and the supply side of the commercial loan market. For the reader's convenience, we first list our notation.

E^N – excess reserves of city member banks

B^N – borrowings of city member banks

S^N – holdings of short-term U.S. Government securities by city member banks

D^N – net demand deposits of city member banks

O^N – holdings of long-term U.S. Government securities by city member banks

T^N – time deposits of city member banks

MUN^N – holdings of municipal securities by city member banks

CL^N – holdings of commercial loans by city member banks

L^N – total loans held by city member banks

RR^N – reserve requirement variable for city member banks[25]

E^C – excess reserves of country member banks

B^C – borrowings of country member banks

S^C – short-term U.S. Government securities held by country member banks

O^C – long-term U.S. securities held by country member banks

D^C – net demand deposits of country member banks

T^C – time deposits of country member banks

MUN^C – municipal security holdings of country member banks

CL^C – holdings of commercial loans by country member banks

L^C – total loans held by country member banks

RR^C – reserve requirement variable for country member banks

s_2, s_3, s_4 – seasonale dummy variables taking on the value one in the quarter indicated by the subscript and zero elsewhere

---

[25] See below, p. 40, for a precise definition of the variable.

r_s – yield on short-term Treasury bills

r_d – Federal Reserve discount rate

r_e – rate charged on commercial loans

r_m – yield on municipal securities

r_3 – yield on three-to-five year U.S. Government securities

r_{10} – yield on long-term U.S. Government securities

$\bar{S}$ – total supply of short-term U.S. securities in the hands of the public

$\bar{O}$ – total supply of long-term U.S. securities in the hands of the public

D^* – potential deposits (demand) of the banking system defined as $(R^u - k_T \cdot T)/k_D$ where R^u is unborrowed reserves, k_T and k_D are the reserve requirements on time and demand deposits respectively and T is the volume of time deposits.[26]

The description of the data with comments on measurement, sources, and methods of derivation from which both single-equation (direct least-squares) estimates and two-stage least-squares are computed may be found in the Appendix. The data used are quarterly, seasonally unadjusted time series beginning in the third quarter of 1950 and ending in the second quarter of 1962, a total of 48 observations. The coverage of the data is restricted to Federal Reserve member-banks. This choice was dictated by the data available and our interests in disaggregation. In a later chapter, we shall extrapolate certain components of member-bank behavior to generate, for purposes of the complete model, estimates of total-bank behavior. All dollar variables are denominated in billions while the interest rate variables are measured in percent. All time subscripts refer to quarterly values. The absence of a subscript indicates the current value of a variable.

The estimates presented in this chapter have been obtained by direct least-squares estimation. One of the main contentions of this study is that the monetary and related sectors must be represented by a simultaneous-equation model. Preliminary use of single-equation pilot investigations runs counter to this view. If these investigations are used to make decisions with respect to inclusion of certain variables, functional form, or lag pattern (and they invariably are), then we are defeating to some extent

---

[26] D^* represents the maximum level of deposits which could prevail given current Fed policy (i.e., R^u), if there were no excess or borrowed reserves. The computation of D^* takes into account the existence of bank class differences for demand deposit requirements.

the virtue of simultaneous-equation techniques. The advantage of single-equation techniques is, of course, that they allow one to experiment on a partial-equilibrium basis without forcing one to specify a complete model all at once. In what follows, we have avoided making any "close" decisions on the basis of single-equation estimates. Nevertheless, grossly unsatisfactory forms were discarded on the basis of single-equation estimates. Implicit in this procedure was the belief that the structural estimates obtained by use of two-stage least-squares would not lead to any new decisions in apparently clear-cut cases. A comparison of certain of the single-equation and structural estimates supported this contention.[27]

There is a second consequence of our contention that the monetary sector must be represented by a structural model. In particular, only asymptotic properties of the structural estimates are known. Thus, strictly speaking, statistical tests which can be used where single-equation models are appropriate do not apply to structural estimates or to these exploratory single-equation estimates. However, because of the need to establish a systematic method of evaluating the results, we shall, with serious reservations, tentatively use some of the usual regression criteria for this purpose. In particular, we shall report parameter estimates and their standard errors (and hence implicitly t-values), R^2, standard errors of estimate, and Durbin-Watson statistics.[28] The inadequacy of the standard t-, F- and Durbin-Watson tests means, however, that one should place a relatively larger degree of reliance on the *a priori* specification of the model. With these qualifications in mind we can now begin specifying our first equation which deals with excess reserves.

2.5.2. *Excess Reserves*

Discussion of the Instrument

Excess reserves comprise, at the cost of income foregone, the most passive and conservative manner of providing for bank liquidity. The larger the volume of excess reserves held by an individual bank the less likely it is that, in order to secure reserves, the bank will have to have

---

[27] This is not to say that another structural estimation technique such as full information maximum likelihood might not produce significantly large changes in the parameter estimates. The fact that it does so, however, also reflects its greater sensitivity to specification error.

[28] In the present context the Durbin-Watson statistic is rendered invalid on another ground since all of the equations reported below contain a lagged value of the stock as an explanatory variable.

recourse to the discount window or to the money market. For small or geographically-isolated banks, these holdings also reduce the reliance on transactions balances at money-market banks.

As figures 2.2 and 2.3 reveal, American bankers hold widely diversified views as to appropriate levels of excess reserves. While country bankers appear to regard them as an appropriate form of liquidity, the evidence is that many city banks minimize their holdings of excess reserves. These differences are, of course, basic to the proper specification of equations explaining holdings of excess reserves.

A bank holding excess reserves bears an opportunity cost which is represented by the yield it could have obtained by holding its funds in another form. With short-term government securities the most obvious alternative to excess reserves, it seems appropriate to approximate this cost by r_s, the yield on Treasury bills. Since country banks hold over 85% of aggregate excess reserves, one may very well doubt the interest sensitivity of their excess reserve holdings. In spite of their high aggregate level, these banks appear, from a rough examination, to have varied excess-reserve holdings quite extensively, both secularly and cyclically. It seems appropriate to examine whether this variation has been in accordance with the opportunity costs involved.

Some city banks, on the other hand, have followed a policy of excess-reserve-minimization throughout the period we are examining. In order to maximize earnings on temporarily idle cash, these banks generally take quite frequent inventory checks on their asset positions. If this type of behavior were uniformly practiced in the city-bank sector, we would have little hope of explaining their excess reserves. It might behave very much like a random error term.[29] However, the breadth of the city-bank classification and the fact that, even within a large city, banks similarly situated behave quite differently with respect to excess reserve-policy, both suggest that we may expect r_s to be a significant variable in explaining both city and country excess reserves.[30]

Equation Estimates
In conformance with the pattern outlined in section 2.4, we included in

---

[29] Of course one might be able to find systematic factors which caused banks to miss the zero excess reserve level at some times moreso than at others. Hence, one could generate an error theory of excess reserve holdings. This idea may have some validity, especially for large New York and Chicago banks, but it was not pursued.

[30] For some limited evidence on differences within a particular city see [37].

addition to the bill rate a lagged value of the dependent variable, seasonal dummy variables and various constraint variables such as deposit flows of various types. In this first approximation, the results for city and country banks are as follows:[31]

$$\Delta E^N = 0.131 + 0.022s_2 - 0.013s_3 + 0.028s_4 - 0.560E^N_{-1} - 0.031r_s$$
$$\quad\quad (0.033)\quad (0.035)\quad (0.048)\quad (0.149)\quad\quad (0.014)$$

$$-0.014\Delta D^N - 0.003\Delta T^N + 0.003\Delta CL^N + 0.0095\Delta D^*$$
$$(0.010)\quad\quad (0.015)\quad\quad (0.014)\quad\quad\quad (0.0046)$$
$$R^2 = 0.357\quad S_e = 0.061\quad (2.1)$$

$$\Delta E^C = 0.206 + 0.067s_2 + 0.152s_3 + 0.162s_4 - 0.415E^C_{-1} - 0.038r_s$$
$$\quad\quad (0.018)\quad (0.016)\quad (0.030)\quad (0.112)\quad\quad (0.010)$$

$$-0.055\Delta D^C + 0.0002\Delta T^C + 0.020\Delta CL^C + 0.004\Delta D^*$$
$$(0.013)\quad\quad (0.014)\quad\quad (0.030)\quad\quad\quad (0.002)$$
$$R^2 = 0.762\quad S_e = 0.030\quad (2.2)$$

A number of interesting comparisons can be made between (2.1) and (2.2). First, we succeed in explaining a much higher proportion of the variation in the country-bank equation. This is, of course, what we would expect on the basis of our previous discussion. Second, despite this difference, both equations produce an appropriately signed coefficient for the bill rate, one several times its standard error in each equation. Third, seasonal factors play a much more important role in the country-bank equation.

In an effort to improve both equations, two refinements were attempted. D^*, since it is constructed by use of an average reserve requirement ratio, does not handle changes in reserve requirements in a wholly satisfactory way. First, reserve requirement changes can be introduced by the authorities in differing amounts for our two classes. Second, it is easy to conceive of offsetting individual class changes which leave the average reserve ratio the same. In view of these difficulties, two types of variables

---

[31] The numbers in parentheses beneath the coefficients are their standard errors. The R^2 and the standard error of estimate (S_e) are both adjusted for degrees of freedom. Finally the Durbin-Watson statistic (DW) appears for only some of the equations. It does, however, appear for at least one equation of each type. This simply reflects the fact that we started to compute it only after the study had been under way.

were constructed for inclusion in (2.1) and (2.2). To describe them we need to introduce some additional notation.

k_1, k_2, k_3 – reserve requirement ratio on demand deposits for central reserve city, reserve city, and country banks respectively

k_4 – reserve requirement ratio on time deposits (the same for all classes)

D_1^N, D_2^N – net demand deposits of central reserve city and reserve city banks

(n.b. $D^N = D_1^N + D_2^N$)

We then define

$$RR_2^N = \Delta \left(\frac{k_1 D_1^N + k_2 D_2^N + k_4 T^N}{D^N + T^N} \right)$$

$$RR_2^C = \Delta \left(\frac{k_3 D^C + k_4 T^C}{D^C + T^C} \right)$$

$$RR_3^N = D_1^N \Delta k_1 + D_2^N \Delta k_2 + T^N \Delta k_4$$

$$RR_3^C = D^C \Delta k_3 + T^C \Delta k_4 \ .$$

RR_2^N and RR_2^C are simply changes in the class average reserve requirements. On the other hand, RR_3^N and RR_3^C are dollar variables measuring the change in required reserves coming about because of requirement changes (assuming the relevant deposits to be the ones for the current period). It should be noted that the former set of variables can change because of deposit redistribution even when requirements (the k's) remain the same.

The second refinement introduced relates to the fact that there is some evidence a structural shift had taken place in the early part of the period under investigation. We decided to deal with this via a shift parameter. In order to do this the shift must be dated. For this reason, let us briefly examine the events of the early part of the period. Until the Treasury-Federal Reserve Accord in the spring of 1951, the Federal Reserve was effectively restrained from practicing active monetary policy. Immediately following the Accord, the Federal Reserve exercised its newfound freedom cautiously, partly because there was considerable uncertainty concerning the market's reaction to the increased flexibility of interest rates. Monetary policy remained cautious throughout 1952. In that period, monetary policy probably did not exert a major influence on the economy. In the early part of 1953, the Open Market Committee introduced several important changes in the concrete ground rules whereby policy was conducted. Henceforth, open-market operations for broad stabilization purposes were to be confined to the short-term market. A second change related to the System's policy with respect to the market for government securities. In particular, the directive was changed from one of "maintaining orderly conditions" to the technically less burdensome one of "correcting a disorderly situation" should one arise. Roughly coincident with these changes was the 1953–1954 recession during which gross national product fell from a peak level of $368.8 billion in the second quarter of 1953 to a low of $358.9 in the second quarter of 1954. The recession, coupled with these revised policy objectives and tools, finally served to bring out the changes envisioned by the Federal Reserve at the time of the Accord. Referring to the period one writer has remarked: "This (June 1953) marked the end of what one might formally consider as the period of transition to flexible market and monetary policy." [78, p. 104]. To take account of this, we have decided to insert a shift variable (d_1, below) which is one (1.) from the beginning of the period until the second quarter of 1953 and zero (0.) after. Below are two single-equation estimates for country and non-country banks. Results including both the shift variable and the reserve-requirement variable follow:

$$\Delta E^N = 0.141 + 0.035s_2 - 0.018s_3 - 0.008s_4 - 1.047E^N_{-1} - 0.020r_s$$
$$\quad\quad (0.028)\quad (0.023)\quad (0.028)\quad (0.126)\quad\quad (0.010)$$
$$+ 0.008\Delta D^* + 0.118d_1 - 0.662RR^N_2 + 0.007\Delta D^*_{-1}$$
$$(0.003)\quad\quad (0.021)\quad (2.213)\quad\quad (0.003)$$
$$R^2 = 0.651\quad S_e = 0.045\quad DW = 2.42\quad (2.3)$$

$$\Delta E^C = 0.212 + 0.062s_2 + 0.136s_3 + 0.148s_4 - 0.437E^C_{-1} - 0.033r_s$$
$$\quad\quad (0.018)\quad (0.022)\quad (0.026)\quad (0.111)\quad\quad (0.009)$$
$$+ 0.0044\Delta D^* + 0.016d_1 - 1.705RR^C_2 - 0.047\Delta D^C$$
$$(0.0022)\quad\quad (0.012)\quad (1.882)\quad\quad (0.011)$$
$$R^2 = 0.771\quad S_e = 0.029\quad DW = 1.82\quad (2.4)$$

Equation (2.3) reveals that the shift variable d_1, substantially increases the explanatory power of the city-bank equation and strongly supports the idea that the same behavioral relationship was not appropriate in an unadjusted form over the entire period.[32] The introduction of the shift variable into the city-bank equation also has the effect of decreasing the coefficient of the lagged excess reserve variable to approximately minus one.[33] As the negative of the speed-of-adjustment, this suggests—somewhat more reasonably than did (2.1)—that city banks adjust their holdings of excess reserves to the desired level within the quarter. This is to be contrasted with an estimated speed of adjustment of 0.44 for the country banks.

Finally, we note that both required-reserve variables are statistically insignificant. Similar results were obtained with RR_3^N and RR_3^C. Although insignificant, the coefficients of these variables were uniformly negative, indicating, reasonably enough, that an increase in reserve requirements led to a decline in excess reserves.[34] Perhaps, therefore, the potential deposit variable D^* which incorporates the average reserve ratio is sufficient to account for reserve requirement changes.

One final point should be noted and that is the negative sign ΔD^C obtains in (2.4) and ΔD^N in (2.1). This indicates an inflow of demand deposits creates a decrease in excess reserves. This seems to come about because we have already accounted for the reserve position of the banking system via D^* and so the actual deposit variables may capture the excess reserves decline occasioned by the expansion of deposits with a given supply of

---

[32] One could, via a covariance analysis, formally test the hypothesis that a different behavioral relationship was appropriate in the two periods. The large contribution to explanation of d_1 suggests that this test would indeed reject the hypothesis. The inclusion of a simple additive shift variable to account for this structural change assumes that the only difference in the two periods was in the level of excess reserves (i.e. a different intercept). There are, of course, other specifications which might explain the change. However, estimating equations similar to (2.3) and (2.4) for the post-53 period produced results sufficiently similar to (2.3) and (2.4) so that we feel confident that d_1 adequately captures the change.

[33] The coefficient of E_{-1}^N in (2.3) is actually slightly bigger than one (in absolute value) although it is not statistically different from unity. A value bigger than one indicates we may have an unstable process. However, in view of the fact that it is not significantly different from one and that (2.3) is merely a preliminary equation, we shall not pursue this further.

[34] An increase of reserve requirements will certainly be expected to decrease excess reserves in the short-run (the reserve computation period of one or two weeks). Within a quarter the results are somewhat less clear. The higher are reserve requirements, the smaller is the consequence, in terms of implied contraction, for the banks of a reserve loss. This would suggest the ultimate effect is in the same direction as the short-run one. On the other hand, the inventory-transactions analogy suggests the result may go the other way.

unborrowed reserves[35] (especially via earning-asset acquisition). Next we turn to a discussion of member-bank borrowing from the Fed.

2.5.3. *Member-Bank Borrowing*

Discussion of Borrowing Theories

As in many areas of dispute, opinion on member-bank borrowing has tended to polarize around two partially conflicting theories which can be termed the need and profit theories, respectively. Intimately connected with this dichotomy is the so-called tradition against borrowing which posits, in its milder versions, that banks have a strong dislike against borrowing and do so only in certain limited circumstances.

The existence of a tradition against borrowing, it is argued, lends support to the need theory which states that member banks borrow merely to meet adverse clearing balances and temporary loan demands of their customers, and that they will repay these debts as quickly as possible. However, as we shall see below, serious doubts can be raised against the strength and extensiveness of the tradition against borrowing.

The profit theory of borrowing emphasizes the possibility of a bank's securing of funds at one rate (the discount rate) and utilizing the funds in another market, thereby increasing the rate of return on bank capital. However, the considerable historical differentials that have existed between the discount rate and open-market money rates attest that, with respect to borrowing, private banks are not motivated exclusively by profit considerations.

At times FRB Chairman Martin has mentioned both factors. As he notes:

> "In the first instance, increasing pressure on bank reserve positions (increased need for borrowing) may be developed through use of the open-market instrument alone. At a point, however, it will become appropriate to support the effectiveness of this open-market action by an increase in the discount rate, strengthening the reluctance of the member banks to remain indebted to the Federal Reserve by making borrowing more expensive as a means of adjusting bank reserve positions."[36]

---

[35] In other words, the increase in required reserves occasioned by deposit expansion is financed out of excess reserves. Another possibility, at least for the rather strong negative effect in (2.4), is the presence of multicollinearity.

[36] Cited in [96, p. 3].

Before we can test the alleged importance of the tradition against borrowing in explaining member-bank behavior, we must first examine the basis for this tradition.

The tradition against borrowing is deeply rooted in the historical development of American banking. In the nineteenth century borrowing under anything but extreme conditions was considered to be an overextension of the bank's asset position. One consequence of the commercial-loan theory (which prevailed until the early 1930's) was that discounts were available only upon the presentation of "eligible" (self-liquidating, short-term) paper. With the advent of the Depression, many banks had exhausted their supply of eligible collateral and thus were unable to borrow from the Fed. As a consequence, even though they had perfectly sound assets on their books, many banks were forced closed down for lack of liquidity. By 1934, the tradition against borrowing could almost be called a phobia.[37] Use of the discount mechanism virtually ceased and was not reestablished until the early postwar years. The real resurgence of the discount mechanism took place following the Treasury-Federal Reserve Accord in the spring of 1951. Borrowings accelerated rapidly, and the Federal Reserve felt a strong need to buttress the apparently weakened tradition against borrowing.[38] Chairman Martin in commenting on the period has noted: "Through a lapse of time some member banks had lost familiarity with the principles of law and regulation relating to the appropriate occasions for borrowing at the Reserve banks."[39]

As a result of this apparent loss of reluctance to borrow from the Fed, Reserve officials undertook a campaign of "reeducation" of bankers, which included both extensive speechmaking and correspondence. The Federal Reserve also began a comprehensive study of its discount function, and this culminated in February, 1955 with the release of a major revision of Regulation A, the preamble to which is reproduced below.

> Federal Reserve credit is generally extended on a short-term basis to a member bank in order to enable it to adjust its asset position when necessary because of developments such as a sudden with-

---

[37] Of course, the limited use of the discount mechanism at this time also reflected profit considerations.

[38] The increased borrowings of the period can to a large extent be attributed to the provisions of the excess profits law then in effect. This law made it profitable for member banks in excess profits tax brackets to borrow to increase their tax base.

[39] Cited in [80, p. 22].

drawal of deposits or seasonal requirements for credit beyond those which can reasonably be met by use of the bank's own resources. Federal Reserve credit is also available for longer periods when necessary in order to assist member banks in meeting unusual situations, such as may result from national, regional, or local difficulties or from exceptional circumstances involving only particular member banks. Under ordinary conditions, the continuous use of Federal Reserve credit by a member bank over a considerable period of time is not regarded as appropriate.

In considering a request for credit accommodation, each Federal Reserve Bank gives due regard to the purpose of the credit and to its probable effect on the maintenance of sound credit conditions, both as to the individual institution and the economy generally. It keeps informed of and takes into account the general character of the loans and investments of the member bank. It considers whether the bank is borrowing principally for the purpose of obtaining a tax advantage or profiting from rate differentials and whether the bank is extending an undue amount of credit for the speculative carrying of or trading in securities, real estate, or commodities, or otherwise.

As indicated by the preamble, the most important general circumstance leading to the use of the discount privilege is an unanticipated loss of reserves through the clearings process. A bank facing this type of reserve loss will be accommodated quite routinely at the discount window. It will, however, be expected to adjust its asset structure in an orderly fashion and to repay the temporary borrowings promptly. Another relatively frequent occasion for borrowing is an unexpectedly large seasonal loss of reserves. The unevenness of seasonal demands on individual member banks means that it is difficult to meet the seasonal requirements of the banking system as a whole by open-market operations. The Fed has emphasized that a bank should not expect to borrow from its Federal Reserve Bank until the seasonal cycle has run its course. Here again they state that borrowing is a temporary expedient to aid in portfolio rearrangement. However, a somewhat more permissive statement was made by one former Federal Reserve official, G. W. McKinney, Jr., who noted:

"The bank may be faced with a seasonal problem substantially greater than that faced by most banks, so that it would be unreasonable to expect the bank to meet its entire seasonal needs from its own resources, even if it were able to predict the extent of those needs." [80, p. 98].

Under certain other circumstances, borrowing may be appropriate for longer periods, but these occasions are considerably less frequent. A bank, for example, located in a community that has been depressed for some time may have a chronic shortage of reserves. In effect, the possibility of long-term borrowing in this context permits the Fed to pursue a regionally-selective monetary policy, perhaps diametrically opposed to its national policies.

On balance, what appears to be relevant in determining "appropriateness" is the highly subjective notion of the "intent of the borrower". The New York Fed's definitive statement on borrowing has declared: "So long as the member bank is making every reasonable effort to operate its business with its own resources, arrangements for temporary accommodation at the discount window can always be worked out." [14, p. 33].

With respect to inappropriate borrowing there are several different types of unwarranted use of the discount facility which vary in the degree of detectability. Thus, for example, a bank tending to borrow from its Reserve Bank during one or more reserve computation periods each month, at the point in the month when total reserves are lowest, would be "systematically" underestimating reserve losses. This, in the eyes of the Fed, would be relying on the discount window to supply part of a predictable need for reserves and is inappropriate regardless of how meritorious the loans made by the member bank may be. This type of behavior, if pursued by a member bank over a relatively long period of time, would presumably be detected by the Fed. In general, however, the matter is not so simple. The Fed has stated that it attempts to establish "whether the 'need' has, so to speak, been created artificially." [14, p. 33]. However, as McKinney has observed, ". . . it is extremely difficult to pinpoint why a bank is borrowing" [80, p. 116]. Other Federal Reserve officials have also indicated skepticism with respect to the success of policing inappropriate borrowing. For example, C. Walker, formerly of the Federal Reserve Bank of Dallas has stated:

"If such policing is effective—and it is an administrative task of considerable proportions during periods of active discounting— there may be some discouragement of the speculative growth of credit. Too much should not be expected of this route, however, partly because of the administrative difficulties involved, and partly because control, even if effective, can be exercised only over the initial use of the funds." [119, p. 232].

With respect to borrowing to earn a rate differential, it is sufficient to note the following statement.

"On the other hand, if a bank borrowed temporarily to meet a commitment to make a loan to a business concern at 4 per cent, with reasonable expectations of having funds at hand shortly to pay out, the bank would not be borrowing to earn a rate differential even though it was borrowing at a lower rate (in one market) and re-lending at a higher rate (in another market)." [80, p. 106].

This pronouncement coupled with the already established difficulty in determining the purpose in borrowing indicates that there is sufficient room (certainly for short periods of time) to take advantage of favorable rate differentials.

Borrowing to gain a tax advantage has not been a problem since the removal of the excess profits tax established during the Korean conflict.[40] A provision of that tax was to allow a proportion (75%) of average borrowing to be counted as capital in computing the rate of return, and this proportionally decreased the amount of earnings subject to the excess profits tax. In effect a bank could borrow at the then prevailing discount rate of 1.75% and could earn approximately 1% net after tax gain even if it allowed the proceeds of the loan to lie idle. As a result of this provision, member-bank borrowings attained extremely high levels in 1952 and 1953 and in fact in December, 1952, attained a level that has not been equalled since. This episode offers additional evidence that member-bank borrow-ing is responsive to changes in the spread between yields on earning assets and the cost of borrowed funds. The 1952–53 experience was one of the major factors leading to the "reeducation" program noted above.

This brief discussion has revealed that, in the aggregate at least when advantageous, banks have historically been willing to put aside their traditions and borrow from the Fed. The aggregate figures, however, conceal a great deal of individual diversity. The tradition against borrow-ing as felt by individual banks and the borrowing habits of banks are to a great extent both matters of management policy and philosophy. Over a period of time, the limited evidence available indicates that most borrow-ing is done by the same group of banks. Some banks, in fact, never borrow, and for them the tradition remains law. Among the borrowing banks, there is an entire spectrum of intensity of use which shifts up as borrowing needs and profitable opportunities present themselves. Of the

---

[40] Tax lock-ins might be an exception to this statement. See MALKIEL and KANE [82].

467 Fifth District member banks in existence in 1957, 224 had not borrowed from the Federal Reserve Bank in the past 21 years. Of those actually borrowing, the volume and period of borrowing varied significantly. There also appears to be an extremely wide divergence in attitude between country and city banks in this district, which further supports our claim on the need for separation of these two categories. Thus, for example, in the Fifth District in 1957, 88% of reserve city banks borrowed at least once, while only 28% of country banks did the same.[41]

In view of the evidence presented thus far, it would appear that: (1) a rather strong tradition against borrowing may be operative for a significant group of banks; (2) but this tradition is clearly not relevant, at least in a rigid form, for another component of the banking system. Despite the existence of these latter banks, however, we still observe that the discount rate is always below the rate obtainable from some asset which the banks could purchase with borrowed funds, if they so chose. In other words, abstracting from transactions costs, the strict version of the profit theory does not hold either. What then provides a limit to member-bank borrowing? From published sources and from discussions with bankers, it would appear that the answer is that banks borrow for what they deem are appropriate needs but the definition of what is appropriate can change from time to time and from bank to bank.[42] Federal Reserve authorities, by what we may term surveillance, play a key role in setting overall standards of reasonable need and in interpreting each specific bank request for funds. Furthermore, by this very process of surveillance the Fed tends to diminish the relevance of the stated discount rate for decisions about borrowing. For example, banks which have been utilizing the discount facility in an inappropriate manner may be subject to Federal Reserve demands for additional records or officer interviews. The objective, politely phrased, of these contacts is to make sure the bank understands the philosophy behind the discount mechanism. Somewhat more grim is Roosa's comment that "we help a bank decide not to borrow from us." These additional activities involving the expense of time and/or effort on the part of the bank add an imputed transactions cost to the discount rate which makes the relevant discount rate higher than the

---

[41] All of the data for the Fifth District were taken from [80, chapter 4].

[42] For example, the "reeducation" program noted above was in part to make clear that borrowing to gain a tax advantage was an inappropriate use of the discount window.

stated rate.[43] On this view the observed differentials between asset yields and the relevant discount rate would narrow and the profit view would be partly redeemed.

The question remains as to how much surveillance is actually necessary to reinforce this effect. In more recent years, it would seem banks have tended sufficiently to restrict their own borrowings so that Reserve Banks apparently did not often find it necessary to suggest to a bank that it was borrowing inappropriately.[44] In this view we can regard the supply schedule of funds available for borrowing by an individual bank as possessing a kink. Up to what the Fed deems as appropriate the schedule is horizontal but after that point it steadily rises perhaps even becoming vertical.[45] It should be noted that Federal Reserve discouragement is apparently quite effective in limiting borrowing. McKinney, having examined Discount Committee records of the Fifth Federal Reserve District (Richmond), has noted: "In practice, once a banker has been contacted, it is rare for him not to take the action necessary to limit his borrowings to appropriate uses of Federal Reserve credit." [80, p. 114].

A common impression fostered by various writings (both official and unofficial) on the discount mechanism is that the member banks are *in practice* subject to a refusal of any given request for loans. For example, the Board's educational handbook describing the Federal Reserve System notes: "When a member bank applies for accommodation, the Federal Reserve Bank is under no automatic obligation to grant the loan. [111, p. 33]. The truth is that while the Reserve Banks could by statute refuse to make loans requested by member banks, they in fact rarely, if ever, do so. McKinney has observed

"Even if it is felt that the bank is abusing the discount privilege, it has been the practice to make the extension of credit in order not to place the bank in an embarrassing position, and then to call on the bank and ask the management to restrict its borrowing activities to appropriate purposes in the future." [80, p. 113].

We have thus arrived at what appears to be at least a partial reconciliation of the need and profit views and in our specification to which we

---

[43] [39, p. 142]. Bankers are reputed to dislike intensely being reprimanded for requesting inappropriate loans as it comes uncomfortably close to complete role reversal.

[44] The difficulty of detection may also account for this.

[45] There are, of course, dynamic problems with this sort of notion. For example, the place of the kink may change with past borrowing and (perhaps) economic conditions.

now turn we shall be guided by elements reminiscent of both points of view.[46]

Specification and Estimation

For a first approximation to specification of our borrowing equations, we can resort to essentially the same variables we utilized in our previous discussion of excess reserves. The one additional matter we must consider is the measurement of the relative cost upon which the choice between discounting and the liquidation of an asset depends. The demand for funds to satisfy the needs that typically induce banks to resort to the Federal Reserve discount facility is probably relatively insensitive to changes in the interest costs involved. However, the extent to which banks actually turn to the Fed to satisfy these needs rather than rely on other sources may be significantly affected by changes in the discount rate. In particular, the choice between discounting and the liquidation of an asset depends on the relationship between the discount rate and the yield on the asset.[47] Given large blank holdings of U.S. Governments, banks are likely to compare the discount rate with a rate on one of the short-term securities to see if they wish to rely on the Fed for funds.[48] We therefore choose to compare r_d with r_s, the rate on three-month Treasury bills. In particular we utilize the rate differential $r_d - r_s$. In view of our discussion

---

[46] For an explicit attempt to introduce, via a utility function, both profit and need notions see POLAKOFF [96]. For related discussions, see also TURNER [115] and MEIGS [83].

[47] In principle, at least, the relevant comparison is between the discount rate and the expected yield over the period of time for which the funds will be required. That is, the comparison should take account of transactions costs and any capital gains or losses. On this point see SMITH [106, p. 172].

[48] In what follows, we are going to make no explicit allowance for the Federal Funds market as an alternative for securing short-term liquidity. The Federal Funds rate is generally lower than the discount rate, and, in addition, the Federal Funds market can aid a bank to avoid becoming a continuous borrower. However, the Federal Funds market has a number of disadvantages which should be noted. For one, the minimum amount that can be borrowed in this market is one million dollars, while the discounting privilege has the advantage that the exact sum, no matter how small, can be secured to cover a reserve deficit. Furthermore, there is no legal limit in borrowing from the Fed, while there is a prohibition against national banks borrowing an amount greater than their capital stocks from other sources. In addition, the early closing of Eastern markets makes it difficult on occasion for Western banks to secure Federal Funds late on the last day of the reserve computation period. For an elaborate description of this market see [13].

of free reserves, we naturally anticipate that the sign of $r_d - r_s$ will be negative.[49]

Utilizing $r_d - r_s$ as our cost measure and including seasonal dummy variables we obtain:

$$\Delta B^N = 0.011 + 0.07 s_2 + 0.12 s_3 + 0.16 s_4 - 0.266 B^N_{-1} \quad -0.076(r_d - r_s)$$
$$\quad\quad (0.08) \quad (0.09) \quad (0.12) \quad (0.097) \quad\quad\quad (0.087)$$
$$+ 0.092 \Delta CL^N - 0.015 \Delta T^N + 0.059 \Delta D^N - 0.067 \Delta D^*$$
$$(0.032) \quad\quad (0.037) \quad\quad (0.024) \quad\quad (0.013)$$
$$R^2 = 0.646 \quad S_e = 0.146 \quad (2.5)$$

$$\Delta B^C = 0.035 + 0.039 s_2 - 0.031 s_3 + 0.122 s_4 - 0.235 B^C_{-1} - 0.045(r_d - r_s)$$
$$\quad\quad (0.015) \quad (0.020) \quad (0.024) \quad (0.074) \quad\quad (0.014)$$
$$- 0.023 \Delta T^C + 0.016 \Delta D^C - 0.006 \Delta D^* + 0.027 \Delta CL^C$$
$$(0.012) \quad\quad (0.011) \quad\quad (0.002) \quad\quad (0.023)$$
$$R^2 = 0.658 \quad S_e = 0.027 \quad (2.6)$$

Equations (2.5) and (2.6) are similar in several respects. For one, each variable, aside from the seasonals, has a coefficient of the same sign in both equations. The equations also indicate that an expansion of actual demand deposits with potential demand deposits remaining the same would lead to an increase in borrowings.[50]

There are, however, also several differences between (2.5) and (2.6). The cost variable, $(r_d - r_s)$, while yielding a negative coefficient in both equations is statistically significant in only (2.6). Second, the seasonal patterns of the two equations are different with the variables in (2.5) being marginal at best. Third, city banks appear to borrow during periods of increased customer loan demand to the extent of about one-tenth of the increase in demand. Country banks, on the other hand, appear to do so to only a small extent. Finally, it should be noted that an expansion of $3 billion in potential demand deposits would lead to repayment of borrowings of about $200 million on the part of the city banks (within the first

---

[49] POLAKOFF, [96], argues that the phenomenon of member-bank reluctance to borrow requires the partial derivative of borrowing with respect to $(r_d - r_s)$ to change sign as borrowing increases. He suggests measuring this by the inclusion of both linear and quadratic terms in the rate differential. This type of behavior may also result from a Federal Reserve enforced reluctance which introduces a higher implicit discount rate. Some sample experiments with a squared rate differential produced no results of interest.

[50] See above, p. 42.

quarter) but only about \$20 million on the part of the country banks.[51]

Various lagged constraint variables were added to both (2.5) and (2.6) but only the lagged stock of excess reserves for country banks proved to be significant. In addition, we experimented briefly with our reserve requirement variables. While they rarely, if ever, achieved statistical significance, they uniformly yielded negative coefficients. This suggests that increased requirements would tend to reduce borrowings.[52] The following results are fairly typical of those obtained.[53]

$$\Delta B^N = 0.164 - 0.428 B^N_{-1} - 0.226(r_d - r_s) + 0.137 \Delta CL^N - 0.156 RR^N_3$$
$$ (0.082) \quad\quad (0.076) \quad\quad\quad (0.030) \quad\quad\quad (0.090)$$

$$-0.035 \Delta D^* \quad\quad\quad\quad\quad\quad\quad\quad R^2 = 0.602 \quad S_e = 0.155 \quad (2.7)$$
$$(0.008)$$

$$\Delta B^C = 0.152 + 0.025 s_2 - 0.057 s_3 - 0.009 s_4 - 0.317 B^C_{-1} - 0.043(r_d - r_s)$$
$$ (0.163) \quad (0.020) \quad (0.024) \quad (0.086) \quad\quad (0.014)$$

$$0.034 \Delta T^C - 0.006 \Delta D^* - 0.012 RR^C_3 + 0.026 \Delta D^C - 0.170 E^C_{-1}$$
$$-(0.013) \quad\quad (0.002) \quad\quad\quad (0.034) \quad\quad\quad (0.010) \quad\quad\quad (0.081)$$
$$R^2 = 0.676 \quad S_e = 0.026 \quad (2.8)$$

Among other things, equation (2.8) indicates that the higher the stock of excess reserves (by country banks) at the start of the period, the smaller will be the increase in borrowings occasioned by other factors. With respect to the city-bank equation, it should be noted that omitting some of the other explanatory variables produces a more significant interest rate coefficient.

---

[51] Open-market operations, via D^*, play a critical role in determining whether there will be an aggregate need for borrowings. There is, however, no assurance that reserves generated by open-market purchases will find their way to banks in need of funds. In fact, since open-market operations are likely to affect country banks only indirectly this may account for some of the differences noted above. We should also note that there is no positivity constraint built into the borrowing (or excess reserve) equations. Hence, there exists some level of flooding of reserves which would force banks off these equations. This has to be taken into consideration in any simulation of the model.

[52] Within the reserve computation period, of course, an increase in reserve requirements would, *ceteris paribus*, cause an increase in borrowing. Within a quarter, however, we get into the same difficulties already noted in the discussion of excess reserves.

[53] We have omitted a number of variables from (2.7) and (2.8). This is not meant to imply that they are permanently removed from our borrowing equations. Those decisions will only be made after the full model is estimated.

One final variable was introduced in line with our decision that the excess-profits tax cited above had served to create a temporary structural shift in the banking sector, and that the inordinate amount of borrowing (relative to apparent need) of the 1952–1953 period had to be dealt with in a special manner. This was done by simply including a shift variable in the regression which served as a proxy for the excess profits tax. Simply adding this variable (*dp* below) to (2.7) and (2.8) produced the following:

$$\Delta B^N = 0.144 - 0.426 B^N_{-1} - 0.189(r_d - r_s) + 0.129 \Delta CL^N - 0.149 RR^N_3$$
$$\qquad\quad (0.074) \qquad (0.069) \qquad\quad (0.027) \qquad\quad (0.082)$$
$$\quad - 0.034 \Delta D^* + 0.339 dp \qquad R^2 = 0.676 \ \ S_e = 0.140 \ \ DW = 2.54 \quad (2.9)$$
$$\quad\ \ (0.008) \qquad (0.104)$$

$$\Delta B^C = 0.195 + 0.019 s_2 - 0.063 s_3 - 0.016 s_4 - 0.378 B^C_{-1} - 0.039(r_d - r_s)$$
$$\qquad\quad (0.014) \quad (0.017) \quad (0.021) \quad (0.077) \qquad (0.012)$$
$$\quad - 0.039 \Delta T^C - 0.006 \Delta D^* - 0.017 RR^C_3 + 0.022 \Delta D^C - 0.235 E^C_{-1}$$
$$\quad\ \ (0.012) \qquad (0.002) \qquad (0.030) \qquad (0.009) \qquad (0.072)$$
$$\quad + 0.065 dp \qquad\qquad\qquad R^2 = 0.765 \ \ S_e = 0.023 \ \ DW = 2.76 \ \ (2.10)$$
$$\quad\ \ (0.018)$$

As is clear from (2.9) and (2.10) the excess-profits tax variable increased the explanatory power of the equations by a considerable amount.

Our pilot investigation has revealed that the basic form of the model is quite capable of producing satisfactory explanations of borrowing behavior.[54] Since we intend to pass on to structural estimates there is little point at this juncture to examining further refinements.

2.5.4. *Bank Security Holdings*

A Supply Complication

It will be recalled that we have decided to disaggregate bank security holdings into two maturity classes, one of securities maturing in five

---

[54] One respect in which the results may seem somewhat puzzling is the relatively slow speed-of-adjustment implied by all of the borrowing equations. Working with weekly data, Edward Kane and the present author have found that the lag coefficients tend to die off after a few weeks. This seems more in accord with standard notions of money-market adjustments. However, it should be remembered that changes in quarterly data may very well reflect long-run considerations such as changes in monetary policy. If this is the case, a quarterly lag becomes more understandable.

years or less and the other of maturities of over five years. While this distinction seemed desirable from a behavioral point of view, one important complication arises from utilizing these data and we shall have to consider this briefly.

In particular, imagine the following situation. The Treasury issues a security with six years to maturity, some percentage of which is purchased by the banks. Within one year, we will reach a point where the issue will change maturity classes as we have defined them. In view of the distinct lumpiness to Treasury issues, we may find that the movement of our class-of-security variables is dominated by these changes. For all practical purposes, a bank's portfolio will change very little when a security with slightly over five years to maturity becomes one of slightly under. The problem, of course, is simply one of accounting for the changing relative supplies of these two types of security. In order to do this we have added to our proposed list of explanatory variables two additional variables, $\Delta \bar{S}$ and $\Delta \bar{O}$, which measure the change in the total supply outstanding in these two categories.[55]

Equation Estimates

Using these two variables, we estimated the following equations for short-term security holdings:[56]

$$\Delta S^N = 1.091 - 0.058s_2 + 0.343s_3 + 0.120s_4 - 0.100S^N_{-1} + 0.152\Delta\bar{S} - 0.275\Delta\bar{O}$$
$$\qquad (0.678) \quad (0.786) \quad (1.018) \quad (0.050) \quad\;\; (0.071) \quad (0.086)$$
$$\quad + 0.159\Delta D^N + 0.958\Delta T^N - 0.492\Delta CL^N + 0.156\Delta D^* - 173.18RR^N_2$$
$$\quad (0.183) \qquad (0.285) \qquad (0.259) \qquad (0.081) \qquad (62.36)$$
$$R^2 = 0.723 \quad S_e = 1.11 \quad (2.11)$$

---

[55] The variables are for all marketable and convertible direct public securities, excluding those held by Federal agencies and trust funds and the Federal Reserve Banks. The data for the period prior to 1960 were taken from OKUN [91], who used them, as we shall below, as explanatory variables in a term structure equation. For 1960 on, the data were taken from the Federal Reserve Bulletin.

[56] No lagged flow variables, other than ΔD^*_{-1} which appears above, added anything to (2.11) and (2.12).

$$\Delta S^C = 0.865 + 0.244s_2 + 0.690s_3 + 0.512s_4 - 0.120S^C_{-1} + 0.120\Delta\bar{S} - 0.095\Delta\bar{O}$$
$$(0.416) \quad (0.455) \quad (0.542) \quad (0.049) \quad\quad (0.044) \quad\quad (0.050)$$
$$- 0.108\Delta D^C + 1.219\Delta T^C + 0.099\Delta CL^C + 0.079\Delta D^* - 0.655RR^C_2$$
$$(0.225) \quad\quad (0.361) \quad\quad (0.508) \quad\quad (0.043) \quad\quad (0.870)$$
$$+ 0.076\Delta D^*_{-1} \quad\quad\quad\quad\quad\quad\quad R^2 = 0.714 \quad S_e = 0.597 \quad (2.12)$$
$$(0.044)$$

The equations bear out the importance of the two supply variables, at least for short-term securities. In addition they reveal a number of interesting aspects of bank behavior. First, time-deposit inflows and inflows of reserves induced by the monetary authorities both produce an increase in bank holdings of short-term securities. Second, city banks appear, in part, to finance the commercial loans they make by selling short-term securities. Third, the reserve-requirement variable shows up strongly for the city bank class but not for country banks. For the former, (2.11) says that a one percentage point decrease in reserve requirements (e.g. from 17% to 16%) will increase bank holdings of securities in the same quarter by $1.7 billion. The inconsequential nature of the reserve-requirement variable in (2.12) suggests that much of the explanatory power of the comparable variable in (2.11) may result from changes in RR^N_2 due to deposit shifts between reserve city and central reserve city.[57]

We have thus far omitted cost considerations from our specification of the short-term security equation. However, *ceteris paribus*, we would expect that short-term securities holdings would be higher, the higher the yield on them and lower, the higher the yields on alternative asset choices. In other words, just as there was an opportunity cost associated with the holding of excess reserves (instead of securities) there is a cost associated with holding short-term securities (instead of higher-yielding loans, municipals, etc.). Since we have adopted a category of 0–5 years it would appear that either the bill rate or the rate on government securities of three-to-five year maturity might appropriately approximate the yield on this category. Our earlier discussion suggested that banks making security decisions look not only at current rates but also at prospects for capital gains. This requires us to construct a variable which measures expected capital losses or gains. One typical approach used in this context is to

---

[57] It will be recalled that our city class is a combination of central reserve city and reserve city and that for most of the period reserve requirements for these two classes were not the same.

posit that investors have in mind some normal rate of interest toward which actual rates are expected to move. Thus, when current rates are above this normal rate, investors expect interest rates to fall (anticipate capital gains). To implement this, we might employ

$$r_3' = \frac{\sum\limits_{i=1}^{n} (r_3)_{-i}}{n}$$

the average of rates over the last n periods as our estimate of the "normal" rate. To make this into a measure of expected capital gains, we could take

$$r_3/r_3' \quad \text{or} \quad r_3 - r_3' \,.$$

Duesenberry has criticized this view, pointing out that the argument could just as easily be turned around: "In many fields trend projection appears to be the dominant influence on expectations. It would not, therefore, be surprising if it turned out that a rise in rates led to an expectation of a further rise and vice versa." [32, p. 318]. On the basis of this argument, it has been suggested that both the relation of the current to a "normal" rate and the relationship of the current to more recent rates might affect expectations of capital gains [29, p. 38]. In addition, the coefficient of the second type of variable should yield a negative sign in contrast to the coefficient of the more traditional type of expectations variable. Variables of both variety can be constructed by varying n in the definition of r_3' above with a larger n corresponding to the "normal" rate. With this in mind, we constructed the following set of variables:

$$\bar{r}_3(L,n) = r_3 - r_3'(n)$$

$$\bar{r}_3(R,n) = \frac{r_3}{r_3'(n)}$$

for $n = 5$, 10, 15 quarters. The notation $r_3'(n)$ simply indicates the dependence of the average rate on n and the L and R symbols are mnemonics for linear and ratio respectively.[58] In addition to these "own" security rates, we added a measure of the return from loans to our security equations. We denote by r_e' the short-term loan rate as reported by the Federal Reserve and by r_e'' a weighted average rate.

---

[58] The same variables were also constructed for the long-term government rate, r_{10}. They are denoted by $\bar{r}_{10}(L,n)$ and $\bar{r}_{10}(R,n)$.

On the whole, the interest rate effects found for the short-term security equations were not terribly strong. The loan rates worked satisfactorily and the expectations variables while producing coefficients with the anticipated signs (and/or sign patterns) never attained statistical significance. Some typical results are as follows:

$$\Delta S^N = 0.715 + 1.12s_2 + 1.27s_3 + 1.48s_4 - 0.113S^N_{-1} + 0.179\Delta\bar{S} - 0.263\Delta\bar{O}$$
$$\qquad\quad (0.53)\quad (0.62)\quad (0.66)\quad (0.050)\qquad (0.075)\qquad (0.086)$$
$$+ 0.938\Delta T^N - 0.332\Delta CL^N - 1.902RR^N_3 - 3.829\Delta r''_e$$
$$(0.278)\qquad (0.256)\qquad\quad (0.799)\qquad\quad (1.601)$$
$$R^2 = 0.735 \;\; S_e = 1.102 \;\; DW = 2.38 \quad (2.13)$$

$$\Delta S^C = 1.207 - 0.15s_2 + 0.56s_3 + 0.32s_4 - 0.124S^C_{-1} + 0.119\Delta\bar{S} - 0.099\Delta\bar{O}$$
$$\qquad\quad (0.31)\quad (0.34)\quad (0.42)\quad (0.047)\qquad (0.040)\qquad (0.044)$$
$$+ 1.178\Delta T^C - 1.033\Delta r'_e + 0.063\Delta D^*$$
$$(0.376)\qquad (0.727)\qquad (0.044)$$
$$R^2 = 0.715 \;\; S_e = 0.578 \;\; DW = 2.38 \quad (2.14)$$

$$\Delta S^C = 0.936 + 0.20s_2 + 0.53s_3 + 0.31s_4 - 0.115S^C_{-1} + 0.132\Delta\bar{S} - 0.090\Delta\bar{O}$$
$$\qquad\quad (0.40)\quad (0.34)\quad (0.42)\quad (0.049)\qquad (0.048)\qquad (0.052)$$
$$+ 1.102\Delta T^C + 0.075\bar{r}_3(L,10) - 0.214\bar{r}_3(L,5) - 0.62RR^C_2$$
$$(0.402)\qquad (0.32)\qquad\qquad (0.36)\qquad\qquad (0.86)$$
$$+ 0.065\Delta D^* + 0.070\Delta D^*_{-1} \qquad\qquad R^2 = 0.716 \;\; S_e = 0.590 \quad (2.15)$$
$$(0.047)\qquad (0.044)$$

Without commenting on these results, we present analogous results for long-term securities.

$$\Delta O^N = 1.309 + 0.56s_2 + 0.39s_3 + 0.37s_4 - 0.042O^N_{-1} - 0.103\Delta\bar{S} + 0.202\Delta\bar{O}$$
$$\qquad\quad (0.31)\quad (0.35)\quad (0.46)\quad (0.030)\qquad (0.037)\qquad (0.039)$$
$$+ 0.132\Delta D^N - 0.219\Delta T^N - 0.205\Delta CL^N - 0.016\Delta D^* - 0.216r''_e$$
$$(0.087)\qquad (0.137)\qquad (0.112)\qquad (0.037)\qquad (0.156)$$
$$R^2 = 0.836 \;\; S_e = 0.507 \quad (2.16)$$

$$\Delta O^C = 0.245 + 0.32s_2 + 0.04s_3 + 0.11s_4 - 0.028O^C_{-1} - 0.085\Delta\bar{S} + 0.136\Delta\bar{O}$$
$$\quad\quad (0.19)\quad (0.25)\quad (0.30)\quad (0.026)\quad\quad (0.023)\quad\quad (0.026)$$
$$\quad + 0.221\Delta D^C - 0.127\Delta T^C - 0.413\Delta CL^C - 0.007\Delta D^*$$
$$\quad (0.123)\quad\quad (0.189)\quad\quad (0.364)\quad\quad (0.024)$$
$$R^2 = 0.847 \quad S_e = 0.332 \quad (2.17)$$

Adding lagged values of flows and/or certain stocks to (2.16) and (2.17) produced no significant changes. Re-estimating (2.16), (2.17) and adding a long-term bond rate to the equations produced the following:

$$\Delta O^N = 0.952 + 0.47s_2 + 0.40s_3 + 0.35s_4 - 0.025O^N_{-1} - 0.108\Delta\bar{S}$$
$$\quad\quad (0.30)\quad (0.36)\quad (0.46)\quad (0.028)\quad\quad (0.041)$$
$$\quad + 0.194\Delta\bar{O} + 0.101\Delta D^N - 0.152\Delta CL^N - 0.217r'_e + 0.171\bar{r}_{10}(L,5)$$
$$\quad (0.040)\quad\quad (0.082)\quad\quad (0.121)\quad\quad (0.146)\quad (0.48)$$
$$R^2 = 0.829, \quad S_e = 0.51 \quad DW = 1.99 \quad (2.18)$$

$$\Delta O^C = 0.559 + 0.26s_2 + 0.18s_3 + 0.25s_4 - 0.030O^C_{-1} - 0.073\Delta\bar{S}$$
$$\quad\quad (0.16)\quad (0.22)\quad (0.25)\quad (0.025)\quad\quad (0.023)$$
$$\quad + 0.135\Delta\bar{O} + 0.076\Delta D^C - 0.132r'_e + 0.118(r_{10} - r_s)$$
$$\quad (0.024)\quad\quad (0.114)\quad\quad (0.083)\quad (0.103)$$
$$R^2 = 0.857 \quad S_e = 0.320 \quad DW = 2.43 \quad (2.19)$$

We also attempted to include a municipal-bond rate in one of the city-bank equations. This produced

$$\Delta O^N = 0.168 + 0.33s_2 + 0.30s_3 + 0.26s_4 - 0.007O^N_{-1} - 0.117\Delta\bar{S} + 0.187\Delta\bar{O}$$
$$\quad\quad (0.30)\quad (0.37)\quad (0.46)\quad (0.024)\quad\quad (0.037)\quad\quad (0.039)$$
$$\quad + 0.136\Delta D^N + 0.331\bar{r}_{10}(R,15) - 0.096r_m - 0.151\Delta CL^N$$
$$\quad (0.081)\quad\quad (1.12)\quad\quad\quad\quad (0.077)\quad (0.108)$$
$$R^2 = 0.824 \quad S_e = 0.524 \quad (2.20)$$

In summary, the above equations do a reasonable job of explaining bank holdings of securities of both maturities. While supply considerations prove extremely important, certain deposit flows and the loan out-flow contribute to the explanation. Interest rate performance, on the other hand, is somewhat disappointing. Although the various interest rate variables produce coefficients which are virtually always of the right sign, they rarely achieve statistical significance. The loan rates (either appears to work) are the most consistent interest variables.

There are several possible ways to account for the failure of interest rates in our security equations. At this juncture we merely note them in passing. First, we may have specification problems.[59] Second, interest inelasticity may be due to the fact that we have estimated by direct least-squares rather than by the more appropriate technique of two-stage least-squares. For both of these reasons, we postpone further discussion until we have estimated the complete model (chapter 5). We turn instead to an analysis of bank holdings of municipal securities.

2.5.5. *Bank Holdings of Municipal Securities*

General Discussion

The postwar growth of public construction, the increased volume of services, and the accommodation of a geographically shifting population have all contributed to the marked increase in spending by state and local governments.[60] The financing of these expenditures has considerably increased the supply of municipal securities.[61] Moreover, these securities have now become an important component of bank portfolios. Commercial banks rank just behind individuals as demanders of municipals, holding about one-quarter of the outstanding securities. In view of the importance of municipals as a bank asset, we pause to describe some of the relevant characteristics of this type of security.

The major feature of municipals is their federal tax exemption. The extent to which a bank finds it desirable to buy tax-exempts naturally varies with its marginal tax rate. For example, a municipal bond yielding 3% will, with a marginal tax rate of 30% be equivalent to a yield of 4.3%, and with a marginal rate of 52% yield 6.25%. In addition, municipals are generally available in serial issues which means that most banks can find

---

[59] We mention one in particular which we shall examine below. Namely, as specified' the equations are not homogeneous of degree one in dollar values. It has been suggested elsewhere [29], that this is a reasonable assumption to impose on bank portfolio equations. Making this assumption would introduce an interest rate variable multiplied by a dollar value. This could make a considerable difference in our findings.

[60] This increase in expenditure is partly accounted for by the fact that public construction costs have increased faster than the general price level.

[61] State and local obligations went from $21.7 billion in 1946 to $81.3 billion in 1962.

a maturity of their choice. Banks can also underwrite municipal securities which further add to their attractiveness. Finally, a bank may choose to hold local municipals as a sign of support for the region in which it is situated. This outward support may often be necessary if the bank wishes to obtain public funds as deposits. This, of course, implies a nonrate benefit can be obtained by holding municipals.

Despite these attractive features municipals retain a number of undesirable aspects. First, they vary enormously in quality. As in the case of a loan account, a bank may have to maintain a careful watch on the credit worthiness of the borrower.[62] Second, because of something akin to a customer relationship which exists between a bank and the local government, a bank may be pressured into buying more than it wants of a lower-quality municipal.[63]

Since municipals possess a relatively undeveloped secondary market, typically they provide a bank with little or no liquidity. The difference between bid and asked prices is substantial—often as much as a year's interest. As a result banks tend to hold tax-exempts until final maturity [101, p. 403].

On balance, at least in recent years, municipals have generally yielded after-tax-income above that available from fully-taxed securities, and banks appear to have found tax-exempts an increasingly attractive asset choice.

Equation Estimates
Utilizing our standard formulation and introducing the rate on municipals, r_m, we have:

$$\Delta MUN^N = -0.162 - 0.446s_2 - 0.190s_3 - 0.551s_4 - 0.016MUN^N_{-1}$$
$$\qquad\qquad (0.098) \quad (0.103) \quad (0.133) \quad (0.024)$$
$$+ 0.170\Delta T^N + 0.044\Delta D^N + 0.041r_m + 0.030\Delta CL^N - 0.001\Delta D^*$$
$$(0.052) \qquad (0.028) \qquad (0.027) \quad (0.013) \qquad (0.013)$$
$$+ 0.141\Delta T^N_{-1} + 0.021S^N_{-1} \qquad\qquad R^2 = 0.739 \quad S_e = 0.171 \quad (2.21)$$
$$(0.050) \qquad (0.008)$$

---

[62] The extent of quality variability can be seen by the following. The net interest cost of 145 new issues sold in May 1958 ranged from 2.09% to 4.74%.

[63] To the extent, of course, that the bank then becomes a repository for public funds it will get additional information about future possible deteriorations in quality.

$$\Delta M U N^C = 0.132 - 0.055 s_2 - 0.029 s_3 - 0.054 s_4 - 0.020 M U N^C_{-1} + 0.185 \Delta T^C$$
$$\qquad (0.027) \quad (0.023) \quad (0.042) \quad (0.009) \qquad\qquad (0.033)$$
$$+ 0.036 \Delta D^C - 0.007 r_m + 0.056 \Delta C L^C - 0.004 \Delta D^* + 0.086 \Delta T^C_{-1}$$
$$(0.019) \qquad (0.007) \quad (0.046) \qquad\quad (0.003) \qquad\quad (0.030)$$
$$R^2 = 0.674 \quad S_e = 0.046 \quad (2.22)$$

In both (2.21) and (2.22), both current *and* lagged time deposit flows play a most important role in explaining bank holdings of municipals. In addition, the city-bank equation portrays a response (appropriately positive) to the lagged stock of short-term government securities. This is consistent with the following chain of events. The banks, receiving an inflow of funds put them first into short-term securities while they decide if the inflows are permanent and if so what to do with them. Part of these funds, if permanent, will be used to purchase municipals and hence the positive sign. This lagged-security variable proved to be of little consequence in the country-bank equation, although to keep the argument symmetric, lagged excess reserves might have been a more appropriate variable to try.

On the other hand, lagged demand deposits did not show up in either equation although lagged potential demand deposits did. Finally, we added r'_e and r''_e individually to both equations. The results, which support the expected negative influence of loan rates on municipals, are not altogether satisfactory. Somehow, as shown below, the loan rate typically caused the speed-of-adjustment coefficient to change sign.

$$\Delta M U N^N = -0.367 - 0.203 s_2 - 0.012 s_3 - 0.277 s_4 - 0.009 M U N^N_{-1}$$
$$\qquad\qquad (0.080) \quad (0.078) \quad (0.076) \quad (0.023)$$
$$+ 0.161 \Delta T^N + 0.136 \Delta T^N_{-1} + 0.023 \Delta D^*_{-1} + 0.031 r_m + 0.024 S^N_{-1}$$
$$(0.045) \qquad (0.048) \qquad\quad (0.012) \qquad\quad (0.026) \quad (0.007)$$
$$R^2 = 0.747 \quad S_e = 0.169 \quad (2.23)$$

$$\Delta M U N^N = -0.032 - 0.218 s_2 + 0.007 s_3 - 0.284 s_4 + 0.035 M U N^N_{-1}$$
$$\qquad\qquad (0.080) \quad (0.076) \quad (0.074) \quad (0.031)$$
$$+ 0.167 \Delta T^N + 0.119 \Delta T^N_{-1} + 0.021 \Delta D^*_{-1} + 0.048 r_m + 0.021 S^N_{-1}$$
$$(0.044) \qquad (0.048) \qquad\quad (0.012) \qquad\quad (0.026) \quad (0.007)$$
$$- 0.124 r''_e \qquad\qquad R^2 = 0.765 \quad S_e = 0.163 \quad DW = 2.19 \quad (2.24)$$
$$(0.063)$$

$$\Delta MUN^C = 0.100 - 0.026s_2 - 0.052s_3 - 0.095s_4 - 0.012MUN^C_{-1} + 0.153\Delta T^C$$
$$\qquad\quad (0.028) \quad (0.028) \quad (0.034) \quad (0.007) \qquad\qquad (0.028)$$

$$+ 0.056\Delta D^C + 0.085\Delta T^C_{-1} + 0.006\Delta D^*_{-1}$$
$$(0.016) \qquad (0.029) \qquad (0.003)$$

$$R^2 = 0.699 \quad S_e = 0.044 \quad (2.25)$$

$$\Delta MUN^C = 0.263 - 0.025s_2 - 0.026s_3 - 0.061s_4 + 0.029MUN^C_{-1} + 0.147\Delta T^C$$
$$\qquad\quad (0.028) \quad (0.028) \quad (0.034) \quad (0.007) \qquad\qquad (0.025)$$

$$+ 0.033\Delta D^C + 0.078\Delta T^C_{-1} + 0.004\Delta D^*_{-1} - 0.084r'_e$$
$$(0.016) \qquad (0.026) \qquad (0.003) \qquad (0.026)$$

$$R^2 = 0.756 \quad S_e = 0.040 \quad DW = 1.68 \quad (2.26)$$

On the whole, the equations perform satisfactorily. Deposit flow variables of various types provide the bulk of the explanation. One final point should be mentioned. In view of the importance of the supply variables in the government security equations, it would seem natural to include a municipal supply variable in the above equation. However, the matter is not easily accomplished. We have already noted the extremely wide divergence of quality among different types of municipals. This means that, in contrast to the straightforward supply series which existed for governments, there is no easy way to characterize the supply of municipals of relevant quality for inclusion in bank portfolios.[64] It is for this reason that no supply variable was utilized.[65]

2.5.6. Supply of Commercial Loans

The Adequacy of the Loan Rate
It will be recalled that in our earlier analysis we designated the loan rate to be the bank's decision parameter. Still there are many ways this parameter could enter a supply formulation. Let us first consider the simplest form of supply mechanism. Namely, the rate on commercial loans is

---

[64] The actual quality composition of bank municipal holdings is fairly difficult to characterize. The American Bankers Association states that banks restrict themselves to the upper end of the quality spectrum but this is not a very useful delineation. ROBINSON [101] feels as we do, that the available evidence is not sufficient to answer the question.

[65] In the final chapter some attempts are made to utilize an aggregate Flow-of-Funds series on changes in municipals outstanding.

functionally related to the demand for these loans and the capacity (measured somehow) of the banking system to meet these loan requests. Such a supply function is consistent with the traditional view of the operation of monetary policy, described by the following sequence of events. In the first instance, open-market sales decrease the price of government securities, inducing asset-holders to substitute securities for money in their portfolios. In consequence, bank liquidity declines. This is partly reflected in the reduction of bank reserves. As a result of these operations, interest rates on private loans increase and the supply of private credit is reduced. In this way, a brake is applied to total expenditures in the economy.

Under the traditional view, the success of monetary policy in curtailing expenditures depended critically on the interest elasticity of various types of expenditures. As economists became increasingly suspect of the strength of the expenditure-interest rate link, the critics of monetary policy gained ammunition with which to attack the supposed effectiveness of traditional monetary techniques. In the last fifteen years, there has developed a new theory (to a significant extent accomplished by individuals connected with the Federal Reserve System) designed to reestablish monetary policy as an acceptable discretionary stabilization device.

The new theory sidesteps the interest elasticity issue. It holds that monetary policy transmits its effects as much by changes in the availability of credit as by changes in interest rates. This "availability doctrine" rests on the dual nature of loan terms: one must consider both the price and non-price aspects of loan decisions. Non-price aspects include credit worthiness, the maturity of the loan, the size of the loan and the guarantees associated with the loan. Stiffer credit standards and/or explicit guarantees for repayment clearly reduce the default risk of any loan, making it more attractive to a bank. Similarly, shorter maturities reduce further uncertainties concerning a particular loan. In addition, a reduced average loan size enables a bank to increase the diversification of its loan portfolio and further reduce risk. What is important for the standard supply formulation is that the price (loan rate) should reflect changing market conditions. To the extent that banks rely on non-price means of affecting loan demand, the observed market rate of interest may be an inadequate indicator of market forces. For example, in times of credit tightness when stiffer credit standards are introduced at unchanged explicit interest rates, this is, in effect, an implicit rate increase. This is so since increasing safety requirements for loans at given interest rates means that loans of a given risk are charged a higher interest rate than before.

It is natural to ask why in times of credit tightness lenders employ non-price rationing techniques rather than resorting to interest rate increases which perform the function automatically. In part, banks may feel that interest rate increases will antagonize customers and be detrimental to long-run account relationships. On the other side, of course, they may feel that the relationship will not be endangered if they scale down the size of loan application or shorten the proposed maturity but continue to meet any urgent need for funds.[66] If market responses are due to a varying mix of the change in rates and the rigidity of non-price limitations, we will mis-specify our system by relying on the loan rate alone. Unfortunately, it is impossible to deal with this matter empirically as there is no satisfactory quantitative estimate of the degree of credit rationing. We must simply rely on the loan rate.

This may not be as restrictive as it first seems. While loan rates are sticky, they do fluctuate and, in fact, do appear to respond to cyclical pressures. P. Samuelson and W. Smith have both argued that the extra stringency of credit rationing immediately after a tightening of credit policy is a temporary phenomenon. After a judicious interval of time, banks will, as Samuelson has stated: ". . . do what any normal prudent commercial-minded man would do: namely, if a thing is in short supply he will gradually raise the interest charges on it, and let the higher prices help him do the rationing."[67] In addition it has recently been asserted: "Pressure of demand on the capacity to meet loan requests causes bankers to welcome a rise in lending rates to ration out the available supply of bank credit to favored borrowers." [20, p. 3].

Thus, we see that the absence of measures of credit availability does not preclude investigation of a supply function for commercial loans. On the other hand, it *does* suggest that there may be lags in the response of the loan rate to demand pressures.

There are several possible data sources from which we could obtain a loan rate series. One of the most commonly used and one which does appear rather sticky is the bank rate on short-term business loans reported for nineteen large cities in the Federal Reserve Bulletin. A second data source is a series constructed by Frank de Leeuw which is weighted-

---

[66] For a formal justification of this position see KANE and MALKIEL [67].

[67] Samuelson quoted in [7, p, 33].

average private security rate.[68] The Federal Reserve rate is a component of this rate but there are other components as well. Of the two the averaged rate appears to be more cyclically sensitive. In view of this greater cyclical variation, the second rate may more accurately reflect the cyclical variations in the entire set of loan terms. It should also be noted that data problems preclude the estimation of country and city supply equations separately.

Specification of the Supply Function

As in the case of portfolio assets, banks are assumed to have a desired level of loan rates. This level depends both on their ability to lend and on the level of various market interest rates. In contradistinction to the other portfolio equations of this chapter, the setting of the loan rate is not subject to the usual flow constraints. Moreover, in view of our earlier discussion of the customer relationship, we shall regard the banks as only partially adjusting the loan rate to its desired level. Hence, quarterly changes in the loan rate will be related to the previous quarter's rate as well. In order to specify the desired level of loan rates, it is necessary to examine the relationship between the loan rate and money-market rates generally.

One example of a linkage between the loan and open-money markets is changes of prime rates, occasioned by changes in open-market money rates. Because most prime borrowers have access to the commercial-paper market, banks must consider their rates relative to, at least, this alternative.[69] Moreover there is an even more fundamental relationship between open-money markets and commercial-loan markets.

With respect to this more basic link, D. Alhadeff has noted:

> "The significance of the open market inheres not in its size, however, but in its marginal nature and in the high sensitivity which that marginal nature implies. The open market simply *measures* the broad forces of supply and demand for short-term funds in the entire country. The margin, in this view, is analogous to the pressure gauge on a boiler." [2, p. 134].

Thus, it is the marginal nature of the open market, the fact that it is the repository for exclusively surplus funds, which creates an essential link

---

[68] See [29], data appendix, for a discussion of the construction of the rate.

[69] Of course, the strength of this link is limited by the fact that, to some extent, the commercial-paper market and loans at commercial banks serve different types of customers.

between the loan rate and other money-market rates. Since the most important submarket of the money market is the Treasury bill market, we follow Alhadeff in using the bill rate to represent the complex of open-market rates.

Besides measuring supply and demand pressures, this rate measures the return on competing short-term assets which are available to the commercial banks. Thus, rate changes in the Treasury bill market are an example of both a direct and indirect influence of the bill market on the commercial-loan market. With respect to the direct influence, bill and loan markets are competing uses of bank funds, which means that bill-market transactions will influence the loan rate. The indirect influence works through effects of changes in the bill rate on expectations.

This suggests that the change in the bill rate would be a suitable explanatory variable. Because open-money markets may be more sensitive to changes in conditions than the commercial-loan markets and reserve pressures may be felt first in the bill market (i.e., only with a lag in the loan market), we ought to experiment with $(\Delta r_s)_{-1}$ the lagged change in the bill rate as well as with the current value.

Changes in the bill rate are only one way in which the effect of interest rate expectations can be introduced. We have already utilized in our security equations several variables designed to capture this effect. It only seems natural to include one or more of these variables here as well. The presumption is that banks would raise their rates more if market rates have been rising recently. Finally, we take as a measure of the banks' ability or capacity to lend, the loan-deposit ratio which we denote by L^*. As the loan-deposit ratio rises we anticipate that banks gradually increase the price of loans.

Equation Estimates

For both the short-term loan rate (r'_e) and the weighted-average rate (r''_e) results appear below.

$$\Delta r'_e = 0.097 - 0.260(r'_e)_{-1} + 0.245\bar{r}_{10}(L,15) + 2.603L^* + 0.068\Delta r_s$$
$$\qquad (0.082) \qquad (0.060) \qquad\qquad (0.973) \quad (0.033)$$
$$R^2 = 0.506 \quad S_e = 0.099 \quad (2.27)$$

$$\Delta r''_e = 0.240 - 0.249(r''_e)_{-1} + 0.358\bar{r}_{10}(L,15) + 2.251L^* + 0.098\Delta r_s$$
$$\qquad (0.049) \qquad (0.043) \qquad\qquad (0.550) \quad (0.023)$$
$$R^2 = 0.782 \quad S_e = 0.067 \quad (2.28)$$

In keeping with our discussion, we added the lagged change in the bill rate to both equations. The results reported below include seasonal dummy variables in the second equation, (2.30).

$$\Delta r_e' = 0.083 - 0.232(r_e')_{-1} + 0.196\bar{r}_{10}(L,15) + 2.357L^* + 0.059\Delta r_s$$
$$\quad\quad (0.077) \quad\quad (0.059) \quad\quad\quad (0.913) \quad (0.031)$$
$$+ 0.080(\Delta r_s)_{-1} \quad\quad\quad\quad\quad\quad R^2 = 0.569 \;\; S_e = 0.092 \quad (2.29)$$
$$\quad (0.030)$$

$$\Delta r_e'' = 0.180 - 0.218(r_e'')_{-1} + 0.313\bar{r}_{10}(L,15) + 1.948L^* + 0.083\Delta r_s$$
$$\quad\quad (0.046) \quad\quad (0.042) \quad\quad\quad (0.522) \quad (0.024)$$
$$+ 0.065(\Delta r_s)_{-1} + 0.090s_2 + 0.043s_3 + 0.025s_4$$
$$\quad (0.024) \quad\quad\quad (0.028) \quad (0.030) \quad (0.027)$$
$$R^2 = 0.820 \;\; S_e = 0.061 \;\; DW = 2.26 \quad (2.30)$$

For both of the rates, these results accord with our *a priori* analysis. First, changes in the loan rate do appear to be explained by a partial adjustment mechanism with a fairly slow speed of adjustment. Secondly, increases in the Treasury bill rate (both current and lagged) are transmitted to the loan market and cause increases in the loan rate. For example, (2.30) says a once-and-for-all increase of one percentage point in the bill rate will increase the loan rate by about one-tenth of a percentage point in the same quarter and about four-tenths of a percentage point in the long run. The relatively slow speed of adjustment indicates, however, that the effect will be drawn out over a number of quarters.

Thirdly, our expectation variable behaves in the way in which we predicted. That is, when interest rates (on long-term government securities in this instance) have been rising recently banks will increase their loan rates by greater amounts. Fourthly, banks definitely respond to increased demand for loans (a higher L^*) be raising their loan rates. Equation (2.30) says, for example, that in the long run an increase of the share of loans in deposits of 10% (a rise in L^* of 0.1) will cause about a one percentage point increase in the loan rate. Again, however, the slow speed of adjustment suggests this increase would be spread out over a number of quarters.[70] Finally, the equations indicate a mild seasonal

[70] Our discussion suggested that both the current L^* and lagged values L^* might be relevant. While we have not included lagged values here they will be utilized when we report our two-stage least-squares estimations.

pattern in the weighted-average rate. None was observed, however, for r'_e.

In addition to this set of variables, we attempted to determine if we could detect a *direct* effect of monetary policy on the loan rate. In particular, we included potential deposit and reserve requirement variables in the above equations anticipating that monetary ease (associated with an increase in potential deposits or a reduction in reserve requirements) would tend to reduce the loan rate. These results were not borne out for r''_e but they were for r'_e as equation (2.31) reveals.[71]

$$\Delta r'_e = 0.108 - 0.184(r'_e)_{-1} + 0.183\bar{r}_{10}(L,15) + 1.777L^* + 0.064\Delta r_s$$
$$\quad\quad (0.081) \quad\quad (0.058) \quad\quad\quad (0.953) \quad (0.031)$$
$$+ 0.069(\Delta r_s)_{-1} + 0.069RR_3^N - 0.007\Delta D^*$$
$$(0.030) \quad\quad (0.056) \quad\quad (0.004)$$
$$R^2 = 0.591 \quad S_e = 0.090 \quad DW = 1.72 \quad (2.31)$$

Finally, as to the choice between the two rates, it is clear that we explain a larger part of the variation in the more-cyclical weighted rate. This is not surprising in view of the relative stickiness of the other rate. Aside from R^2, however, both rates would seem to lead to eminently satisfactory results. Any final decision will have to be made on the basis of which proves to be more satisfactory in the other equations of the model. Once again, we reserve judgment until later.

2.6. Summary

We have completed preliminary specification and estimation of the bank portfolio equations. On the whole, the results are in accord with the theoretical relationships described at the outset. Because these equations neglect simultaneity we refrain from further discussion of these results at this point. In the next chapter, we investigate the public demand side of the monetary sector.

[71] For r''_e the standard errors proved to be many times the coefficients of these variables although they did typically obtain the correct signs. It should also be noted that the variables introduced into this all-bank equation actually refer to the city measures for these variables. However, the loan rate as reported by the Federal Reserve represents an average of nineteen large cities, and it seems appropriate to attempt to maintain homogeneity by using the city measures. This is further supported by the fact that the larger banks, which are naturally located in the major non-country financial and market-areas, account for the bulk of the commercial and industrial loans

Appendix

We have already discussed, in section 2.2.1 above, the sources of uncertainty facing a bank. Two of these sources are deposit variability and loan demand. When a bank grants a loan it simultaneously creates a demand deposit. In general loan-induced deposits are volatile deposits. This means that a bank can only count on retaining some fraction of deposits generated in this way. Given this last point, it can be demonstrated quite simply that increasing loans serves to increase the chance of failing to meet the reserve test.

From a consolidated bank balance sheet, we can write

Deposits + Other Liabilities = Total Reserves + Loans + Investments

or
$$D + OL = R^T + L + I .$$

Total reserves is the sum of required (R^R) and excess reserves (E) while required reserves is obtained by multiplying the reserve requirement by the level of deposits.[72] We thus have

$$R^T = R^R + E$$

and
$$R^R = kD .$$

Substituting into the balance sheet identity yields

$$(1 - k)D + OL - L - I = E .$$

The volume of deposits can, of course, be controlled to some extent from within by an individual bank. In part, D depends on the overall asset structure of the bank. In particular, when a bank makes a loan to a customer, it simply credits his account, and hence D varies with the volume of loans.

The extent to which a bank can expect to retain loan-created deposits depends on several factors including its size and location. Let $D_L = \varrho(L)$, known as the deposit retention curve, represent the deposit level corresponding to a given volume of loans. Since a bank will retain some fraction of its loan-created deposits, we have that $0 \le \varrho'(L) \le 1$. Let us now introduce uncertainty into the example. Tobin has noted

"The consequence of deposit withdrawals, against which the bank protects itself by excess reserves, is not the disaster of insolvency but the additional cost, including perhaps inconvenience and damage to

---

[72] We are abstracting from bank classes and time deposits.

prestige, involved in meeting the reserve test. Given these costs, uncertainty about the future level of deposits will lead to a lower volume of lending and a higher volume of reserves than (the) profit maximization." [114, chapter 9, p. 16].

Of course, the presence of uncertainty means that for each L we have a probability distribution of D_L. To include this case, we write $D_L = \varrho(L) + x$ where x is a random variable with mean zero. There may, in fact, be additional influences which will tend to increase or decrease deposits over time but which are not related to asset holdings. Let A represent the effects on the expected level of deposits of nonrandom influences other than L. Then we can write deposits as

$$D = A + \varrho(L) + x .$$

Substituting this for D above yields

$$E = (1-k)[A + \varrho(L) + x] + OL - L - I ,$$

where everything but L and E are given. Now, the probability of E being less than zero is equal to the probability of x being less than Z where

$$Z = -[A + \varrho(L)] + \frac{L + I - OL}{1-k} .$$

More precisely $\Pr(E \leq 0) = \Pr(x \leq Z) = F(Z)$ where F is the cumulative distribution of x. If $x > Z$ the bank has positive excess reserves and if $x < Z$ the bank has a negative net reserve position. We have

$$\frac{\partial Z}{\partial L} = \frac{1}{1-k} - \varrho'(L)$$

but since $0 < k < 1$ and $0 \leq \varrho'(L) \leq 1$ we have that

$$\frac{\partial Z}{\partial L} > 0 .$$

Thus, as a bank expands its loans, the increase in leakage of loan-created deposits raises the probability of having a negative reserve position. As Tobin has expressed it,

"Every increase in loans thus increases the probability that the bank will be subject to the special costs of meeting a negative reserve position. If the costs of lending are reckoned as the expected costs of providing the funds, the expected special costs must be included. They contribute to the marginal as well as to total expected costs. Indeed, if the probability distribution has the general . . . S-shaped cumulative . . . , marginal expected costs will normally increase with the volume of lending." [114, chapter 9, pp. 18–19].

One qualification to this suggestive exercise is in order. Namely, We made the deposit retention curve ϱ depend only on L. In actuality ϱ may depend on other factors such as age distribution of loans. Loan accounts are probably relatively active ones. In particular, it is possible that new loans are more likely to be an active drain on deposits. Also loans maturing, depending on their frozenness, may or may not be repaid. Thus, whatever factors influence frozenness may also influence deposit retention.

CHAPTER 3

THE DEMAND FOR FINANCIAL ASSETS AND THE TERM STRUCTURE OF INTEREST RATES

3.1. Introduction

By examining bank portfolio behavior, the previous chapter provided the basis for a formulation of the supply of money. This chapter examines the demand side of financial markets. In particular, we examine the determinants of the demand for money at various levels of aggregation. We also specify a time deposit demand equation. Following this, we investigate the demand for commercial and industrial loans. It is these various demand equations which make endogenous the constraint flows discussed in the last chapter. The final part of this chapter discusses the term structure of interest rates.

Additional notation is introduced as needed. As before, all dollar variables are measured in billions of dollars and all interest rate variables in percent. Furthermore, the flow variables are at quarterly rather than annual rates.[1]

3.2. Demand for Currency, Time Deposits and Demand Deposits

3.2.1. *General Considerations in the Demond for Money*

Discussions of the demand for money (defined in various ways) and estimation of equations explaining this demand have been increasingly common in the literature of recent years.[2] In view of this we shall be rather brief both in our discussion and in the extent to which we conduct single-equation experiments. For our purposes, money will be defined in

---

[1] The one exception is the GNP variable in the second section which is at annual rates. Final estimates of the demand for money contain this variable at quarterly rates.

[2] For a review of these efforts see JOHNSON [64] and TEIGEN [110].

the most conventional manner as the sum of currency and demand deposits. Some investigations include time deposits in the definition but this seems undesirable since it prejudges the substitution issue and confounds the interest rate effects.[3]

In what follows, we first examine an individual economic unit's transactions demand for money. We then briefly discuss the asset demand for money and the specification of an aggregate demand function for money.[4] Following this, we separate the demand function for money into its two component demands. We conclude with an examination of the demand for time deposits.

Money, either in the form of currency or as checks written on a demand-deposit account at a commercial bank, retains, among all assets the unique characteristic of serving as a generalized means of payment in economic transactions. Individual economic units are typically faced with a lack of synchronization between payments and receipts. Hence, at first glance it seems reasonable to assume that these economic units will choose to hold some of their assets in the form of money in order to facilitate meeting their payment commitments. In general, however, an economic unit can predict with fair accuracy its future *net* income stream.[5] This fact, coupled with the existence of almost perfectly liquid, riskless, income earning assets (e.g., time deposits or short-term government securities), makes it feasible to invest transactions balances in one of these assets when surplus balances exist and to convert back to money when needed.

Thus, it might appear that we have concluded that money *per se* need not be held, except at the precise instant of transaction. The assumption which enables us to draw this conclusion is that movements into and out

---

[3] In particular, as we see below, the demand for money will be negatively related to various interest rates but the demand for time deposits is presumably positively related to its yield. Hence, with a broader definition of money these opposing effects may be offsetting. It should be noted that we have not established why conventional money should be called *money* and the extended definition not.

[4] The initial discussion of this section is quite similar to that of TEIGEN [110], who in turn made extensive use of some of the ideas of Tobin. See, for example, [113] and [114].

[5] Patinkin in fact refers to the transactions motive as resulting from certain but imperfectly synchronized payment and receipt streams. The precautionary motive is the result of the uncertainty of the timing of these payments and is introduced in his model by imposing social opprobium on economic units who default in their payments. For a more detailed discussion of this point, see [94, chapter 7].

of liquid income-earning assets are costless. In a more realistic setting, of course, there will be brokerage charges, bank service charges, and the like.[6] The existence of these costs suggests that there is an economic tradeoff between holding yieldless cash on the one hand and holding income-earning assets for which there is an associated service charge on the other. We now investigate the optimal cash holdings implied by this tradeoff.

Tobin has dealt with this investment decision problem quite thoroughly in the sources noted above. In these, he has derived expressions for an individual's average holdings of what he terms bonds (the riskless interest-yielding alternative to cash) and the revenue and total profit from such holdings. He has done so, however, on the assumption that the income payment is received at the start of the period and is paid out evenly throughout the period. Modigliani and Ando have extended this discussion to the case of income being received in installments over the year, and it is from this generalization that we shall derive a function expressing the individual's demand for money.

The actual derivation will not be reproduced here, although we shall state the assumptions and conclusions below.[7] In particular, we assume an individual to receive an income of Y per year which is paid to him in f equal installments and hence $y = Y/f$ is the income received at the beginning of each decision period. Let r ($\%$ per annum) represent the rate of interest on bonds and hence the effective rate for decision over the period is r/f. We further posit a fixed charge a for each transaction into and out of bonds.[8] Under these assumptions, it can be shown that the optimal cash holding during the decision period will be

---

[6] In the U.S., for example, the holder of time or savings deposits is not formally entitled to withdraw funds without first giving the bank sixty or thirty days' notice, respectively. Banks seldom exercise their right to such notice although they might demand notification if the frequency of transaction on an account were to become excessive. Secondly, it is only recently that the practice of giving "instant interest" has gained some prominence. Most banks continue to compute time-deposit yields on the basis of the minimum balance per accounting period. Under both these procedures, especially if the accounting period is extensive, one would expect that the movements into and out of time deposits will be lessened. Similar remarks apply to deposits held at mutual savings banks.

[7] [110] contains the derivation.

[8] It is quite simple to incorporate variable charges into the analysis. See [110] or [114].

if bonds are not held, $\bar{C} = Y/2f$ (i)

otherwise $\bar{C} = \sqrt{\dfrac{Ya}{2r}}$.   (ii)

Thus, if either (a) the frequency of payment is high; (b) annual income is low; or (c) if r is small relative to a, it may not be profitable to hold bonds at all. When it does become profitable, (ii) applies.

One way to derive an adequate macroeconomic relationship from these expressions is to make a set of successive approximations, gradually adapting a formulation suitable for estimation. We first note that aggregation of individual demands will, in all likelihood, comprise summing individuals who are following different rules.[9] In addition, in a more realistic setting we cannot expect to satisfy exactly the assumptions implicit in the derivation of these rules. Therefore we rewrite the individual's demand for money as

$$C_i = \Omega_0 \, r^{\Omega_1} \, y_i^{\Omega_2}$$

in which we have subsumed both f and a as institutionally determined constants. Ignoring the aggregation problem we write the following approximation:

$$\Sigma \, C_i = M \cong \gamma_0 r^{\gamma_1} y^{\gamma_2} \, . \qquad \text{(iii)}$$

Next we assume the demand for money can be written as the product of a function of r and a function of Y. In particular, holding Y constant, we can obtain a relationship between M and r by expanding (iii) in a Taylor series and truncating the higher order terms. This yields:

$$f(r|y) \cong r_0^{\gamma_1} + \gamma_1 \, r_0^{\gamma_1 - 1} (r - r_0) = B_0 + B_1 r \, .$$

There is some evidence that in the aggregate the relationship between the income velocity of money and the interest rate is approximately linear over a fairly wide range.[10] At a given interest rate, this would imply a constant velocity and a proportional relationship between M and Y.

---

[9] That is, some individuals will be following (i) and others (ii).

[10] For some evidence on the wide range of linearity see LATANE [70].

Hence, we can write $M = B_2 Y$ where r is held constant.[11] Multiplying the two segments of the monetary demand schedule, we have:

$$M = (B_0 + B_1 r)(B_2 Y) = \gamma'_1 Y + \gamma'_2 (rY).\qquad\text{(iv)}$$

Teigen has used a function of this form with some success. However, while the derivation sketched is suggestive, by no means does it restrict us to a form of the demand function as given by (iv). As another possibility, we try below a function which is linear in the logarithms of the variables.[12]

Furthermore, we still must specify several details before (iv) becomes suitable for estimation. For example, we must choose particular interest rate variables. In addition, since the analysis is somewhat stylized, there exists sufficient latitude for the inclusion of an additional variable in (iv). We have in mind a measure of wealth, a variable which has been widely regarded as influencing the demand for money.[13] In a loose sense, wealth may influence the amount of assets people feel they can afford to hold in cash, i.e., it may influence some of the parameters of the money demand function. In addition, while money may not be demanded as an investment asset, it will also be related to wealth because of transactions on capital account. That is, reallocations of portfolios requiring asset shifts which are spread out over time may lead to temporary changes in money holdings.[14] In view of this, we expect that money holdings may indeed be positively related to wealth.[15] Of course, income and wealth variables, because of their high intercorrelation, are notoriously difficult to work with in a single equation. This difficulty is borne out below.

---

[11] TEIGEN [110], has a somewhat more detailed explanation of this step.

[12] Edward Kane has informed the author that he has used the logarithmic form with considerable success in estimating money demand functions for about ten countries.

[13] The demand for money can be viewed in a formal way as part of the general portfolio problem facing an individual. It should be clear that, when looked at in this manner, money demand will depend on total portfolio size or wealth. See, for example, BAILEY [9] and TOBIN [114].

[14] This will be reinforced if "broker's charges" for moving into and out of time deposits are sufficiently large relative to the return on these assets to justify occasional accumulations of cash in the permanent portfolio. Thus, if transactions on capital account are expected to occur in the near future, the analysis outlined above may apply. See, on this, TOBIN [114, chapter 4, pp. 23–25].

[15] The influence of wealth on the demand for money is not to be confused with the "asset" demand for money posited by Keynesian liquidity preference. According to the latter, when a rise in the interest rate (a decline in the price of bonds) is expected, individuals holding bonds will shift out of them and into money. Thus money is assumed to be demanded as a portfolio asset, and consequently the stock of money net of trans-

3.2.2. *Equation Estimates*

Let us now turn to some single-equation estimates of the demand for money. We shall make use of the following additional notation:

M – stock of money

C – currency

D – demand deposits (n.b. $M = C + D$)

T – time deposits

Y – gross national product (throughout this section measured at annual rates)

r_s – yield on Treasury bills

r_p – yield on time deposits

W – net worth of public

P – implicit price deflator for GNP

As in the bank equations of the last chapter, we modify (iv) above to allow for a partial-adjustment mechanism. Also, we include the time-deposit yield and the bill rate in the money-demand equation. We first estimated:

$$\Delta M = 2.814 + 3.99s_2 + 4.85s_3 + 8.38s_4 - 0.139M_{-1} + 0.039Y$$
$$\quad\quad (0.60) \quad (0.58) \quad (0.88) \quad (0.062) \quad\quad (0.019)$$
$$-0.0015(r_s Y) - 0.0033(r_p Y) \quad\quad\quad R^2 = 0.949 \quad S_e = 0.836 \quad (3.1)$$
$$(0.0005) \quad\quad (0.0022)$$

Although highly tentative, it is instructive to note income and interest elasticities implied by (3.1). The long-run income elasticity can be calculated from the following expression:

$$\frac{\partial M}{\partial Y} = 0.281 - 0.011r_s - 0.024r_p \, .$$

Hence, the income elasticity depends on the two interest rates as well. Evaluating the elasticity as the means of the respective interest rates we get

$$\frac{\bar{Y}}{\bar{M}} \frac{\partial M}{\partial Y} = 0.67 \, .$$

The interest elasticities calculated in a similar manner are about 0.1 with respect to both the bill rate and the yield on time deposits. If we add a

---

actions requirements will vary inversely with the interest rate. However, given the existence of assets which dominate money (e.g., time deposits) as a store of value we would then expect the "asset" demand for money to be negligible in a "rational" economy. As a matter of fact, as modern portfolio theory makes clear, we cannot operationally distinguish the three Keynesian sources of the demand for money (precautionary, speculative, transactions).

wealth variable to (3.1), it obtains a positive and significant coefficient. But, as (3.2) reveals, it seems to interact with several of the other explanatory variables.

$$\Delta M = 9.11 + 3.71s_2 + 4.44s_3 + 8.44s_4 - 0.242M_{-1} + 0.029Y$$
$$\quad\quad (0.55) \quad (0.55) \quad (0.80) \quad (0.066) \quad\quad (0.017)$$
$$-0.0015(r_sY) - 0.006(r_pY) + 0.010W$$
$$(0.0004) \quad\quad (0.002) \quad\quad (0.003)$$
$$R^2 = 0.957 \ \ S_e = 0.762 \ \ DW = 1.87 \quad (3.2)$$

Estimating a logarithmic form of the function produces:

$$\ln M = 0.173 + 0.031s_2 + 0.038s_3 + 0.066s_4 + 0.896 \ln M_{-1} + 0.058 \ln Y$$
$$\quad\quad (0.004) \quad (0.004) \quad (0.005) \quad (0.048) \quad\quad (0.039)$$
$$-0.008 \ln r_s - 0.011 \ln r_p \quad R^2 = 0.992 \ \ S_e = 0.006 \ \ DW = 1.47 \,(3.3)$$
$$(0.003) \quad\quad (0.013)$$

For (3.3) the coefficients themselves are the elasticities (short-run). The long-run elasticities from (3.3) are therefore seen to be quite similar to those given above. We reserve judgment as to which form is preferable. Tentatively, the linear version seems somewhat superior. On the whole, however, both formulations capture the positive influence of income and wealth variables and the negative influence of the two interest rates.[16]

Disaggregation of Money Demand

While an aggregated equation appears to explain money holdings in a satisfactory manner, we decided to investigate whether we could successfully explain the two components of money demand, i.e., currency and demand deposits.[17] We simply separate the dependent variable into its two components, and attempt to utilize roughly the same set of explanatory variables. This has the virtue of allowing different income and interest elasticities for currency and demand deposits, but is justifiable only to the extent that the public regards these two assets as distinct items.

---

[16] We have not reported a version of (3.3) which included a wealth variable. However one was estimated and the wealth variable yielded the correct sign.

[17] As we shall see below, our monetary policy variable is the sum of unborrowed reserves plus currency. Since it is unborrowed reserves which are relevant for bank behavior, we must explain currency holdings in order to translate monetary policy into bank behavior.

A priori reasoning and the extremely limited empirical evidence suggest that this assumption is a reasonable one.

The most careful study of the demand for currency, that of Philip Cagan, was mainly concerned with the long-run relationship of currency to the total money stock [17]. Despite this long-run emphasis, some of his distinctions between currency and demand deposits are suggestive. Briefly, currency is a more widely-acceptable means of payment. Therefore, the greater the volume of cash-and-carry transactions in an economy, the greater would be the share of currency in the money supply. On these grounds, one might expect a direct relationship between currency and the volume of retail transactions and (perhaps) an index of travel.[18] Holding money in the form of currency also avoids the service charges on demand deposits.[19] On the other hand, with currency there is a risk of loss in transit and dangers in keeping large quantities of currency on hand. Furthermore, checks provide receipts for all transactions. The various reasons suggest that there may indeed be different income elasticities for currency and demand deposits and that disaggregation may be desirable.

Our estimates for currency equations follow:

$$\Delta C = 2.85 + 0.77 s_2 + 0.80 s_3 + 1.18 s_4 - 0.220 C_{-1} + 0.008 Y$$
$$ (0.10) \quad (0.09) \quad (0.12) \quad (0.053) \quad\quad (0.003)$$

$$- 0.0007 (r_p Y) - 0.0001 (r_s Y)$$
$$ (0.0003) \quad\quad (0.0001)$$

$$R^2 = 0.930 \quad S_e = 0.158 \quad DW = 1.19 \quad (3.4)$$

---

[18] The implicit assumption is that retail transactions involve currency to a greater extent than other transactions. Cagan suggests that variations in retail trade account for much of the seasonal variation in currency holdings. An article in the Review of the Federal Reserve Bank of St. Louis [30] also suggests that when sales which typically use currency rise then currency holdings also rise.

[19] In the long period which Cagan considered, the default risk of banks was also a relevant factor. He found further that the sharp wartime (WW II) increase in currency holdings was attributable to the motivation to evade income taxes on the part of certain unincorporated businesses and individuals in independent professional practice. See CAGAN [17, pp. 312–15]. Another factor which can be expected to influence the choice between currency and demand deposits is the convenience associated with the former as compared with the latter. On a cross-section basis it has been suggested one might measure this by the number of bank branches in a region. However, the growth of supermarkets and similar institutions as check cashers means that convenience and acceptability are much more elusive concepts. In the equations presented above, since we are interested in short-run behavior, we have made no attempt to quantify the various factors mentioned in this and the previous footnote.

In logarithmic form we found:

$$\ln C = -1.321 + 0.028s_2 + 0.029s_3 + 0.041s_4 + 0.815 \ln C_{-1}$$
$$ (0.003) \quad (0.003) \quad (0.004) \quad (0.047)$$

$$+0.118 \ln Y - 0.035 \ln r_p - 0.0004 \ln r_s;$$
$$ (0.031) \qquad (0.011) \qquad (0.0026)$$

$$R^2 = 0.988 \quad S_e = 0.005 \quad DW = 1.14 \quad (3.5)$$

Before commenting on these results, let us present the corresponding equations for demand deposits:

$$\Delta D = -0.613 + 3.46s_2 + 4.31s_3 + 7.65s_4 - 0.085D_{-1}$$
$$ (0.56) \quad (0.55) \quad (0.84) \quad (0.069)$$

$$+0.022Y - 0.0015(r_s Y) - 0.0017(r_p Y);$$
$$ (0.018) \quad (0.0004) \qquad (0.0021)$$

$$R^2 = 0.938 \quad S_e = 0.778 \quad (3.6)$$

In logarithmic form we have:

$$\ln D = -1.204 + 0.033s_2 + 0.042s_3 + 0.074s_4 + 0.931 \ln D_{-1}$$
$$ (0.004) \quad (0.004) \quad (0.004) \quad (0.048)$$

$$+0.024 \ln Y - 0.011 \ln r_s \qquad\qquad R^2 = 0.991 \quad S_e = 0.007 \quad (3.7)$$
$$ (0.021) \qquad (0.003)$$

The addition of the yield on time deposits to (3.7) produced a correctly signed but insignificant coefficient and the result is not reproduced. We also experimented with the measure of wealth, W, in the currency and demand deposit equations. As with (3.2) above, it interacted with other explanatory variables. For example, we have:

$$\Delta D = 6.38 + 3.00s_2 + 3.66s_3 + 7.43s_4 - 0.252\, D_{-1}$$
$$ (0.50) \quad (0.50) \quad (0.73) \quad (0.075)$$

$$+0.017Y - 0.0014(r_s Y) - 0.005(r_p Y) + 0.012W$$
$$ (0.016) \quad (0.0004) \qquad (0.002) \qquad (0.003)$$

$$R^2 = 0.954 \quad S_e = 0.675 \quad DW = 1.95 \quad (3.8)$$

Being highly preliminary, these results are suggestive at best. Still, it is interesting to examine the effect of disaggregating the two money components. For one, while aggregate money holdings appear to be influenced by both the Treasury bill rate and the yield on time deposits, we have found that in the main currency holdings respond to the latter and demand-deposit holdings to the former. In addition to these differing interest elasticities, the currency and demand deposit equations imply different income elasticities. For example, from (3.4) and (3.6) the long-run income elasticities evaluated at the means of the relevant variables are 0.43 and 0.72, respectively. The lower elasticity for the currency equation is in accord with Cagan's investigation.[20]

3.2.3. *Demand for Time Deposits*

The final equation of this section explores the public's holdings of time deposits. The form of the equation is exactly the same as those above. Now, of course we anticipate that the yield on time deposits will obtain a positive coefficient. We also include in the time deposit equation a variable expressing the expected return from holding longer-term government securities on the grounds that these securities are probably substitutes for time deposits.[21] We first estimated:

$$\Delta T = 3.87 - 0.32s_2 - 0.67s_3 - 1.24s_4 - 0.028T_{-1} + 0.004(r_p Y)$$
$$\quad\quad (0.35)\quad (0.34)\quad (0.45)\quad (0.062)\quad\quad (0.002)$$

$$-0.010\bar{r}_{10}(R,15)Y + 0.002Y \quad\quad\quad R^2 = 0.560 \quad S_e = 0.83 \quad (3.9)$$
$$\quad (0.004)\quad\quad\quad\quad (0.013)$$

As can be seen from (3.9) the coefficient of the income variable is only a fraction of its standard error. Substituting a lagged value of Y produced

$$\Delta T = 0.612 + 0.50s_2 - 0.05s_3 - 0.43s_4 - 0.063T_{-1} + 0.003(r_p Y)$$
$$\quad\quad (0.48)\quad (0.42)\quad (0.47)\quad (0.054)\quad\quad (0.002)$$

$$-0.014\bar{r}_{10}(R,15)Y + 0.019Y_{-1} \quad\quad R^2 = 0.611 \quad S_e = 0.78 \quad (3.10)$$
$$\quad (0.003)\quad\quad\quad\quad (0.008)$$

Estimating the same equation in logarithmic form, yielded

$$\ln T = \text{const} + 0.002s_2 - 0.005s_3 - 0.015s_4 + 0.863 \ln T_{-1} + 0.086 \ln r_p$$
$$\quad\quad\quad (0.007)\quad (0.006)\quad (0.005)\quad (0.043)\quad\quad\quad (0.032)$$

$$-0.106 \ln \bar{r}_{10}(R,15) + 0.015 \ln Y_{-1} \quad\quad R^2 = 0.998 \quad S_e = 0.012 \quad (3.11)$$
$$\quad (0.027)\quad\quad\quad\quad\quad (0.011)$$

---

[20] See CAGAN [17].

[21] A variable expressing the yield on savings and loan shares, if a suitable one were available, might also be included in a time deposit equation. See [42].

The behavior of the income variable is rather interesting. Equation (3.10) suggests that lagged income is more appropriate than current income. Of course, it should be remembered that current income does enter positively in (3.9) in two places, once in a product term with the time deposit yield and once by itself. For what they are worth, both (3.10) and (3.11) imply elasticities of about 0.6, -0.8 and 1.0 for the time deposit yield, the expected security yield, and GNP. These estimates are, on the whole, reasonable and we suspend further estimation until the entire model is specified.

3.3. Demand for Commercial and Industrial Loans

3.3.1. *Discussion of the Instrument*

Before discussing the theoretical aspects of the demand for bank loans, let us look at some data exhibiting business uses of such funds. Although the principal source of funds for American business has been equity finance, between 35% and 40% of business assets have been obtained via borrowed funds. Of this, business loans of commercial banks accounted for roughly half or 19% of the indebtedness at the end of 1959. In addition, the Federal Reserve has estimated that in the fall of 1957 there were between 1.75 and 2 million separate bank loans outstanding, this in a total business population of about 4 million firms. These data suggest that an extensive number of businesses rely on banks for at least part of their credit [4, pp. 123–124].

In discussing the demand for business loans, one is faced with twin issues. First, one must consider the factors which generally necessitate the securing of external funds by business. Second, one must inquire after the reasons for choosing bank financing rather than some alternative means of external finance. The demand for external funds on the part of business is the result of a complex set of economic calculations coupled with, or rather constrained by, a set of beliefs concerning the efficacy of external finance. A firm's current cash outflow is a result of numerous factors including its wage bill, its decisions with respect to the level of inventories deemed desirable, and its current and past decisions with respect to the volume of capital outlays on plant and equipment. The inflow items (retained earnings and depreciation allowances) depend in part on profits and serve to determine, when considered relative to expected outflows, a firm's capital requirements. It seems natural to presume, as other writers have, that there exists a causal relationship between the strain on a firm's cash position and the pressure to secure external finance [86].

There is, of course, a variety of external sources of funds available to business. In addition to bank loans, there are opportunities for trade credit, bond financing, and direct placement of commercial paper. Strictly speaking, one cannot look at the nominal rates of these various alternatives in order to determine their relative costs, but these rates are suggestive. Trade credit appears to be the most costly method. Under typical terms 2% may be deducted from a bill if cash is paid within ten days; otherwise the face amount is due in thirty or sixty days. If due in thirty days, the effective rate is 36.5% per annum and if due in sixty days, the rate is reduced to 14.5%. However, in some cases payment can be deferred for longer periods of time, or suppliers can make special arrangements with customers, which further reduce the effective rate.[22]

Bond financing requires, in addition to payment of the nominal rate, that a firm cover the cost of the flotation. More serious, however, is the fact that the success of bond placement operations depends to a marked extent on the reputation of the issuing company. This naturally presents a problem for a wide class of firms, especially for newer and smaller businesses.

Finally, the securing of funds by the issuance of commercial paper is available typically to only a relatively few firms of widely-recognized standing. It should be noted, however, that the prime commercial paper rate is generally lower than the bank loan rate and this enhances the attractiveness of finance by commercial paper.[23]

Bank loans, while carrying a higher rate than some of the alternatives noted above, are available to a wider class of borrowers. In particular, it will be recalled that surveys have found the typical business firm borrowing from a bank to be of less-than-average profitability. Thus, to some extent, alternative financing methods serve different types of customers. While the extension of bank credit may be more important to small businesses (in terms, perhaps, of their very existence), this is not to suggest that bank loans are unimportant to larger businesses. In particular, borrowing for intermediate periods of time from banks may be more convenient for bigger businesses than offering bonds or equities. For example, the needs for funds in plant construction arise only gradually.

---

[22] See [4, chapter 4] for more extensive discussion of this point.

[23] There are, of course, issuing costs and (for direct-placement companies) overhead to be considered as well.

Thus, firms may choose to initially obtain these funds by bank finance. After some time has elapsed and the exact long-term needs are known, firms may then refinance via bonds or equities.[24]

There are certain other features of bank borrowing which should be mentioned. For one, to the extent that receiving a loan demonstrates that a firm has met certain objective standards, the proven ability of a firm to borrow from a bank may enhance its reputation. Second, there is the feature of the compensating balance by which we mean deposit balances required of a borrower by a bank as a condition for granting a loan. Such balances, to the extent they exceed the average balance a firm would voluntarily choose to hold, serve to increase the effective rate of interest charged on loans.[25] The existence of these balances may present a problem in using the loan rate as an adequate measure of the price of obtaining a loan.[26] The American Bankers Association has noted that required balances are likely to be higher and more rigidly enforced when interest rates are high. Voluntary balances are likely to decrease in times of credit stringency, and since the rate equivalent of a compensating balance depends on the required balance considered relative to the voluntary balance, it seems probable that under such conditions the loan rate will be understating the cost of obtaining a loan.

Finally, there are many helpful services which a bank makes available to its loan customers, such as advice on the current local business outlook. However, this type of "service" becomes undesirable to a firm whenever it turns into a form of bank control. In the case of a term loan, for example, the firm may be required to enter into formal agreements which impose certain conditions and restrictions on the operations of the borrower. Firms may be required to maintain a specified working capital position, to submit regular financial reports, and may have limits placed on other borrowing and capital expenditures or sales of assets. It is precisely these sorts of restrictions which make internal financing attractive to many firms.

---

[24] It has been noted that one-half of total capital expenditures of public utilities ultimately financed in the securities market were initially financed in banks. See BUDZEIKA [16, p. 68]. Budzeika also suggests that the increase in internal funds of the 1958–1962 period led to an increase in bank loans. He argues firms expecting internal flows repaid long-term debt and substituted bank loans.

[25] These balances may, under certain assumptions, actually be irrational from the point of view of the bank. See for example, [28] and the references cited therein.

[26] Another and perhaps more serious, inadequacy of the loan rate as a cost measure is suggested by the recent development of a credit availability theory which emphasizes nonprice rationing methods.

3.3.2. *Specification and Estimation*

Bankers have generally found variations in the demand for bank loans, arising from changes in inventory, accounts receivable, and equipment requirements, with inventory fluctuations being the dominant factor. In addition to these sources of demand, there are numerous seasonal and other short-term factors which contribute to bank loan demand. For example, financing interest payments on bond issues or, as we have noted, coverage of capital outlays while long-term financing is being secured can also generate a demand for bank loans. A summary of bank credit conditions taken from a recent Federal Reserve Bulletin serves to point up the factors to which loan demand is generally attributed and also indicates the nature of the competing financial arrangements available. In particular, it is noted:

> "The slower growth in business loans may reflect in part the less rapid rise in inventory investment in the current upswing than in earlier ones. Plant and equipment outlays also have increased more slowly. And with the expansion in retained earnings and the continued growth in depreciation allowances, substantial amounts of internal funds have been available to cover financing requirements. Furthermore, with rates on financing in capital markets more favorable than on bank loans, corporations have relied to a considerable extent on long-term financing, and some firms—particularly public utilities—have funded bank debt." [41, July 1962, pp. 793–794].

A speech by Chairman Martin of the Board of Governors of the Federal Reserve System before a subcommittee of the Joint Economic Committee, dealing with inventory changes, is also reprinted in the same issue of the Bulletin. In it, he asserts:

> "Additionally, bankers have traditionally regarded inventory needs as one of the most legitimate reasons for borrowing, and they consider the meeting of such needs as one of the most appropriate forms of bank lending." [41, July 1962, p. 810].

The formal specification of the loan demand function can best be thought of in a framework analagous to the one utilized by W. L. Anderson.[27] Briefly speaking we consider that a firm has already made produc-

---

[27] See [8]. This framework has been applied in a different context by the author to explain business holdings of cash, time deposits, government securities, and other types of debt. See [54].

tion decisions and decisions about current and capital inputs. The effect of these decisions is to produce a given need for funds which can be financed by either increasing various types of debt or decreasing various stocks of liquid assets. The optimum financial mix depends on interest rate considerations, initial-period stocks and the various components producing the need for funds. More particularly, we would anticipate the following types of variables to be positively related to the demand for commercial loans: fixed investment, inventory investment, sales (as an indicator of transactions requirements), dividends, yields on various types of liquid assets and yields on other types of debt.[28] The variables negatively related to commercial loan demand include the cost of bank loans and the supply of various types of liquid assets.

We estimated several equations with various measures of these variables. For example, we had the two measures of the loan rate discussed earlier, two different measures of inventory investment and two types of transactions (sales variables).[29] On the whole, using these different types of variables produced no interesting contrasts. Introducing the following additional notation,

CL – volume of commercial and industrial loans
ΔH – inventory investment (all business)
I – fixed investment
DIV – dividend payments
SA – sales,

we can write a typical equation as follows:

$$\Delta CL = -3.02 + 0.76s_2 + 0.70s_3 + 1.20s_4 - 0.179CL_{-1} + 0.011SA$$
$$\quad\quad (0.29)\quad (0.27)\quad (0.33)\quad (0.044)\quad\quad (0.019)$$

$$-0.019r_e' + 0.209r_s + 0.185\Delta H + 0.198I + 1.85DIV$$
$$(0.468)\quad (0.168)\quad (0.080)\quad\quad (0.138)\quad (0.43)$$

$$R^2 = 0.717\quad S_e = 0.45\quad (3.12)$$

---

[28] It should be noted, however, that the inclusion of an inventory variable in the loan demand equation is an issue separate from the inclusion of a credit-cost variable in an inventory-investment equation. An inventory-demand schedule which is interest inelastic within the relevant range of operation is still consistent with inventory-induced loan demand. It will, of course, create problems for the traditional implementation of monetary policy.

[29] For the loan rate variables, see the supply discussion, above, p. 64. The two inventory measures are manufacturing inventory investment and an all-business measure, while the transactions measures were manufacturing sales and GNP less inventory investment (final sales). On these last four measures, see below, pp. 121–122.

A number of features of this equation deserve attention. On the favorable side, all variables enter with appropriate signs, although not all are statistically significant. On the other hand, the dividend variable produces an unreasonably large coefficient. It says a $1 billion increase in dividends per quarter increases loans in the same quarter by more than $1 billion and by considerably more in the long-run. There are several possible explanations for this. In the first place, actual dividends paid have never varied by this much per quarter and hence in terms of actual loan variation explained, the dividend variable does not contribute as much as the coefficient seems to imply.[30] Secondly, there appears to be multicollinearity difficulties. The coefficient on the lagged stock of loans changes considerably when the dividend variable is introduced. Finally, there is the possibility that the dividend variable is serving as a proxy for some other variable. For example, loan demand might be related to anticipated investment needs. If these are more stable than actual requirements, the dividend variable might capture their effect.

Other features of (3.12) emerge when we compare it with (3.13) below, an equation which includes sales and interest rate variables only.

$$\Delta CL = -1.7 + 0.65s_2 + 0.70s_3 + 1.37s_4 - 0.05CL_{-1} + 0.076SA$$
$$\quad\quad\ (0.25)\ \ \ (0.26)\ \ \ (0.29)\ \ \ (0.05)\quad\quad\ (0.021)$$

$$-0.92r'_e + 0.48r_s \quad\quad\quad\quad\quad\quad\quad R^2 = 0.49 \quad (3.13)$$
$$\ \ (0.56)\ \ \ (0.17)$$

As can be seen in (3.13), sales and the two interest variables produce considerably higher t-values than in (3.12). The addition of investment and dividend variables tends to diminish the importance of the other variables.

In the case of sales, this seems to be a reasonable occurrence. We have included sales as a somehwat vague measure of transactions but, the more one specifies variables which are related to transactions (such as investment and dividends), the less important we would expect sales to become. The diminished significance of the interest variables, on the other hand, may reflect simultaneous-equations bias. Interest rates and investment, as we shall argue below and as national-income textbooks take for granted, are related via investment decisions. In view of this, we performed no further preliminary tests to secure a more adequate loan demand equation. We turn instead to a discussion of the term structure of interest rates.

---

[30] Annual dividends, for example, from 1956 to 1962 were 12.1, 12.6, 12.4, 13.7, 14.5, 15.2 and 16.5 billions respectively.

3.4. Term Structure of Interest Rates

In our discussion thus far, we have introduced three distinct interest rates on government securities, namely the bill rate, the rate on 3–5 year securities and the long-term bond rate. The determination of these various rates is presumably the net result of the interaction of both lender and borrower preferences. At a minimum, in considering lender behavior, one should examine the portfolio-selection decisions of the several economic groups who are the major holders of both government and private securities. For example, one should investigate the behavior of commercial banks, of savings and loan associations, of pension and trust funds, and of life insurance companies. These various demand functions would be of the type we have already described for the banks. In other words, the demand for a security would be a function of its own yield, the yields on competing assets, and various flow constraints. For government securities the total supply of each type of security can be viewed as given by consolidated Federal Reserve-Treasury actions. Hence, all the demand relationships and the usual equilibrium conditions (equating demand and supply for each type of security) would suffice to determine all demands and all the yields on government securities.[31]

Quite clearly, such a general-equilibrium approach is beyond the scope of this study. However, it is still desirable to treat these government rates as endogenous within a complete system. Furthermore, we want to examine how monetary-policy actions influence these rates. We do this by resorting to two "term-structure" equations which reflect the consolidated behavior of the financial sector as well as the behavior of the nonfinancial public.

3.4.1. *A Brief Review of the Expectations Hypothesis*

The explanation of the term-structure of interest rates, while of considerable interest to the practioners in the market, has received relatively scant treatment in the academic literature both at the theoretical and applied levels.[32] Fisher's *The Theory of Interest* (published in 1930),

---

[31] Such an approach would still treat as exogenous the yield on private securities. These could only be made endogenous by specifying the nature of the supply of all private types of debt.

[32] For an extensive review of the literature see CONARD [23] and for more recent references see MALKIEL [81].

developed the relationship between short and long rates under conditions of perfect foresight. Later this became the basis for the expectations theory of the term structure. One version of the expectations theory contends that the interest rate on long-term debts tends to equal the average of the short-term rates expected to exist over the duration of the long-term debt.[33] Expectations types of hypotheses have a great deal of intuitive appeal since investors do appear to compare the alternatives of investing for short periods of time and then reinvesting with the alternative of investing over longer periods of time.[34] The difficulty in subjecting the expectations hypothesis to a rigorous empirical test is that very little is known about how expectations are formed. They are, of course, unobservable.

In addition to this lack of verifiability, another major defect of the strict expectations hypothesis is that it assumes perfect arbitrage between securities, leaving no role for lender preferences and the influence of relative supplies of different types of debt. Once risk, differing expectations, and transaction costs are allowed for, we would expect that relative supplies of different types of debt would matter. Holding a portfolio of short-term securities would provide little chance of variation in capital value, but the investor might incur large transactions costs as he reinvested his frequently maturing portfolio. In addition, at each reinvestment, the holder of shorts would be subject to variation in yield. Hence, the short portfolio has considerable income risk. The long portfolio has assurance of income, but may be subject to variation in market value. In view of the differing liability structures of many institutions and the tendency of institutions to place funds in investments whose maturities are similar to their own liabilities, we would expect lender preferences to make securities of differing maturities imperfect substitutes. For example, we have already discussed above, in the context of bank liquidity, the factors which make short-term securities more liquid than long-term ones, and also the reasons for banks' needing to hold liquid assets. On the other side, insurance companies and pension and trust funds which have longer-term liabilities should have preferences for longer-term securities. Following Conard, we hold that the expectations theory should be modified to include the influence of relative supplies. In the last analysis, of course, the actual importance of relative supplies in influencing the term structure is

---

[33] See CONARD [23] and [62], [77].

[34] CONARD [23] and MALKIEL [81].

an empirical question, one which can only be settled by recourse to empirical investigation.[35]

One other theory of the term structure should be mentioned. In particular, Culbertson observing the concern for liquidity of many institutions offered a liquidity theory to explain movements of long and short rates. He argues that short rates are more volatile, because the volume of outstanding private short-term debt declines by a far greater proportion in a recession than does long-term debt. Hence, if many investors have preferences for holding short claims, they will accept much smaller returns on those assets which are available. At the margin then, liquid securities command a premium. Thus Culbertson notes: "Abnormally low yields on liquid short-term debt during a depression may be an indication that the economy is starved for liquidity, and abnormally high yields on such debt during prosperity may indicate that the supply of liquidity is excessive for the time." [24, p. 517].

To account for this same phenomenon the expectations theory invokes the explanation of inelastic expectations. That is, expected short rates are altered by only a fraction of the current change in short rates so that the long rate displays a smaller change. Culbertson argues strongly against the expectations theory. However, it would seem that there is nothing inherent in his emphasis on the importance of private debt which necessarily invalidates the expectations hypothesis. As Conard suggests, it is not clear why both the qualifications of the importance of the supply of public and private debt cannot be added to the expectations analysis. Actual implementation of the modification with respect to private debt is, unfortunately, currently impossible as there exists no adequate quarterly series of private debts by maturity category. In what follows we therefore only include supply variables for federal debt. While this is not entirely satisfactory it is the only feasible alternative.[36]

3.4.2. *Econometrics of the Term Structure*

As noted above, there has been only limited econometric implementation of term structure theory. Meiselman has provided an indirect test of the

---

[35] The concentration of investors in different types of securities, or market segmentation as it is called, does not logically mean that perfect arbitrage is not possible. MEISELMAN [84] points this out and indicates that investors with overlapping interests and security dealers do provide the market with continuity.

[36] MEISELMAN [84] criticizes this consolidation of private debt. However, OKUN [91] and DE LEEUW [29] also adopt a similar procedure.

expectations hypothesis. Wood and de Leeuw have incorporated both expectational and supply influences.[37] In addition, Okun, in a recent interesting paper, has advanced a model in which he relates the level of both short and long rates to money, income, and the existing stocks of government securities of various maturities [91]. We briefly examine his findings. A sample of Okun's results is presented below where $M*$ is a potential money variable, Y is an income variable, S and O are the supply of short- and long-term securities, T is the mean maturity of the outstanding long-term securities, and the Q's are seasonal factors.

$$\text{long rate} = -2.21 - 0.0066M* + 0.0219S + 0.0187O + 0.0105Y + 0.0046T$$
$$\qquad (0.69)\ (0.0021) \qquad (0.0042)\quad (0.0029)\quad (0.0014)\quad (0.0023)$$
$$R^2 = 0.935$$

$$\text{short rate} = -1.57 - 0.307M* + 0.0567S + 0.0410O + 0.0227Y - 0.62Q_1$$
$$\qquad (0.65)\quad (0.0051) \qquad (0.0074)\quad (0.0068)\quad (0.0025)\quad (0.14)$$
$$-0.47Q_2 - 0.21Q_3$$
$$(0.13) \qquad (0.13) \qquad\qquad\qquad\qquad R^2 = 0.899$$

With respect to inclusion of the income variable, Okun states that it is designed to reflect private transactions demand for liquidity [91, p. 342]. It is clear, of course, that this does not get at the Culbertson liquidity effect. In fact, Okun's estimates yield a larger coefficient for income in the short-rate equations than in the long-rate one. An increase in income would narrow the differential between the two rates, while Culbertson's liquidity hypothesis says an increase in the demand for liquidity would widen the differential.

As to the inclusion of a potential money variable rather than an actual money variable, Okun reasons as follows [91, pp. 336–337]. A quantitative explanation of interest rates in terms of the components of private balance sheets (such as the stock of money) does not provide an estimate of the way in which interest rates are affected by monetary policy. In order to achieve this, one must link the balance-sheet items to variables of a policy nature. The alternative is to relate interest rates directly to variables under public control. By experimenting with two potential money stock variables as well as with the actual stock of money, Okun incorporates this approach into his investigation. He finds that the

---

[37] See [84], [123] and [29].

policy-linked variables are more satisfactory in explaining the two interest rates.

There are various difficulties with the equations presented above. First, Okun, as he realizes, is working with several highly correlated variables. This creates some difficulty in the interpretation and stability of his results. Second, his results are subject to simultaneous-equations bias. Although we might interpret Okun's specifications as representing reduced-form equations, it is hard to imagine a properly-specified structural system which has income for an exogenous variable and yet simultaneously determines both the long and short rates. Third, there is some difficulty with the dimensional consistency of the equations. For example, the equations state that long-run growth in the dollar value of both security variables will lead to a secular increase in both interest rates, but a secular decline in the differential of the long rate over the short rate. This dimension problem is also exhibited with respect to the income and potential money variables. Finally, while security supplies should be introduced, using only two (S and O) categories may obscure much interesting variation. The short-term category is an under-five-year group and it has been suggested that a division of this category into 0–1 and 1–5 year categories may be desirable.[38] We now turn directly to the specification of our term-structure equations.

3.4.3. *Specification and Equation Estimates*

Rather than use the levels of the intermediate and long-term rates as dependent variables, we have decided to utilize various rate differentials. As shall become clear when we specify the entire model, we need only two term structure equations to assure that we have a fully-determined system. There are, however, three possible rate differentials, namely $r_{10} - r_s$, $r_{10} - r_3$ and $r_3 - r_s$. The introduction of equations explaining any two of these is sufficient for our purposes. Except perhaps on empirical grounds, it makes little difference which two we choose. We report preliminary results using all three differentials and reserve judgment as to a final choice until later.

In keeping with our previous discussion, we experimented with several explanatory variables. In particular, we included interest-rate-expecta-

---

[38] Okun reports experimenting with this finer division, but he rejects it on empirical grounds. SCOTT [103], and DE LEEUW [29] both suggest the finer breakdown is more appropriate.

tions variables, an income variable, a potential-money variable, and relative-supply variables. As a measure of expectations, we employed the variables described in the discussion of bank security equations. As in the setting of the loan rate, we made use of first differences and lagged first differences of the bill rate. For an income variable, we used ΔY and for a potential money variable we used ΔD^*. Finally, as supply variables we used a breakdown into 0–1 and 1–5 year categories:

S_1^* – proportion of government debt in 0–1 year category
S_2^* – proportion of debt in 1–5 year category
$\bar{S}_1$ – dollar amount of debt, 0–1 year
$\bar{S}_2$ – dollar amount of debt, 1–5 years (n.b. $\bar{S} = \bar{S}_1 + \bar{S}_2$).

On the whole the results support a role for all types of variables, although the expectations and supply variables performed the most consistently. A sample of the results follows:

$$r_{10} - r_s = 1.213 - 0.483(\Delta r_s)_{-1} - 4.289\Delta S_1^* - 2.018\Delta S_2^* + 0.003\Delta Y$$
$$\qquad\qquad (0.124) \qquad\quad (2.704) \qquad (2.370) \qquad (0.002)$$

$$-0.769\bar{r}_{10}(L,15) \qquad\qquad\qquad R^2 = 0.496 \;\; S_e = 0.38 \quad (3.14)$$
$$(0.251)$$

$$r_{10} - r_s = 3.545 - 0.500(\Delta r_s)_{-1} - 2.45\Delta S_1^* - 0.66\Delta S_2^*$$
$$\qquad\qquad (0.115) \qquad\quad (2.56) \qquad (2.15)$$

$$-6.068\bar{r}_{10}(R,10) + 3.831\bar{r}_{10}(R,5) \qquad R^2 = 0.612 \;\; S_e = 0.33 \quad (3.15)$$
$$(1.239) \qquad\qquad (1.493)$$

$$r_{10} - r_3 = 0.529 - 0.919\bar{r}_{10}(L,15) - 1.15\Delta S_1^* - 1.73\Delta S_2^*$$
$$\qquad\qquad (0.158) \qquad\qquad (1.73) \qquad (1.45)$$

$$+0.019\Delta D^* + 0.025(\Delta D^*)_{-1} \qquad R^2 = 0.573 \;\; S_e = 0.243 \quad (3.16)$$
$$(0.012) \qquad (0.012)$$

$$r_{10} - r_3 = 3.13 - 0.012\Delta\bar{S}_1 - 0.018\Delta\bar{S}_2 + 0.024\Delta D^* + 0.026(\Delta D^*)_{-1}$$
$$\qquad\qquad (0.012) \quad (0.009) \qquad (0.013) \qquad (0.012)$$

$$-0.008\bar{S}_1 - 0.005\bar{S}_2 - 2.064\bar{r}_{10}(R,15)$$
$$(0.004) \quad (0.003) \quad (0.488)$$
$$R^2 = 0.601 \;\; S_e = 0.235 \quad (3.17)$$

$$r_3 - r_s = 1.21 + 2.74\Delta S_1^* + 3.23\Delta S_2^* - 1.947\bar{r}_3(\mathrm{R},10) + 1.6.6\bar{r}_3(\mathrm{R},5)$$
$$\quad\quad\quad (2.44) \quad\quad (1.90) \quad\quad (0.456) \quad\quad\quad\quad (0.563)$$
$$\quad - 0.207\Delta r_s - 0.315(\Delta r_s)_{-1} \quad\quad\quad\quad R^2 = 0.389 \;\; S_e = 0.30 \quad (3.18)$$
$$\quad (0.119) \quad\quad (0.107)$$

The above five equations reveal several interesting features. First, ΔS_1^* and ΔS_2^*, the changes in the proportion of debt in the 0–1 and 1–5 year categories, produce consistently negative signs in equations (3.14)–(3.16). Hence, an increase in the proportion of securities in either of these categories leads to a narrowing of the rate differential of a long rate over a shorter rate. This is precisely what is expected. An increase in the supply of shorter-term securities can be expected to decrease their price (raise their yield); hence, narrow the differential. Equation (3.17) uses the actual dollar values of the variables rather than the proportions but also reveals the expected negative influence.[39] In (3.14) and (3.15), the 0–1 year category is somewhat more important than the 1–5 year category, but the situation is reversed in (3.16) and (3.17). Of course, this is eminently consistent with the fact that the former equations use $r_{10} - r_s$ as a dependent variable and the latter equations use $r_{10} - r_3$. In fact, in (3.18) the supply variables both produce positive signs. The sign on ΔS_2^* should be positive as S_2^* is the 1–5 year category and r_3 is the rate on 3–5 year securities. The sign on ΔS_1^* is less clear since the 0–1 category does not correspond to either the 3–5 year rate or the 3-month bill rate. Hence, a positive sign does not seem unreasonable.

As for expectation variables, they too perform as anticipated. With only one of the "barred" variables (e.g. $\bar{r}_{10}$ or $\bar{r}_3$) in an equation, it receives the appropriate (negative) sign. For example, (3.14), (3.15) and (3.17) all indicate that if rates are high relative to normal rates and capital gains are expected, the rate differential will be smaller than otherwise. However, (3.16) and (3.18) also reveal that the Duesenberry-de Leeuw suggestion of including two expectation rates in an equation appears to account for both expected losses and expected gains.[40] In addition to these constructed

---

[39] (3.17) also uses the levels of the supply variables as well as the changes in these levels and all four variables yield negative coefficients. The levels suffer from the dimensional consistency problem noted above. The levels of the proportions S_1^* and S_2^* do not have this feature. These are employed in the two-stage estimation.

[40] It will be recalled that when a rate is high relative to a long-term average, we expect capital gains. If high relative only to a short-term average, then capital losses may be expected. See above, p. 56.

variables, changes in the bill rate also appear to enter in with the appropriate (negative) sign.[41] Interestingly enough, lagged changes work distinctly better than current changes.

As for the potential money variable, ΔD^*, it produces a positive sign in (3.16) and (3.17), but did not show up in the other equations. *A priori*, this sign is the correct one. We expect an easing of monetary conditions to lead to increased ease in the financial markets and a consequent widening of the rate differential.

In terms of goodness-of-fit, the equation explaining the differential $r_3 - r_s$ is the poorest performer. This tentatively suggests that we should eliminate this differential, but we leave the matter until later.[42,43]

----

[41] Under the expectations hypothesis, changes in the bill rate will be introduced into the calculation of averages which yield the long-term rates. Under the assumption of inelastic expectations, however, changes in the short rate will cause smaller changes in the long rate. Here, this will narrow (for an increase in the bill rate) the rate differential, and should produce a negative sign.

[42] One other type of specification produced uniformly better fits for the three differentials ($r_3 - r_s$ was still the least satisfactory). This involved including the discount rate and other lagged rates. For example one result was

$$r_{10} - r_s = 0.495 - 1.86\Delta S_1^* - 0.67\Delta S_2^* + 0.46(r_{10})_{-1} - 0.52(r_s)_{-1} + 0.85(r_d - r_s)$$
$$\quad\quad (1.65) \quad\quad (1.35) \quad\quad (0.09) \quad\quad (0.07) \quad\quad (0.11)$$
$$R^2 = 0.819 \quad S_e = 0.23$$

Aside from its superior explanatory power, due largely to $(r_{10})_{-1}$ and $(r_s)_{-1}$ the equation has little to recommend it.

[43] In addition to the government security rates we tried briefly to explain the differential of the municipal rate over the bill rate. The former has up to now been treated as exogenous, but for simulation purposes it makes sense to try some crude attempts at making it endogenous. One such equation was:

$$r_m - r_s = 1.31 + 0.093\Delta D^* + 0.143(\Delta D^*)_{-1} + 0.381(r_m)_{-1} - 1.80\bar{r}_3(R,10)$$
$$\quad\quad (0.048) \quad\quad (0.046) \quad\quad (0.124) \quad\quad (0.83)$$
$$\quad - 0.013\Delta r_s - 0.390(\Delta r_s)_{-1}$$
$$\quad (0.286) \quad\quad (0.295) \quad\quad\quad\quad\quad\quad\quad R^2 = 0.479 \quad S_e = 0.89.$$

CHAPTER 4

INVESTMENT AND CONSUMPTION FUNCTIONS

4.1. Introduction

The two previous chapters have concentrated on financial or monetary matters. In view of our interest in ultimately integrating these financial factors with the behavior of national income, in this chapter we concentrate on explaining several of the components of gross national product. In particular, we examine demand functions for four categories of expenditure: fixed investment, inventory investment, durable consumption and nondurable consumption. While we examine all proposed determinants of these expenditure components, our major interest remains, of course, the role of financial variables in these expenditure decisions. Before investigating these components individually, we wish to make several brief points.

First as will become clear, we intend to ignore the supply side of investment and consumption, concentrating instead on effective demand. Our procedure delineates particular demand relationships and combines them into an aggregate model. In order to do this we must, in effect, assume that there are no bottlenecks on the supply side which feed back to demand. This procedure has obvious shortcomings, but is probably appropriate for a quarterly short-run model.[1]

Second, there is the question of whether (and by what prices) one should deflate the different variables under discussion below. The demand for fixed investment is typically expressed in real terms. Despite this, the

---

[1] For a similar 'demand model' see T. C. LIU, [72]. One way in which the supply side could be brought in would be to make capacity utilization itself an endogenous variable. See the discussion of fixed investment below. One also might introduce production functions explicitly. This would certainly be a prerequisite to a model investigating growth over a longer period.

question of what is an appropriate deflator for fixed investment remains unsettled. For inventory investment, price correction is also a quite tricky problem because of the variation in accounting and valuation practices. Similarly, as is indicated below, consumption hypotheses have been framed in both current and real terms.[2] As is well known, the problem of deflation is tied up with the use of accounting identities. What we have done below is to follow a middle course. In particular, we have estimated all relations in both nominal and real terms and have examined the resulting differences. However, the real variables are constructed by dividing all dollar variables by the implicit GNP deflator. We thus allow for general price effects, but do not incorporate relative price changes. Whatever its shortcomings, this procedure is simple and it allows the income identities to hold in real as well as money terms. In view of the difficulties noted above in securing theoretically appropriate deflators, this procedure seems to be a natural expedient. Moreover, it has found recent support in the theoretical literature.[3]

A third problem arises from the fact that in certain instances we introduced seasonally-adjusted explanatory variables into an equation which contained seasonal dummy variables, e.g., disposable income figures are only available on an adjusted basis. To see the approximate effect of this, consider the following alternatives where the subscript s indicates that the data have been adjusted and where D stands for the matrix of dummy variables:

$$Y = b_1 X + a_1 D + e_1 \tag{i}$$

$$Y_s = b_2 X_s + e_2 \tag{ii}$$

$$Y = b_3 X_s + e_3 \tag{iii}$$

$$Y = b_4 X_s + a_4 D + e_4 \tag{iv}$$

$$Y_s = b_5 X + a_5 D + e_5 . \tag{v}$$

Lovell has proved that if the seasonally-adjusted data are obtained by a least-squares procedure with D as the matrix of explanatory variables,

---

[2] See pp. 124–127.
[3] See ANDO [6] and SAMUELSON [102].

then the regression coefficients obtained by the application of least-squares to (i)–(v) imply [75]:

$$b_1 = b_2 = b_3 = b_4 = b_5$$

$$a_4 = a_1 + b_1 a_x \qquad \text{where } a_x = (D'D)^{-1} D'X$$

$$a_5 = a_1 - a_y \qquad \text{where } a_y = (D'D)^{-1} D'Y.$$

Since $b_1 = b_4$ the inclusion of, say, seasonally adjusted disposable income in an unadjusted consumption function will produce the same marginal propensity to consume but a different estimate of the seasonal factors from that obtained with unadjusted disposable income. Hence, none of the results will be seriously changed by this substitution. Of course, the validity of this conclusion depends on the extent to which the seasonal-adjustment procedure embodied in the disposable-income variable resembles the least-squares adjustment procedure of the theorem. While the Commerce Department utilizes a different technique to adjust income figures, the effect of this difference is likely to be small.[4]

4.2. Fixed Investment

4.2.1. *Financial Considerations*

In this section, we examine the determinants of aggregate fixed investment with special emphasis on the relationship between investment and the monetary sector. More precisely, we want to isolate the effects of monetary variables (such as interest costs) on expenditures on plant and equipment, with an eye towards investigating the policy implications of such linkages. There are numerous lags which occur between the initial actions of the monetary authorities and the subsequent effect (if any) of these actions on income. In particular, there is the lag from the initial policy action to its effect on the relevant monetary policy variable. Secondly, there is a lag between a change in this variable and its effect on investment decisions. And finally there are lags between the decision to invest

---

[4] Certain series, e.g., GNP, are available in both seasonally adjusted and unadjusted form. Hence, some evidence on the size of the above effect can be obtained by estimating equations in two ways. This was done for several of the equations and the resulting differences in the income coefficients were quite small. This offers some indirect support for the statement in the text.

and the actual production of capital goods and consequent investment outlays. This section examines the final two links, leaving it to a later section to deal with the first one.

There are two possible modes of attack. The first is to relate monetary variables to investment expenditures directly; the second focuses on the two links separately, generating a two-echelon explanation of the influence of monetary variables on expenditures. The latter approach is the one adopted in the CMC study paper by Ando, Brown, Kareken and Solow [15]. Each approach has its empirical shortcomings. For example, the first suffers from the fact that investigators adopting it have frequently failed to detect a significant interest elasticity of investment demand, while the second must somehow approximate an investment-decision variable, something not statistically measurable from available data.[5] In what follows, we take the direct approach. Before presenting our results, let us review some of the general arguments concerning the interest-investment links and examine possible explanations for the lack of empirical evidence supporting the existence of a significant interest rate effect on investment.

While voluminous, the literature on fixed investment and its interest elasticity is inconclusive. We simply do not know the precise determinants of investment nor the role that interest costs play in that determination. Early survey information tended to minimize the role of interest rates.[6] More recently it has been argued:

> "In view of the general nature of investment decisions, there are some lines of theoretical reasoning which would suggest *a priori* that the effects might be expected to be weak. And, finally, there are some features of the institutional framework within which investment activity is conducted which tend to weaken the effects of interest rates on investment." [116, pp. 368–369].

One argument proceeds from a crude examination of the basic data. Since over the business cycle, interest rates and investment tend to move in the same direction, it is concluded that interest rates do not affect investment. It is, of course, clear that this partial analysis does not yield valid conclusions concerning the interest-investment link. In particular,

---

[5] National Industrial Conference Board data represent a major exception to this. They provide observations on certain types of investment decisions (e.g., appropriations). While these data are inappropriate for our purposes, they merit independent investigation. See ALMON [3].

[6] The studies are reprinted in [93].

one might explain the phenomenon by noting that investment depends on many other factors. At times of high interest rates these factors are likely to lead to increased investment demand which might have been greater had not interest rate increases slowed down the expansion.

Institutional change in the form of heavy reliance of firms on internal finance is also said to weaken the effect of interest rates and hence monetary policy on business investment. In principle, firms should make an opportunity cost calculation, comparing the return on internal funds obtained by a capital good expansion with the return obtainable in alternative uses. These alternative returns clearly depend on prevailing interest rates, but it is argued that in practice, such comparisons are rarely made. For example, it has been stated:

"Prospective returns from capital projects that might be under consideration are so high relative to returns on safe financial assets (such as government securities) that the comparison is of little relevance and outside investments involving substantial risk require continuous attention and divert the energies of management away from the firm's main line of business." [16, p. 371].

In addition it has been assumed:

"The high uncertainty about the outcome of an investment — particularly about the results after the first year or so — made the expectation of very high returns a prerequisite to the undertaking of any project. The minimum acceptable rates of return would be so high and subject to so wide a margin or error that changes of one or two percentage points in the cost of (money) capital could be neglected. In fact, it could be rationally concluded that the great height of required returns made efforts at quantification superfluous: acceptable projects were obviously acceptable; borderline cases were by definition unacceptable." [120, p. 1].

Despite all these claims, it appears that uncertainty or at least the role it plays in decision-making has diminished somewhat since the depression-dominated prewar and early postwar periods. One of the more vocal proponents of the interest sensitivity of investment, William H. White, has further stressed the rapid increases in the use of scientific management techniques that have occurred since 1955. He has cited broad survey evidence to support the hypothesis that elaborate financial, sales and capital spending planning has been undertaken by many of the larger firms. This extensive evidence suggests that the conditions under which economists originally investigated investment determinants have changed, and that the widely-cited empirical evidence has lost some of its validity for the present. White argues that advanced management techniques coupled with financial pressures lead to the acceptance of lower rates of return, thus creating a more favorable environment for an interest rate effect on investment. For example, as early as 1955 a survey found that 41% of the respondents took account of the interest rate in calculating the profitability of self-financed investments, and it can be assumed that many more did so where investments using borrowed funds were concerned [120, p. 20].

More recently a growing number of investigators have reported finding a significant interest elasticity of investment demand in a variety of contexts.[7] For example, Meyer and Glauber note: "The interest variables' coefficients consistently agree with the usual *a priori* hypothesis by being negative in sign." [49, p. 148]. They go on to conclude that:

"An adequate theory of investment behavior also seems to require the incorporation of monetary or interest rate effects, at least under certain circumstances. Specifically, the interest rate was an integral part of any model that provided a good empirical explanation of investment when high interest rates prevailed late in the upswing of the business cycle. Since good forecasts and structural understanding tend to be even more essential for public policy purposes late in the business cycle than at other times, this interest rate behavior pattern must be considered relevant if not highly significant." [49, p. 248].

In addition to this new empirical evidence, an increasing number of theoretical formulations of the investment decision have allowed interest rates to play an important role. While the matter of the interest sensitivity of investment is still in a state of flux, recent evidence makes us hopeful that we can formulate a model exhibiting a significant interest rate variable.

In addition to examining a period in which negative conclusions concerning interest rates may have been justified, early empirical studies further suffered from certain technical difficulties, which tended to add to the strength of the negative conclusions. Before turning to our own investigation, it is appropriate to indicate briefly some of the difficulties with these early regression model studies.

In the early postwar period, interest rates were pegged. Consequently,

---

[7] [48], [31], [49] and [59]. In view of the rough coincidence in time of these studies they understandably note that this result has not been found in many previous empirical studies. At this writing, however, a statement of this sort no longer seems appropriate.

they exhibited very little movement of either a cyclical or secular variety. Moreover, they remained at relatively low levels. The rate on long-term U.S. bonds was 2.09% in the first quarter of 1949. Its peak value in the pre-Korean War period was 2.45% in the third quarter of 1948. This was not exceeded until the second quarter of 1951 which, it will be recalled, marks the data of the Treasury-Federal Reserve Accord. This limited variability of interest rates and their low levels (relative to the return on other opportunities available to postwar firms who, in addition, possessed large supplies of liquid assets) probably contributed, in part, to their lack of success as an explanatory variable. However, recent movements of this variable should lessen this difficulty in contemporary investigation.

In later periods, interest rates began to rise and to exhibit increased cyclical variability, but regression studies examining investment typically found profits and sales to be the major explanatory variables. Such studies still found no role for an interest rate. However, in using profits, sales, and interest rates in a single equation, investigators were working with strongly intercorrelated variables, which lead to problems of multi-collinearity and consequent difficulty in disentangling the individual effects of the different variables. In order to allow an interest variable a fair chance to exhibit explanatory power, one must insure that this variable can be clearly identified in a regression equation. Early studies often made this identification extremely difficult. In addition, early studies paid little attention to the appropriate functional form for the interest rate. As we shall see shortly, this can be of paramount importance.

Another qualification to early studies of investment behavior is that they ignored the simultaneous nature of the problem, producing both biased and inconsistent estimates. Thus, for example, an autonomous increase in total demand might lead to an increase, via the accelerator, in fixed investment. This autonomous increase would be likely to produce a roughly coincident increase in interest rates, thus producing a positive association between investment and interest rates. In fact, in order to have a meaningful relation between interest rates and investment, or more generally between monetary policy and investment, it is necessary for the relevant rates of interest to be determined elsewhere in the model and to be functions, in part, of parameters controlled by the monetary authorities. Furthermore, the model should be estimated by techniques providing consistent estimates.

A final difficulty relates to the fact that early studies necessarily used investment expenditures rather than investment decisions as a dependent variable and yet simultaneously worked with roughly contemporaneous interest rate effects. A decision to acquire a capital good initiates a sequence of events which may include some or all of the following: the drawing up of engineering plans; the announcement of bids and the awarding of contracts; the placement of orders; the setting up of financial arrangements, the actual production of the capital good, delivery, and payment. This decision, therefore, will generate an expenditure stream from the point of the decision on. In view of this, it seems more reasonable to expect that interest rate effects (and the effects of other variables as well) will be felt, on investment at the time of the decision-making process. Actually, as we shall see below, the relevant rates may include the entire constellation of rates from the point of the decision to the completion of the expenditure. One can deal with this problem in two ways. Interest rate variables of various lags may be included as independent variables or, alternatively, one can graft a distributed lag structure onto the investment equation. However one chooses to deal with the problem, it is clear that to the extent early investigators ignored this lag issue they had further misspecified their models.

In passing we might note that the use of expenditure data may account for part of the success of internal funds as an explanatory variable. Once a firm has made a decision to invest, it knows it will have to disburse funds at future dates. It may begin immediately to accumulate internal funds for this purpose. This after-the-fact accumulation may then show up as a variable explaining investment. One could argue, however, that the investment decision was influenced by the expected future availability of internal funds, and the truth is probably a combination of these two effects. With all these considerations in mind we turn to the specification of our investment equation.

4.2.2. *Some Theoretical Underpinnings*

Let us, somewhat informally, imagine that at a certain time businessmen have an objective function which they seek to maximize. Let us assume further that this maximization yields a level of desired capital stock K^d, given by:

$$K_t^d = B_t O_t \tag{i}$$

where O_t is, strictly speaking, a measure of expected output. In one sense, this says very little, for K_t^d and O_t are merely numbers at a given point of time, and one can definitionally find a series B_t which makes this equation hold for all t. The substantive element in (i) comes from the dependence of B_t on the economic variables in the problem, such as the cost structure of the firm. The precise functional dependence is a consequence of the maximization procedure. The usefulness of (i) depends on the nature of this relationship and, in particular, on the stability of B_t as a function over time.

The firm now compares its desired level of capital stock with the level anticipated to be on hand at the beginning of period t, say K_{t-1} and we can let

$$\Omega_t = K_t^d - K_{t-1} = (B_t O_t - K_{t-1}) \tag{ii}$$

represent the gap between desired and actual capital stock. We might view the firm as "deciding" or appropriating the funds to invest amount Ω_t. The investment, of course, will not take place all in the current period but will be distributed over future periods as well. It is probably more realistic to modify (ii) so as to regard firms as appropriating only a fraction, b, of the gap. Under this (ii) becomes:

$$\Omega_t = b(K_t^d - K_{t-1}) = b(B_t O_t - K_{t-1}). \tag{iii}$$

Several comments about (iii) are in order. First, in passing from (i) to (iii) we have actually covered up several important steps. More specifically, we referred to a maximization procedure which led to equation (i), but posited further costs which would lead to a departure of behavior from that result, In actuality, profit-maximizing results should incorporate these additional costs into the decision procedure, deriving a result analogous to (iii) directly. This procedure is described by Eisner and Strotz, who posit an expansion cost function which makes the cost of a given firm size depend on how fast the additions to capital take place.[8] There are numerous reasons which could contribute to the existence of costs of expansion which depend nonlinearly on the rate of expansion. The most obvious would be limited capacity in the capital goods industry

---

[8] In particular let $\varrho[s(t)]$ be the rate of profit for a plant of size s at time t, and the cost-of-expansion function be $c[ds/dt,\, t]$ where c depends nonlinearly on ds/dt and also depends on the elapsed time between the decision and the actual addition to plant. Then for a given rate of discount r the firm is assumed to maximize the functional

$$\Phi = \int_0^\infty e^{-rt} \{\varrho[s(t)] - c[ds/dt,\, t]\}dt = \Phi\{s(t)\}$$

by choosing an optimal $s(t)$. For a complete discussion of this and some interesting distinctions between what they term the "interequilibrium approach" and the "intertemporal allocation" approach see [35]. For another example of this type of analysis, see ANDO [5].

but there are numerous others. It should also be mentioned that fractional reactions may result because of uncertainty. If the expected demand for output in (i) has a high variance associated with it, investors are likely to discount changes that would imply large alterations of the capital stock. In view of this, firms may adjust only a little at a time in order to see if the conditions which imply a significantly different capital stock will actually persist.

Leaving aside the explicit determinants of b we now attempt to implement (iii). We are immediately faced with a difficulty since Ω_t refers to decisions or appropriations and not to the observed investment expenditures for which data are available. Hence, Ω_t is not an observable variable. We noted above that these decisions generate a future stream of expenditures. To formalize this, we write:

$$I_t = \sum_{i=0}^{\infty} k_i \Omega_{t-i} \qquad\qquad \text{(iv)}$$

where I_t represents expenditure, and the k's are a set of weights.[9] In order to utilize (iv), one must specify the weights exactly. We shall use a distribution consisting of a geometrically declining series of weights for the k's.[10] Thus we write:

$$k_i = aq^i$$

where a and q are constants, and hence

$$I_t = a\Sigma q^i \Omega_{t-i} \; ; \; qI_{t-1} = a\Sigma q^{i+1} \Omega_{t-i-1}$$

and finally we have

$$I_t = qI_{t-1} + a\Omega_t . \qquad\qquad \text{(v)}$$

We have thus translated the dependence of current investment expenditures on current and past Ω's into a dependence of current invest-

---

[9] Strictly speaking, (iv) represents the consolidation of two distinct distributed lags. In particular, we have combined the distributed lag between the capital stock gap and appropriations on the one hand, and between appropriations and expenditures on the other. As will be clear from our end result, however, the same functional form can be arrived at by different routes.

[10] It might be more realistic in (iv) to terminate the summation after a finite number of periods. The geometrically declining weights may be viewed as an approximation to this.

ment on past investment expenditure and on the current size of the capital stock gap.[11]

Let us rewrite (v) as:

$$I_t = abB_tO_t - abK_{t-1} + qI_{t-1} . \tag{vi}$$

Now the influence of the interest rate and other economic variables enter, in this formulation, through either the capital coefficient B and/or the speed-of-adjustment b. The simplest hypothesis concerning the interest rate would make B_t a linear function of the interest rate r and make b a constant. Setting

$$B_t = b_1 + b_2 r_t ,$$

substituting into (vi) and combining constant terms produces:

$$I_t = A_1 O_t + A_2 r_t O_t + A_3 K_{t-1} + A_4 I_{t-1} . \tag{vii}$$

This, however, far from exhausts the possibilities. For example, b could be made a function of r as well and this would produce terms in O_t, $r_t O_t$ and $r_t^2 O_t$. In addition, b might also depend on the firm's supply of liquid assets. Unlike the interest variable, there is less theoretical justification for making B a similar function. It seems more reasonable to include liquidity variables in such a way so as to allow their influence to eventually die out.[12] In any event, however, one goes about introducing interest rates into (vi), it is clear that the variable will enter multiplicatively with output with perhaps additional types of nonlinearities.[13] In view of this, it is not surprising that on the basis of their empirical investigation Meyer and Glauber report: "In short, the relationship between invest-

---

[11] Meyer and Glauber have suggested another way to derive a function like (v). They state "An equally plausible hypothesis about the lagged adjustment might be that it is the rate of investment itself that is difficult to increase. Accordingly, the delay in adjustment would not be proportional to the gap between desired and actual stock but to the gap between the desired rate of investment and the previously achieved rate." [49 p. 27]. For a contrary view denying the existence of a desired flow see GRILICHES, [57, p. 116].

[12] For a similar view see GRILICHES [57, p. 117].

[13] Other possibilities include writing $K^d = A_t + B_t O_t$ and making A and B functions of r (or equivalently b). This would introduce terms in $r_t O_t$ and r_t. Another possibility would be to make K^d a linear function of r_t and O_t which introduce linear terms in these variables.

ment demand and interest rates seems to be nonlinear and multiplicative with levels of business activity and liquid assets." [49, p. 249].

With (vii), we have arrived at what appears to be a tractable investment equation. Before we proceed to estimate this, an important caveat is in order. Much of the logic behind the flexible acceleration model is derived from the behavior of the firm. We intend, however, to apply the model to highly aggregative data. Unfortunately, the operation of many unknown interactions and nonlinearities make it impossible to express the aggregate coefficients in terms of microeconomic parameters. This implies that the macroeconomic version of (vii) is not behavioral in the same way as the microeconomic version. Furthermore, it indicates that (vii) should be regarded only as a highly suggestive starting point, one to be modified in the light of the eclectic theorizing necessary at the aggregative level.[14]

4.2.3. *Specification Details*

Capital Stock versus Capacity
We now turn to some additional considerations in connection with the specification of (vii). First, we have yet to indicate clearly the nature of the capital stock variable. Virtually all theorizing about investment and the desired capital stock rests on technological considerations derived from production function theory. In this framework the relevant capital stock notion is a quantity—a homogeneous *physical* magnitude. In this case output (via a production function), and investment, may bear no stable relation to the *value* of capital. However, value data are the only types available. Formally, one could treat this problem by using many heterogeneous capital goods and a programming type of analysis. We do not propose to examine fully the usefulness of an aggregate value concept. The recent theoretical literature is replete with the making of a debate on the subject. Some of the disputants, while recognizing its shortcomings, have argued in favor of qualified use of an aggregated capital concept.[15] Others have argued vehemently against the concept.[16]

---

[14] We have thus far ignored investment demand which results from changes in the composition of final output or from technological considerations. One could presumably introduce these via *B* but we shall not do so, preferring to deal only with what has been termed "aggregative investment demand" [35]. This can presumably be justified in this context since we are interested in explaining quarter-to-quarter variations in investment and these other considerations are likely to change only slowly over time.

[15] See, for example, ANDO [6], SAMUELSON [102] and SOLOW [107].

[16] See KALDOR [66] and ROBINSON [99].

The attitude among econometricians has typically been a schizophrenic one. Namely, they recognized the need for a capital-like concept and yet were bothered by whatever measure they used.[17] In what follows we shall sidestep the entire issue by introducing a different type of measure and, of course, a different set of problems.

More particularly, there is in the literature another approach to the problem, and that is to substitute the concept of capacity for that of capital stock.[18] Capacity, however, like capital stock, is a concept beset with definitional arbitrariness.[19] For example, capacity is often defined loosely as the flow of output per unit time obtainable from existing facilities. Does obtainable output refer to maximum output independent of cost (engineering capacity) or does it refer to some minimum average cost notion (economic capacity)? While economic capacity seems the more relevant of the two, problems of multiple shifts and the like make it a harder concept to define. On balance, there is little to choose between the capital stock and the capacity notions since both, as indicated above, have their respective shortcomings. Capacity data are somewhat easier to come by and hence, in what follows, we have decided to attempt an explanation of investment, using a function similar to (vii) in which we have replaced the capital stock variable by a measure of capacity. The actual measure of capacity utilized was constructed by Frank de Leeuw [30]. It will be used in a variety of forms to be made more explicit below.

Interest Rate Variables

A second set of problems surrounding the specification of (vii) center on the appropriate interest rate to use. In view of our desire to minimize the number of distinct interest rate variables, we initially restrict our choice to the rates thus far introduced. Assuming we will choose one of the

---

[17] For a careful, almost soul-searching, study on this subject see GRILICHES [57]. This study, interestingly enough, suggests that it may be appropriate to include two different types of capital stock measures in an investment equation. Ideally one would capture the adjustment effect and hence have a negative coefficient while the other would capture the replacement effect and have a positive coefficient.

[18] See, for example [15] and [89].

[19] While one can present a capital-stock adjustment model or a capacity-adjustment model, one should emphasize that the two are different concepts—especially in the long run. Capacity, in the sense of obtainable output, is a function of capital stock and all other factors of production. For example, if we admit labor substitutability, there will be a difference between the two principles, although it may not be very significant for short-run fluctuations.

government rates reduces the problem to one of determining the appropriate maturity. The most common argument is that the relevant term for the rate of interest is one which roughly corresponds to the horizon of the investment commitment. This sort of argument leads Eisner and Strotz to state unequivocally that the relevant rate is "the" long-term rate [35, p. 132].

It has recently been argued that what is relevant for the investment decision of a firm is its cost of capital considered in relation to the market rate of return, and that interest rates may provide a poor approximation to this comparison. For example, changes in interest rates may affect the cost of capital and the market rate of return in different ways and with different lags.

If this is the case not only is it no longer clear which interest variable is the relevant one, it is not even clear if any measured interest rate will reflect the actual cost considerations facing the firm. In fact, Modigliani has suggested that one might include both a long-term and a short-term rate in an investment equation. The latter, while probably inappropriate if perfect capital markets prevailed, may serve to account for some of the credit availability effects not reflected in the longer rates. Another possibility which suggests itself is to use some of the interest rate expectations variables discussed earlier.

The need for expectations variables in explaining investment has long been stressed. This suggests that other types of proxies for expectations may be appropriate. One possibility is to include directly a variable reflecting the actions of the monetary authorities. Monetary policy presumably influences businessmen's expectations both directly and indirectly by affecting the nature of risks facing the decision-makers. Perhaps a potential deposit variable could also be included in the investment equation. Another particularly promising expectational variable is some measure of stock prices. This, it would appear from scattered evidence, might usefully serve as a measure of business confidence.[20]

4.2.4. *Equation Estimates*

Let us now turn to some single-equation estimates of investment demand

---

[20] MEYER and GLAUBER [49, p. 152] report success with a stock price variable primarily in expansions when there was a tendency to underestimate investment. HAMMER [59] and MEYER and KUH [86] also utilize stock price variables of various types. These variables might also pick up part of the cost-of-capital considerations which have been noted above as potentially important.

functions. We utilize the symbol K_t for capacity utilization (expressed as a fraction between 0 and 1). In addition we denote by Y^* the *previous* peak value of GNP. Following (vii) we first introduce K_{t-1} and Y. In addition, we include $(Y-Y^*)$, a catch-all variable to pick up any residual accelerator or expectational influences of income on investment. If GNP is steadily rising then $(Y-Y^*)$ behaves like ΔY. In the first period when GNP declines, the variable is also equal to ΔY but thereafter $(Y-Y^*)$ will exceed ΔY (in absolute value). This type of timing pattern with its built-in delays may be more appropriate to explain investment behavior. In any event we have:

$$I = -2.45 + 0.292s_2 I_{-1} + 0.141s_3 I_{-1} + 0.239s_4 I_{-1} + 0.724I_{-1}$$

[undeflated] $\quad\quad (0.014) \quad\quad (0.010) \quad\quad (0.010) \quad\quad (0.047)$

$$+2.75K_{-1} + 0.081(Y-Y^*) + 0.009Y \quad\quad R^2 = 0.977 \quad S_e = 0.19 \quad (4.1)$$

$\quad (0.63) \quad\quad (0.017) \quad\quad\quad (0.003)$

$$I = -1.98 + 0.285s_2 I_{-1} + 0.137s_3 I_{-1} + 0.239s_4 I_{-1} + 0.702I_{-1}$$

[deflated] $\quad\quad (0.014) \quad\quad (0.010) \quad\quad (0.011) \quad\quad (0.050)$

$$+2.27K_{-1} + 0.070(Y-Y^*) + 0.010Y \quad\quad R^2 = 0.954 \quad S_e = 0.18 \quad (4.2)$$

$\quad (0.66) \quad\quad (0.018) \quad\quad\quad (0.004)$

Several points can be briefly noted about (4.1) and (4.2). First, seasonal factors enter in multiplicative fashion to allow for nonstationarity in the seasonal.[21] Since the factors are multiplied by lagged investment, the lag pattern allowed for is a more sophisticated one. Second, the capacity variable enters both equations with a significant positive coefficient. This sign, of course, is to be contrasted with the negative sign expected from a capital stock variable. In this instance, the positive sign is appropriate. We expect higher capacity utilization to induce investment. Finally, there does not appear to be much difference between deflated and undeflated forms.

We attempted to introduce a stock price index into (4.1) and (4.2). While it yielded a positive and significant coefficient in the absence of Y, whenever both were included the stock price variable became insignificant. We also tried introducing the capacity variable in yet another way. We constructed

---

[21] An examination of the investment series and a comparison of (4.1) and (4.2) with equations containing additive seasonals suggests that the nonstationarity is effectively captured by the above device.

$(Y/K - Y_{-1})$ where Y/K can be interpreted as potential output. This variable should, of course, produce a negative coefficient since the more potential output deviates from last period's output, the less incentive there is to invest. Some illustrative results including this variable are as follows:

$$I = -0.30 + 0.289s_2 I_{-1} + 0.139s_3 I_{-1} + 0.242s_4 I_{-1} + 0.753I_{-1}$$
[undeflated]
$$\quad\quad\quad (0.013) \quad\quad (0.009) \quad\quad (0.010) \quad\quad (0.046)$$

$$+0.071\Delta Y + 0.014Y - 0.029(Y/K - Y_{-1}) \quad R^2 = 0.979 \; S_e = 0.18 \; (4.3)$$
$$(0.021) \quad (0.003) \quad (0.004)$$

$$I = -0.47 + 0.283s_2 I_{-1} + 0.136s_3 I_{-1} + 0.241s_4 I_{-1} + 0.723I_{-1}$$
[deflated]
$$\quad\quad\quad (0.013) \quad\quad (0.009) \quad\quad (0.010) \quad\quad (0.050)$$

$$+0.053\Delta Y + 0.019Y - 0.029(Y/K - Y_{-1}) \quad R^2 = 0.961 \; S_e = 0.17 \; (4.4)$$
$$(0.023) \quad (0.004) \quad (0.004)$$

Finally, we turn to the question of incorporating monetary variables into our investment equations. Following the suggestion of equation (vii) above, we include a long-term rate in a multiplicative fashion. In addition, we include a commercial-loan funds variable. With these we have:

$$I = -2.31 + 0.28s_2 I_{-1} + 0.13s_3 I_{-1} + 0.22s_4 I_{-1} + 0.72I_{-1} + 2.33K_{-1}$$
[undeflated]
$$\quad\quad\quad (0.013) \quad\quad (0.01) \quad\quad (0.01) \quad\quad (0.04) \quad (0.57)$$

$$+0.044(Y - Y^*) - 0.00066(r_{10} Y) + 0.014Y + 0.159\Delta CL$$
$$(0.018) \quad\quad\quad (0.0011) \quad\quad\quad (0.009) \quad (0.043)$$
$$R^2 = 0.982 \; S_e = 0.16 \quad (4.5)$$

$$I = -2.33 + 0.30s_2 I_{-1} + 0.15s_3 I_{-1} + 0.25s_4 I_{-1} + 0.68I_{-1} + 1.44K_{-1}$$
[deflated]
$$\quad\quad\quad (0.01) \quad\quad (0.01) \quad\quad (0.01) \quad\quad (0.04) \quad (0.59)$$

$$+0.050(Y - Y^*) - 0.0019(r_{10} Y) + 0.0285Y + 0.149\Delta CL$$
$$(0.016) \quad\quad\quad (0.0009) \quad\quad\quad (0.0097) \quad (0.036)$$
$$R^2 = 0.965 \; S_e = 0.15 \quad (4.6)$$

Both (4.5) and (4.6) reveal a negative role for the interest rate and a positive role for the commercial-loan variable. Equation (4.6), for example, implies an interest elasticity of approximately -0.5 at the means of the relevant variables. Several other variants of interest rates were briefly assessed. Each told essentially the same story as (4.5) and (4.6).[22] Since most of the simultaneous-equations bias probably works against monetary variables it appears tentatively that we shall be able to allow a role for monetary variables in the context of the complete model.

4.3. Inventory Investment

Even a cursory examination of postwar national income statistics reveals that inventory investment has fluctuated widely over the business cycle. In describing its volatility a Commerce Department publication says "changes in business inventories often account for a major portion of quarterly increments in the entire gross national product."[23] Clearly no econometric model can purport to describe short-run movements of the economy and to allow evaluation of alternate stabilization policies unless it contains a reasonable explanation of inventory behavior.

In dealing with inventory investment as with each of the other components of our model, it is clear that a complete examination of the subject would require a relatively extensive amount of disaggregation. In particular, one might provide separate explanations for inventories of retailers, wholesalers, manufacturers, and others; separate durable goods from non-durable goods; and treat work-in-process, raw material, and finished good inventories separately. Nevertheless, in view of the resources and time which constrain this investigation, it was decided to concentrate on a single, aggregate-inventory equation and to devote our energy instead to an examination of the influence (if any) of monetary variables on inventory investment.[24] Before turning to the actual model, let us examine current thinking on the relationship between interest rates, monetary policy, and inventory investment.

---

[22] One somewhat curious result was obtained when the bill rate was added to (4.5). or (4.6). For the deflated case we have

$$I = -2.25 + 0.29s_2 I_{-1} + 0.14s_3 I_{-1} + 0.24s_4 I_{-1} + 0.62 I_{-1} + 1.26K_{-1}$$
$$\quad\quad (0.01) \quad\quad (0.01) \quad\quad (0.01) \quad\quad (0.05) \quad\quad (0.57)$$
$$+ 0.037(Y - Y^*) + 0.0013(r_s Y) + 0.127\Delta CL - 0.004(r_{10} Y) \quad\quad\quad R^2 = 0.97$$
$$\quad (0.017) \quad\quad\quad (0.0006) \quad\quad (0.036) \quad\quad (0.001)$$

As this reveals, the long-term rate is now highly significant but the bill rate yields a positive sign.

[23] U.S. Income and Output [118, p. 98].

[24] This, of course, may be misguided since it is possible that monetary variables only exhibit a discernable influence for suitably disaggregated data.

4.3.1. *Financial Considerations*

A wide variety of arguments have been offered to explain why, even on *a priori* grounds, interest rates will not influence inventory investment. As with fixed investment, the first bit of evidence stems from early survey studies. While information gathered from businessmen on what they respond or do not respond to is certainly relevant, there are various reasons for questioning the relevance of these particular survey results for our analysis. Since White discusses a number of their shortcomings, we shall not pursue the matter any further here [120].

A second argument relates to the fact that interest cost is claimed to be only a small fraction of all other costs involved in carrying inventories, leading businessmen to ignore these interest considerations. Moreover, since inventories are held for such a short period of time, capital costs are a small fraction of total costs.

Thirdly, it has been argued that expectations of rising prices offset much of the deterent effect of rising interest rates. In the same vein, it is argued that other uncertainties tend to swamp interest rate considerations. For example, the risks associated with being unable to fill an order for a long-standing customer (and the implied loss of an account) may counteract any reduction in inventories because of an increased interest rate.

Fourthly, it has been suggested that certain inventories (e.g., work-in-process inventories) may be technically fixed in ratio to plant and equipment utilization and to other factors of production. To the extent that this is true, interest effects may not influence inventory investment.

Finally, it has been suggested that while interest rates may affect desired inventory holdings, the translation to actual inventories obscures the relationship [35]. It is not clear whether this is meant to be an empirical or theoretical argument. It may apply at both levels.

Besides these pure-interest arguments, critics offer another set of arguments based on an assumed proposition that credit-availability effects are more important than actual interest cost changes. These arguments try to demonstrate that, broadly conceived, monetary policy cannot influence inventory investment. First, it is suggested that the availability of bank loans to business may be relatively insensitive to changing credit conditions over the cycle. That is, banks, by virtue of viewing business loans as their most appropriate form of loan, may absorb the prevailing credit tightness in other components of their portfolio. As Chairman Martin has noted:

"Banks often elect to provide for such needs by reducing portfolios of liquid and even long-term securities and, on occasion, by limiting mortgage, security, and other non-business lending. Business loans are the bread-and-butter business of many banks and it is evident to them that a dissatisfied business customer can be lost forever to competing lenders." [41, July 1962, p. 910].

Second, it is argued that, even if bank loans are restricted by monetary policy, this may not curtail inventory investment. Since inventories can also be financed by internal means, by non-bank finance, or by trade credit, there may be cyclical offsets due to the extension of trade credit, the growth of internal funds, and of accounts receivable, simultaneous with the accumulation of inventories. For example, Meyer and Kuh cast some doubt on the need for bank finance when they note: "It seems, moreover, that the financing of inventories in the phase of most rapid accumulation, (early recovery) even though assisted by bank lending, could proceed at a rapid rate without much borrowing because of a very large coincidental generation of internal funds."[25]

In addition to cyclical offsets to credit policy, there has probably been a secular offset in the postwar period (at least the early parts). Corporations have had surplus liquidity which they have gradually decreased to help, in part, the financing of inventory accumulation. This liquidity, it is argued, has made corporations relatively immune to credit conditions.

Despite these arguments, there are some *a priori* reasons for believing that interest rates and/or other monetary variables may influence inventory investment. Some of these reasons have been cited above in the discussion of fixed investment. As with fixed investment, the pertinent cost for inventory investment financed out of retained earnings, depreciation allowances, or reduction of liquid assets, is the opportunity cost associated with alternative uses of these funds. For example, if the opportunity cost moves like the Treasury bill rate, it will fluctuate more than bank lending rates. Hence, changes in opportunity costs may have more of a leverage on inventory investment. In addition to the general investment-interest arguments posed above there are several distinguishing characteristics of inventory investment which increase the likelihood of an impact by monetary variables. For one, inventory decisions in con-

---

[25] [86, p. 366]. EISNER and STROTZ [35, p. 133] also seem doubtful about the ability of monetary policy to influence inventory investment in the face of a posited significant interest elasticity of trade credit. For some empirical evidence on this, see MELTZER, [85].

trast to those concerning fixed investment, are divisible in nature, and this facilitates small adjustments appropriate to relatively small changes in credit conditions. Second, the short-run nature of the decision may aid monetary policy to the extent that interest rate changes will be less swamped by risk considerations. Third, businessmen can reduce the level of their inventories (whereas gross capital fixed investment must be non-negative), and this facilitates adjustments in inventory positions.

If these arguments have any merit and policy-controlled variables influence the relevant monetary variables, there may be a role for monetary policy in the inventory-income nexus. Monetary policy would presumably be further aided by the fact that the average lag between inventory decisions and the purchase of materials is relatively short. After adding up the yeas and nays, Chairman Martin of the Federal Reserve contends:

"... it seems to me that credit conditions do at times significantly influence inventory policies. Moreover I think it reasonable to believe that the potential influence of these conditions is greater now than in earlier postwar years, because interest costs are a larger proportion of total inventory costs and firms have generally become less liquid and therefore more dependent on credit." [41, July 1962, p. 810].

Meyer and Kuh, on the other hand, feel:

"Manufacturing firms are ordinarily in a comfortable position to finance the greatest part of their requirements from internal sources because a rapid inflow of internal funds and a very sharp increase in accounts payable normally coincides with inventory accumulation. A tight monetary policy at this juncture of events not only would normally be considered undesirable but if put into operation would presumably have small effect." [86, p. 370].

Along these lines, one might argue that when the Fed becomes restrictive in the early stages of the cycle, they may produce results different in both timing and magnitude from those anticipated. For example, if diminished external credit forced firms to use internal funds for inventory accumulation, this might curtail expansion in plant and equipment at some future time. The exact effect would depend on the lag of monetary policy, the predictive ability of the monetary authorities, and the nature of the credit restrictiveness. This effect clearly complicates monetary policy. On balance, definite conclusions regarding both the sensitivity of business inventory decisions to monetary variables and the feasibility of exploiting this link, if it exists, by monetary policy cannot be firmly established by theoretical reasoning alone. Some recourse to empirical evidence is required.[26]

Empirical Evidence

It should be stated at the outset that most empirical studies of the inventory decision have found little role for interest rates or for other monetary variables.[27] There are a number of possible explanations for this finding (assuming, of course, that financial factors do influence inventory investment). First, most previous studies were subject to the purely statistical problems cited previously in the context of fixed investment (e.g., multicollinearity, simultaneous-equations bias, lag structure, etc.). Second, there are problems connected with inventory data themselves. In particular, inventory data not only reflect conscious management decisions, but also reflect involuntary changes. In fact, intended inventory changes tend to bring along with them unintended changes in the opposite direction. For example, planned reductions by one firm can cause an unintended decrease in sales and consequent increase in inventory of the firm's suppliers. Third, as we shall see, there are important problems connected with how one specifies a firm's expected sales.

Finally, another major issue is how one chooses what monetary variable to include in the model. One could simply settle for a commercial-loan rate or some other short-term interest rate,[28] but this may not capture all of the opportunity cost suggested to be relevant. It is widely held that monetary policy works as much through nonprice rationing of loans by the banks as through changes in interest rates. Unfortunately, as we noted earlier, there is no numerical measure of the degree of credit

---

[26] This section only concentrates on the first half of the problem: interest sensitivity We pursue the question of the efficacy of monetary policy at a later point. However, one point which might be mentioned here is the question of whether, in the implementation of monetary policy, credit restrictions can be suitably directed towards the industries or firms whose inventory behavior is contributing destabilizing effects to the economy. The question of the possible need for selective stabilization may make an aggregate inventory equation inappropriate for policy purposes. See EISEMANN [34].

[27] For a review of various studies and their findings with respect to the financial determinants of inventory investment see LOVELL [73] and McGOULDRICK [79].

[28] Given the short-run nature of inventory decisions a short-term rate seems the most relevant. A rise in the long-term rate could conceivably cause an increase in inventories if they are substituted for fixed capital.

rationing characterizing the market for bank loans. One possible alternative to the loan rate is simply to use a monetary policy variable (e.g., D^*). Both approaches are employed in the Ando *et al.* CMC paper referred to above. This paper finds a significant role for the loan rate, but its statistical significance appears to be sensitive to the lag structure utilized. In addition, attempts to make direct use of a monetary-policy variable (a constructed series measuring maximum earning assets of the banks) met with distinct failure. The variable proved to be statistically significant with a sign counter to *a priori* expectations. A study by T. C. Liu and one by Michael Lovell and Paul Darling have also reported statistically significant (although admittedly marginally so) and appropriately signed coefficients for interest rate variables.[29] Liu utilized a "real" rate of interest (the bill rate less the rate-of-change of the GNP deflator) to get at the risk problem while Lovell and Darling used the loan rate.

The most extensive study to date, by Paul Kuznets, came to the author's attention only after this work was essentially completed [69]. Kuznets includes variables measuring internal funds, external funds, and interest rates in his equation. Rejecting the standard liquidity variable typically measured by the stock of quick assets (cash plus government securities), he focuses instead on internal finance. His measure is essentially the sum of net retained earnings and depreciation flows. With respect to external finance, he criticizes bank-availability measures as both too narrow and too broad. They are too narrow since availability also depends on the financial strength of the borrower and business conditions; they are too broad since bank lending capacity is not fully available to finance inventory investment. His measure of external finance, decided upon after some experimentation, includes net trade credit, long-term debt, equity finance and bank loans. The interest variable is the short-term business loan rate. Kuznets finds a significant role for all three financial variables although the results appear to be sensitive to the lag structure, the choice of data, adjustment procedures, and the definitions of both the financial and nonfinancial variables. It is not clear why existing external finance should capture the availability of funds for business borrowers. If used on a contemporaneous basis, there would be a clear case of simultaneous-equations bias involved. On a lagged basis (which is how it is actually used), one might argue that a level of existing external finance is consistent

[29] [72] and [26].

with any level of credit availability.[30] Thus, for example, high outstanding external finance could mean tight credit conditions and reduced inventory investment. The variable actually yields a positive coefficient. Despite these difficulties, the Kuznets study appears to provide one of the first careful analyses of the financial determinants of inventory investment.

4.3.2. *Some Theoretical Considerations*

Let us now turn to the general specification of our inventory equation. We make use of a flexible-accelerator model. Since this has become quite standard in the literature, we summarize only the essentials of the model.[31] Our notation follows:

S_t – sales during period t

$\hat{S}_t$ – anticipated sales during period t
(formed during period $t-1$)

H_t – inventories at end of period t

H_t^{P} – inventories planned for the end of period t

H_t^{e} – equilibrium level of inventory

U_t – unfilled orders.

The firm is assumed to have a desired or equilibrium stock of inventories which, in the simplest version, is simply taken to depend on anticipated sales. Thus we write

$$H_t^{\mathrm{e}} = \alpha + \beta\hat{S}_t . \tag{i}$$

It is further postulated that the firm will plan to adjust only partially to the discrepancy between the equilibrium level and last period's stock. This can be written as

$$H_t^{\mathrm{P}} = H_{t-1} + \delta(H_t^{\mathrm{e}} - H_{t-1}) \tag{ii}$$

where δ is the reaction coefficient. There exists a wide variety of justifications for such partial-adjustment. Among the more common explanations are the following: (a) time is required to renew stocks of purchased materials; (b) economies of scale in the placement of orders may lead to lumpiness in ordering; (c) an increase in inventories may

---

[30] Kuznets is, of course, aware of some of these difficulties. See [69, pp. 345–346]

[31] For a more complete discussion see LOVELL [73] and [74] and the references cited therein.

require new warehouse space, the acquisition of which may introduce lags; and (d) if the variance of expected sales is high, firms may proceed cautiously at first. In any event substituting (i) into (ii) yields

$$H_t^{\mathrm{P}} = \delta\alpha + \delta\beta\hat{S}_t + (1-\delta)H_{t-1} . \tag{iii}$$

This last relationship is still unsuitable for empirical use. It contains two nonobservable quantities, namely anticipated sales and planned inventories. Leaving aside for a moment the question of $\hat{S}_t$, let us translate planned inventories into actual inventories. The deviation between actual inventories and planned inventories will be taken to depend on the error in anticipating sales, i.e., on $\hat{S}_t - S_t$. More explicitly we write

$$H_t = H_t^{\mathrm{P}} + \lambda(\hat{S}_t - S_t) = \delta\alpha + \delta\beta S_t + (\delta\beta + \lambda)(\hat{S}_t - S_t) + (1-\delta)H_{t-1} . \tag{iv}$$

The term λ has been called the "production adaptation coefficient". If λ equals one, then the firm does not compensate at all for errors in sales prediction; while if λ is less than one, firms partially offset these errors. Two other extreme values of λ are $\lambda=0$ which implies that inventory plans are always carried out and $\lambda=-\delta\beta$ where firms fully compensate for prediction errors [73, p. 194].

Finally, with respect to the problem of anticipated sales, two main tacks have been followed in the literature. The first is to substitute actual sales for anticipated sales. This procedure makes sense if we assume that errors of prediction are random, i.e., the expected value of $\hat{S}_t$ is S_t. In that case the term $(\hat{S}_t - S_t)$ in (iv) can be subsumed in the (unwritten) stochastic component of (iv). The other procedure is one suggested by Lovell where anticipated sales are made a linear combination of lagged and actual sales, i.e.,

$$\hat{S}_t = \varrho S_{t-1} + (1-\varrho)S_t . \tag{v}$$

The case $\varrho=0$ corresponds to the previous case, while $\varrho=1$ corresponds to what has typically been termed naive expectations. Substituting (v) into (iv) yields:

$$H_t = \delta\alpha + \delta\beta S_t - (\delta\beta + \lambda)\varrho\varDelta S_t + (1-\delta)H_{t-1} . \tag{vi}$$

It should be noted that estimation of (vi) would enable one to estimate δ, α, and β separately but not λ and ϱ.

4.3.3. *Specification Details*

Equation (vi) is suitable for empirical work. Implicit in (vi) however, is the fact that sales (or expected sales) is the sole determinant of the equilibrium stock of inventories. In view of recent empirical work and our own discussion of financial influences on inventory investment, it seems reasonable to specify that equilibrium inventories may depend on additional factors.

In the first instance, we may introduce one or more financial variables into the model. As with fixed investment, this could be done in a number of ways. An interest-rate variable might enter linearly in the determination of equilibrium inventories or it could enter via β, the marginal desired inventory-sales ratio, in (i). The last specification would, of course, lead to a multiplicative interest-sales variable. This same multiplicative relationship would evolve if the reaction coefficient, δ, were made a function of the interest rate. As for other financial variables (e.g., funds variables) it makes slightly more sense to introduce them via δ but even here the matter is unclear.

A second variable often introduced as a determinant of desired inventories is unfilled orders. A variety of explanations has been offered rationalizing this link between unfilled orders and inventory investment. An increase in demand may, given the nature of production lags, lead to an increased volume of goods-in-process inventories. The expansion of this type of inventory will be partially offset by both a reduction in the stocks of inputs (held by the firm's suppliers) and by a reduction of finished-goods inventory. However, it is clear that unfilled orders will not accumulate if the new orders are met in this way. In other words, an increase in demand will produce an increase in inventories precisely when unfilled orders are increasing. Hence, the change in unfilled orders should appear with a positive coefficient in an inventory equation. Another reason for the inventory-orders link may result from entrepeneurs having an extended horizon in deciding upon the change in stocks to be made in the current period. As Lovell has expressed it:

> "If unfilled orders represent an established demand, indeed a possible committal to deliver at some future date, entrepreneurs may well consider it advisable to carry additional stocks when unfilled orders are large as a hedge against possible shortage and price commitments." [74, p. 297].

Stanback has provided another explanation for the influence or orders upon inventories [108]. In his explanation, the desired inventory-sales ratio is taken to depend on market tightness. More explicitly, when supply conditions are tight and deliveries of purchased materials necessary for production are subject to many vagaries, firms will hold higher (raw-materials) inventories to avoid costly stoppages of the production process. The final step in this argument is to identify the ratio of unfilled orders to sales, since it approximates the average delivery lag, as a measure of market tightness. With H^e/S dependent on U/S, actual inventory investment becomes a function of unfilled orders.[32]

On the basis of Stanback's market tightness argument, another variable may be expected to influence desired inventories: the level of capacity utilization. It is quite clear that market tightness and high levels of capacity utilization tend to occur at roughly the same points of time. Reasoning from a production-smoothing concept, Lovell and Darling have offered an additional argument for including a capacity variable [26]. In order to avoid overtime and other abrupt changes in production, firms typically accumulate stocks of finished goods inventories to meet seasonal demands. If the firm is experiencing high capacity utilization, they will start accumulating further in advance of the seasonal peak than is ordinarily necessary. Aggregating firms with different seasonal demand patterns will therefore produce a higher level of inventory stocks when capacity utilization is high.[33]

4.3.4. *Equation Estimates*

In trying to implement our inventory equation, we experimented with two sources of inventory data. The first was the business inventory investment category of the national income accounts (denoted simply by H); the second was a series on manufacturers' inventory investment (denoted by H'). In addition, we experimented with two types of sales variables:

---

[32] RUTH MACK [73], has objected to the *ad-hoc* addition of an unfilled-orders variable to what is supposed to be a flexible accelerator (sales) model, especially since the variable typically turns out to be so important. She suggests that the change in unfilled orders reflects the eventual impact of price expectations and further argues that the orders variable must itself be explained. CHILDS [19], in fact provides a good example of a somewhat more detailed model which considers both production and inventory decisions and their interactions and which simultaneously explains both unfilled orders and inventory investment.

[33] There is a possibility that high capacity utilization will increase the difficulty in obtaining inputs and may exert a negative effect on inventory investment. The empirical evidence, [26] and below, seems to suggest that the positive relationship is dominant. The production-smoothing argument would further suggest that a purely seasonal increase in sales may lead to a reduction in inventories rather than the increase implied by the accelerator model. Hence, if there is a reasonable basis for predicting the seasonal pattern in sales, we may want to utilize seasonally-adjusted sales changes in our inventory equation.

(a) a measure of manufacturers' sales (SA), (b) $(Y-\Delta H)$ or GNP less inventory investment as a measure of final sales.[34] Finally, following a suggestion given in an article by Duesenberry, Eckstein, and Fromm, we also added ΔH_{t-1} to the inventory equation [33]. Some sample results are as follows:[35]

$$\Delta H = -2.71 - 2.91s_2 - 2.06s_3 - 3.27s_4 - 0.149H_{-1} + 0.250\Delta H_{-1}$$
[undeflated]
$$\qquad\quad (1.17) \quad (0.74) \quad (1.17) \quad (0.061) \qquad (0.109)$$

$$+0.140\Delta U_{-1} + 0.085(Y-\Delta H) - 0.071\Delta(Y-\Delta H) + 0.381\Delta CL$$
$$\quad (0.038) \qquad\quad (0.033) \qquad\qquad (0.065) \qquad\qquad (0.184)$$

$$R^2 = 0.842 \quad S_e = 0.69 \quad (4.7)$$

$$\Delta H = -8.36 - 3.95s_2 - 2.53s_3 - 4.31s_4 - 0.217H_{-1} + 0.338\Delta H_{-1}$$
[deflated]
$$\qquad\quad (1.37) \quad (0.88) \quad (1.42) \quad (0.061) \qquad (0.127)$$

$$+0.157\Delta U_{-1} + 0.170(Y-\Delta H) - 0.046\Delta(Y-\Delta H) - 0.215\Delta CL$$
$$\quad (0.039) \qquad\quad (0.048) \qquad\qquad (0.089) \qquad\qquad (0.193)$$

$$R^2 = 0.827 \quad S_e = 0.70 \quad (4.8)$$

$$\Delta H' = -4.51 + 0.70s_2 + 0.07s_3 + 1.76s_4 - 0.081H'_{-1} + 0.332\Delta H'_{-1}$$
[undeflated]
$$\qquad\quad (0.48) \quad (0.36) \quad (0.51) \quad (0.034) \qquad (0.090)$$

$$+0.101\Delta U_{-1} + 0.032(Y-\Delta H') - 0.112\Delta(Y-\Delta H') + 0.246\Delta CL$$
$$\quad (0.026) \qquad\quad (0.012) \qquad\qquad (0.035) \qquad\qquad (0.123)$$

$$+5.45K \qquad\qquad\qquad\qquad R^2 = 0.865 \quad S_e = 0.44 \quad (4.9)$$
$$\;(1.94)$$

$$\Delta H' = -6.48 + 0.91s_2 + 0.13s_3 + 1.91s_4 - 0.094H'_{-1} + 0.228\Delta H'_{-1}$$
[deflated]
$$\qquad\quad (0.55) \quad (0.42) \quad (0.62) \quad (0.038) \qquad (0.101)$$

$$+0.100\Delta U_{-1} + 0.038(Y-\Delta H') - 0.119(Y-\Delta H') + 0.055\Delta CL$$
$$\quad (0.028) \qquad\quad (0.012) \qquad\qquad (0.046) \qquad\qquad (0.122)$$

$$+7.48K \qquad\qquad\qquad\qquad R^2 = 0.827 \quad S_e = 0.47 \quad (4.10)$$
$$\;(2.01)$$

---

[34] This variable has been used by KLEIN [68] as a measure of sales.

[35] The GNP inventory figures are actually reported in flow fashion so one has to construct a stock figure. This was done by adding up all the previous flow figures for each time period. This means the stock variable is actually $H_{t-1} - H_0$ where H_0 is the initial period stock. In view of this the estimates of the constant term in the equations using different sources of data are not comparable.

Briefly speaking (4.7)−(4.10) support the flexible-accelerator model quite well. The variables of the form $(Y-\Delta H)$ capture the sales effect and ΔU_{-1} picks up the influence of unfilled orders. It should be mentioned that the level of unfilled orders proved to be of little value in the above equations. There are at least two differences between the deflated and undeflated forms worthy of note. First, the commercial loan variable only shows up in the undeflated version; second, the explanatory power of deflated forms seems consistently lower than for the undeflated counterparts. This, of course, is eminently sensible. Price correction removes some trend elements common to all the variables. Finally, the only contrast between H' and H variables seems to be that the capacity variable (K) proved to be significant only for the narrow definition of inventory investment.

As for financial influences, as already indicated the commercial-loan variable gives mixed results. We report below the results of including interest-rate variables along with the other sales measure. Similar results were obtained when the interest variables were included in the above equations. We have:

$$\Delta H = -4.65 - 2.84s_2 - 1.30s_3 - 1.94s_4 - 0.113H_{-1} + 0.293\Delta H_{-1}$$
[undeflated] $\qquad$ (0.35) $\quad$ (0.32) $\quad$ (0.34) $\quad$ (0.028) $\qquad$ (0.097)

$$+0.139\Delta U_{-1} + 0.115SA + 0.067\Delta SA - 0.448\Delta r_s$$
$\quad$ (0.030) $\qquad$ (0.026) $\qquad$ (0.037) $\qquad$ (0.204)

$$R^2 = 0.904 \quad S_e = 0.54 \quad (4.11)$$

$$\Delta H = -4.33 - 2.86s_2 - 1.24s_3 - 1.86s_4 - 0.055H_{-1} + 0.354\Delta H_{-1}$$
[deflated] $\qquad$ (0.37) $\quad$ (0.35) $\quad$ (0.37) $\quad$ (0.020) $\qquad$ (0.112)

$$+0.135\Delta U_{-1} + 0.078SA + 0.094\Delta SA - 0.365\Delta r_s$$
$\quad$ (0.034) $\qquad$ (0.028) $\qquad$ (0.041) $\qquad$ (0.220)

$$R^2 = 0.879 \quad S_e = 0.59 \quad (4.12)$$

$$\Delta H' = -2.25 - 0.50s_2 - 0.73s_3 + 0.82s_4 - 0.062H'_{-1} + 0.228\Delta H'_{-1}$$
[deflated] $\qquad$ (0.33) $\quad$ (0.28) $\quad$ (0.35) $\quad$ (0.037) $\qquad$ (0.100)

$$+0.133\Delta U_{-1} + 0.087SA - 0.039\Delta SA - 0.311r'_e$$
$\quad$ (0.028) $\qquad$ (0.023) $\qquad$ (0.031) $\qquad$ (0.202)

$$R^2 = 0.808 \quad S_e = 0.49 \quad (4.13)$$

As the above results reveal, both the loan rate and the bill rate (the two short-term rates we used) produce negative coefficients, thus supporting the expected *a priori* effect. Various other formulations including multiplicative interest rates also generally produced negative (and insignificant) coefficients. Equations (4.11) and (4.12) yielded a positive coefficient for ΔSA, but this coefficient is negative in (4.13). This may reflect the fact that the sales variable more strictly corresponds to the H' definition of inventories. On the whole, the preliminary results can be construed as encouraging as to the possibility of building links between monetary factors and inventory investment.

4.4. Consumption Expenditures

4.4.1. *General Considerations*

In contrast to the relative paucity of empirical investigations on aggregate investment behavior, consumption behavior has received extensive attention at the empirical as well as at the theoretical level. Consumption functions have been estimated for a wide variety of time periods, levels of aggregation and specifications and much work has been devoted to interpretation and reconciliation of the various bits of evidence.

Post-Keynesian developments in consumer theory have developed along several discernable although not independent lines.[36] The hypothesis that aggregate consumption expenditure depends on current aggregate disposable income has been revised in various ways. A number of investigators have proposed the notion that a long-run consumption function expresses the relationship between a gradually-changing standard of living and some longer-run measure of resources available to support this standard. A variety of resource measures have been proposed including, for example, Friedman's "permanent income" notion. In a similar spirit, other writers have suggested that net worth or consumer wealth is also a relevant determinant of consumer expenditure. The Modigliani-Brumberg-Ando model, for example, starts from an individual consumer's utility function which is assumed to depend on his own current and future consumption. The individual maximizes his utility subject to a constraint on resources available over his lifetime: the sum

---

[36] SUITS [109] contains an extensive review of the current state of consumer theory. References to the standard works in consumer theory which are not cited here can be found in that source.

of current and future (discounted) earnings and current net worth. After obtaining individual consumption functions in this way, they can be combined to produce an aggregate consumption function in which consumption (in current prices) depends on income and net worth (also in current prices) [7].

A second direction of investigation has included various analyses of the determinants of short-run variations in consumption expenditure. In the postwar period, it has become widely recognized that there are short-run changes in consumption which are unrelated to changes in current income. This, of course, follows in part from the long-run evidence mentioned above. Duesenberry, for example, has proposed a "previous peak income" ratchet effect which cushions the effect of a decline in income on current consumption. Furthermore, in the short-run, since the money market is not accessible to most consumers, the timing of expenditures may be significantly influenced by liquidity considerations.

The concern with short-run fluctuations in consumption has naturally led into a variety of dynamic problems. Resolution of these has often resulted in the inclusion of one or more lagged values of consumption in a consumption function to represent the influence of past consumption on present consumption. Practically speaking, the inclusion of lagged consumption variables allows the consumption function to recognize shifts in consumption once they have occurred and consequently may pick up the effects of omitted variables. Another consequence of paying increased attention to dynamic considerations is a growing recognition that for short-run purposes it is important to distinguish between durable and nondurable consumption.[37] Many of the short-run fluctuations in consumption expenditure arise from purchases of consumer durables. What one might expect to bear a systematic relationship to some long-run resource measure is the stream of current services of existing durables. Since small increases in services desired can lead to considerable increases in consumer durable expenditures, it is not surprising that there are fluctuations in durable expenditures. There are obvious problems of timing involved. Strictly speaking, the definition of what is a durable should depend on the time units of the analysis.

Finally, other directions of post-Keynesian consumer research have involved less disaggregated analyses of consumer behavior. These

---

[37] SUITS [109] stresses the durable-nondurable distinction quite strongly and suggests that even an aggregate durable category may be too heterogeneous.

analyses have often relied on survey information and have investigated the influences of demographic factors, expectations, and consumer attitudes on consumer expenditures. This type of analysis has typically been of the cross-section variety. Consequently, a reasonable amount of effort has been aimed at integrating time-series and cross-section results.

As is quite clear even from this brief sketch, a vast and diverse literature has developed in the area of consumer behavior. Our interest in this section is somewhat removed from these developments. We are mainly interested in the influence of various monetary variables on consumption. We briefly assess current thinking on this subject and then report some empirical attempts to include monetary variables in one of the garden variety of consumption functions. We consider the following types of variables:

(1) *Interest Rates*   According to the classical notion, high interest rates increase incentives to save, thereby decreasing consumption. For a target saver, of course, the opposite would be true. Other possibilities include high interest rates leading to restricted consumer-credit conditions and, in this way, to reduced consumption. On the whole, the empirical evidence has not supported an interest effect on consumption.[38,39]

(2) *Prices*   Most consumption hypotheses are specified in real terms although, (as we have seen) the Modigliani-Ando hypothesis is expressed in money terms. In addition, other writers have argued that money illusion may be an important component of consumption behavior. Furthermore, the expected course of prices may influence consumption behavior by generating speculative changes in expenditures. Finally, changing relative prices may affect consumption behavior. As indicated earlier, we report our own results in both nominal and real terms. We also include a speculative price variable.

(3) *Wealth*   The positive dependence of consumption on wealth has been emphasized by various writers including those noted above. Reasoning from a utility function in which wealth has diminishing marginal utility, this dependence simply expresses that, as an individual's wealth

---

[38] Consumer credit, when included, has often proved to be a significant variable in explaining (durable) consumption behavior. Typically, this has been accomplished by including a volume-of-credit variable or a repayment variable, not an explicit interest cost.

[39] Interest rates changes do enter indirectly in formulations including net worth or wealth variables because these change as interest rates vary.

increases, his motivation to save is reduced. On the whole, empirical evidence regarding a wealth effect is mixed.

(4) *Liquid Assets*   To the extent that liquid assets are used as an index of wealth, the argument for its conclusion rests on grounds noted above. Some writers have suggested, however, that changes in liquid asset holdings with wealth constant, will also influence consumption. An observed relation between consumption and liquid assets may simply reflect timing patterns, but as Suits has observed "it is hardly correct to speak of an 'effect' on consumption of liquid balances that are deliberately saved up to be spent." There is, of course, the possibility that liquid assets allow an individual to maintain expenditures in the face of declining income.

4.4.2. *Equation Estimates*

In what follows, we make use of the following additional notation:

C^T – total consumption expenditures
C^D – durable consumption expenditures
C^{ND} – nondurable consumption expenditures
W – net worth of consumers
P – GNP implicit price deflator
Y^d – disposable income.

Turning directly to results in current prices, for total consumption, nondurable consumption and durable consumption, we observe:

$$C^T = -4.53 + 3.36s_2 + 2.12s_3 + 9.09s_4 + 0.818Y^d + 0.002W$$
$$ (1.33) \quad (0.95) \quad (1.05) \quad (0.176) \quad (0.005)$$
$$+0.082C^T_{-1} + 53.4(\Delta P)/P \qquad\qquad R^2 = 0.993 \quad S_e = 0.98 \quad (4.14)$$
$$(0.138) \qquad (24.7)$$

$$C^{ND} = -4.97 + 4.65s_2 + 3.40s_3 + 8.67s_4 + 0.374Y^d + 0.004W$$
$$\phantom{C^{ND} =} (0.89) \quad (0.67) \quad (0.71) \quad (0.120) \quad (0.003)$$
$$+0.458C^{ND}_{-1} + 30.5(\Delta P)/P \qquad\qquad R^2 = 0.997 \quad S_e = 0.61 \quad (4.15)$$
$$(0.125) \qquad (16.5)$$

$$C^D = -1.00 + 1.75s_2 + 0.84s_3 + 2.76s_4 + 0.105Y^d - 0.001W$$
$$ (0.43) \quad (0.33) \quad (0.47) \quad (0.078) \quad (0.004)$$
$$+0.289C^D_{-1} + 35.03(\Delta P)/P \qquad\qquad R^2 = 0.857 \quad S_e = 0.64 \quad (4.16)$$
$$(0.146) \qquad (16.7)$$

Equations (4.14)–(4.16) reveal once again that it is easier to explain economic aggregates than it is to explain the components. In particular, as (4.16) reveals, consumer durable consumption is more difficult to explain than either total or nondurable consumption. Long-run marginal propensities to consume (out of disposable income) implied by the three equations are 0.89, 0.69, and 0.15 respectively.[40] Although it is not statistically significant, the wealth variable does best in nondurable consumption. In the durable equation, it is slightly negative, perhaps reflecting the negative influence of the pre-existing stock of consumer durables. The lagged consumption term shows up in both (4.15) and (4.16) although not in (4.14). Finally, all three equations produce a positive coefficient for the percentage change in prices. Rather than being an indication of speculative price behavior, however, this may simply reflect the fact that the variables are measured in money terms. We experimented with including liquid asset variables in all three equations. The variables tried were the conventional definition of money and money plus time deposits. The asset variables yielded perverse (negative) though insignificant coefficients in total and nondurable consumption. In the durable equation, both variables were positive with the narrow definition seemingly superior.[41] In addition, we included both ΔY and $(Y - Y^*)$ in the durable equation on the grounds that deviations of income from recent or peak levels might play a role in influencing durable consumption behavior. Both variables proved highly positively significant. For example, we have[42]

$$C^D = -0.99 + 2.02s_2 + 1.06s_3 + 2.98s_4 + 0.059Y^d + 0.461C^D_{-1} + 0.214\Delta Y$$
$$\qquad (0.37) \quad (0.28) \quad (0.32) \quad (0.015) \quad (0.125) \qquad (0.054)$$
$$R^2 = 0.889 \quad S_e = 0.57 \quad (4.17)$$

Corresponding results in real terms are as follows:

$$C^T = -5.30 + 4.14s_2 + 2.66s_3 + 9.32s_3 + 0.729Y^d + 0.002W$$
$$\qquad (1.18) \quad (0.85) \quad (0.94) \quad (0.168) \quad (0.003)$$
$$+0.198C^T_{-1} + 46.8(\Delta P)/P \qquad\qquad R^2 = 0.987 \quad S_e = 0.80 \quad (4.18)$$
$$(0.132) \qquad (21.2)$$

---

[40] The propensities obtained by simply regressing the dependent variable on Y^d are 0.93, 0.83 and 0.11.

[41] We have not presented an equation in current prices including a liquid-asset variable. For a similar result, see the deflated case below, equation (4.21).

[42] Somewhat more appropriate might be the inclusion of ΔY^d rather than ΔY.

$$C^{ND} = -4.89 + 5.23s_2 + 3.80s_3 + 8.86s_4 + 0.265Y^d + 0.004W$$
$$\quad\quad (0.73) \quad (0.54) \quad (0.57) \quad (0.102) \quad (0.003)$$
$$+ 0.591C^{ND}_{-1} + 5.01(\Delta P)/P \quad\quad\quad\quad R^2 = 0.995 \quad S_e = 0.46 \quad (4.19)$$
$$(0.108) \quad\quad (11.5)$$

$$C^D = -1.41 + 1.77s_2 + 0.88s_3 + 2.67s_4 + 0.125Y^d + 0.353C^D_{-1}$$
$$\quad\quad (0.39) \quad (0.30) \quad (0.34) \quad (0.083) \quad (0.144)$$
$$-0.002W + 33.3(\Delta P)/P \quad\quad\quad\quad R^2 = 0.760 \quad S_e = 0.60 \quad (4.20)$$
$$(0.003) \quad (16.3)$$

Equations (4.18)–(4.20) tell pretty much the same story as their undeflated counterparts. In fact, the explanatory power of the consumer durable equation is reduced even further in the deflated form. Surprisingly enough, the price variable continues to be significant in (4.18) and (4.20) although not in (4.19). This suggests that some sort of speculative price response may indeed be operative for consumer durables. Long-run marginal propensities are 0.91, 0.65, and 0.19 for the three equations respectively.[43] As in (4.17), ΔY and $(Y - Y^*)$ were added to (4.20), each producing a significant coefficient. In addition, liquid-asset variables produced the expected positive sign in the durable equation. For example, we have:

$$C^D = -7.58 + 2.01s_2 + 1.07s_3 + 2.64s_4 + 0.057Y^d + 0.538C^D_{-1}$$
$$\quad\quad (0.32) \quad (0.25) \quad (0.32) \quad (0.017) \quad (0.114)$$
$$+ 0.205\Delta Y + 0.049M \quad\quad\quad\quad R^2 = 0.827 \quad S_e = 0.57 \quad (4.21)$$
$$(0.055) \quad\quad (0.025)$$

This concludes our discussion and preliminary estimation of the various components of gross national product. We are finally in a position to combine the various bits and pieces of the last three chapters into a unified model. In the next chapter we now turn to this task.

---

[43] The results with just Y^d were 0.93, 0.84 and 0.10 respectively.

CHAPTER 5

ESTIMATION AND APPLICATION OF A COMPLETE MODEL

5.1. Introduction

In this chapter we draw together all of the previously-examined relationships, supplement them with a number of identities, and specify a complete thirty-two equation model of the postwar United States economy. In order to take full account of simultaneity, the model is estimated by structural methods. Then, in the context of our estimates, we attempt to resolve a number of questions left outstanding in earlier chapters. For example, we examine the influence of financial factors on investment and consumption expenditures and the quantitative impact of monetary policy on both financial and nonfinancial variables.

The chapter is organized as follows. For the convenience of the reader, we first present final estimates of the complete model. Next, we discuss several technical issues which logically precede the choice of the final model, but which are best understood after the model has been presented. Following this, we examine alternative behavioral hypotheses on an equation-by-equation basis, presenting estimates for alternative specifications of the various equations. We then use the final estimates of the model (1) to make predictions outside the sample period, (2) to compare structural and ordinary least-squares estimates and (3) to assess the impact on the endogenous variables of several monetary and fiscal policies. The chapter concludes with an examination of some miscellaneous issues. We summarize our findings in chapter 6.

Before turning to the final estimates, the following points which are relevant for the interpretation of the results are noted.

(a) All estimates in this chapter were obtained by two-stage least-squares. The R^2 and the standard error of estimate of each equation were adjusted for degrees of freedom.

(b) The variables G (government expenditure), Tx (taxes less transfers), F (business income), Z (unborrowed reserves plus currency), $\Delta\overline{MUN}$ (supply of municipals) and UN (unemployment rate) are new to this chapter.[1]

(c) The reserve-requirement variables (RR_2^N, RR_2^C) are measured as fractions between 0 and 1.

5.2. The Model: Estimation and Alternative Specifications

5.2.1. *Final Equation Summary*

The final form of the model consists of the following thirty-two equations.

$$\Delta E^N = 0.142 + 0.052s_2 - 0.004s_3 + 0.004s_4 - 1.093E_{-1}^N$$
$$(0.027) \quad (0.022) \quad (0.029) \quad (0.122)$$
$$- 0.00020r_s \, (D^N + T^N) + 0.0076\Delta D^* + 0.0096\Delta D_{-1}^* + 0.114d_1$$
$$(0.00008) \qquad\qquad (0.0039) \qquad (0.0034) \qquad\quad (0.019)$$
$$R^2 = 0.700 \quad S_e = 0.041 \quad DW = 2.34 \quad (5.1)$$

$$\Delta E^C = 0.316 + 0.048s_2 + 0.080s_3 + 0.077s_4 - 0.595E_{-1}^C - 0.034r_s$$
$$(0.023) \quad (0.018) \quad (0.025) \quad (0.123) \qquad (0.011)$$
$$+ 0.0041\Delta D^* + 0.0048\Delta D_{-1}^* + 0.013d_1$$
$$(0.0033) \qquad (0.0028) \qquad\quad (0.012)$$
$$R^2 = 0.670 \quad S_e = 0.035 \quad DW = 1.70 \quad (5.2)$$

$$\Delta B^N = 0.049 + 0.081s_2 + 0.077s_3 + 0.187s_4 - 0.411B_{-1}^N + 0.117\Delta CL^N$$
$$(0.080) \quad (0.099) \quad (0.133) \quad (0.088) \qquad (0.035)$$
$$- 0.153(r_d - r_s) + 0.311dp - 0.049\Delta D^* - 11.42RR_2^N$$
$$(0.106) \qquad\qquad (0.104) \quad (0.015) \qquad (7.477)$$
$$R^2 = 0.705 \quad S_e = 0.133 \quad DW = 2.34 \quad (5.3)$$

$$\Delta B^C = 0.026 + 0.044s_2 - 0.011s_3 + 0.034s_4 - 0.299B_{-1}^C + 0.055\Delta CL^C$$
$$(0.013) \quad (0.013) \quad (0.019) \quad (0.060) \qquad (0.020)$$
$$- 0.040(r_d - r_s) - 0.022\Delta T^C - 0.0066\Delta D^* + 0.061dp$$
$$(0.016) \qquad\qquad (0.013) \qquad (0.0024) \qquad (0.019)$$
$$R^2 = 0.722 \quad S_e = 0.024 \quad DW = 2.27 \quad (5.4)$$

---

[1] As the equations below reveal, the G and Tx variables are actually somewhat broader than this brief description implies.

$$\Delta S^{N} = 2.441 - 1.656s_{2} - 0.587s_{3} - 1.742s_{4} - 0.103S^{N}_{-1} + 0.101\Delta\bar{S}$$
$$\quad\quad\quad (0.512) \quad (0.512) \quad (0.681) \quad (0.034) \quad\quad (0.049)$$
$$- 0.330\Delta\bar{O} + 0.830\Delta T^{N} + 0.672\Delta D^{N} - 0.848\Delta CL^{N} - 160.0RR^{N}_{2}$$
$$\quad (0.059) \quad\quad (0.207) \quad\quad (0.097) \quad\quad (0.217) \quad\quad\quad (44.6)$$
$$R^{2} = 0.881 \;\; S_{e} = 0.740 \;\; DW = 2.20 \quad (5.5)$$

$$\Delta S^{C} = 0.332 - 0.779s_{2} - 1.206s_{3} - 1.335s_{4} - 0.121S^{C}_{-1} + 0.011\Delta\bar{S}$$
$$\quad\quad\quad (0.396) \quad (0.507) \quad (0.565) \quad (0.038) \quad\quad (0.043)$$
$$- 0.171\Delta\bar{O} + 1.961\Delta T^{C} - 0.644\Delta CL^{C} - 101.61RR^{C}_{2} - 1.071\Delta D^{C}$$
$$\quad (0.043) \quad\quad (0.469) \quad\quad (0.581) \quad\quad\quad (36.82) \quad\quad (0.229)$$
$$+ 0.158\Delta D^{*} + 0.094\Delta D^{*}_{-1} + 0.030\bar{r}_{3}(R,15)(D^{C} + T^{C})$$
$$\quad (0.054) \quad\quad (0.041) \quad\quad\quad (0.011)$$
$$R^{2} = 0.823 \;\; S_{e} = 0.478 \;\; DW = 2.43 \quad (5.6)$$

$$\Delta O^{N} = 0.466 + 0.767s_{2} + 0.694s_{3} + 0.855s_{4} - 0.036O^{N}_{-1} - 0.124\Delta\bar{S}$$
$$\quad\quad\quad (0.236) \quad (0.337) \quad (0.376) \quad (0.029) \quad\quad (0.044)$$
$$+ 0.213\Delta\bar{O} - 0.0014r'_{e}(D^{N} + T^{N}) - 0.122\Delta CL^{N} + 0.0056\bar{r}_{10}(L,5)(D^{N} + T^{N})$$
$$\quad (0.040) \quad\quad (0.0007) \quad\quad\quad\quad\quad (0.134) \quad\quad\quad (0.0051)$$
$$R^{2} = 0.821 \;\; S_{e} = 0.529 \;\; DW = 2.02 \quad (5.7)$$

$$\Delta O^{C} = 0.159 + 0.476s_{2} + 0.334s_{3} + 0.554s_{4} - 0.011O^{C}_{-1} - 0.091\Delta\bar{S}$$
$$\quad\quad\quad (0.168) \quad (0.178) \quad (0.209) \quad (0.032) \quad\quad (0.027)$$
$$+ 0.141\Delta\bar{O} - 0.0079r'_{e}(D^{C} + T^{C}) + 0.421\Delta CL^{C} + 0.0094r_{10}(D^{C} + T^{C})$$
$$\quad (0.024) \quad\quad (0.0049) \quad\quad\quad\quad\quad (0.319) \quad\quad\quad (0.0067)$$
$$R^{2} = 0.838 \;\; S_{e} = 0.341 \;\; DW = 2.27 \quad (5.8)$$

$$\Delta MUN^{N} = -0.282 - 0.373s_{2} - 0.078s_{3} - 0.333s_{4} - 0.019MUN^{N}_{-1}$$
$$\quad\quad\quad\quad (0.074) \quad (0.071) \quad (0.072) \quad (0.021)$$
$$+ 0.192\Delta T^{N} + 0.105\Delta T^{N}_{-1} + 0.024S^{N}_{-1} + 0.132\Delta\overline{MUN}$$
$$\quad (0.055) \quad\quad (0.051) \quad\quad (0.008) \quad\quad (0.104)$$
$$R^{2} = 0.732 \;\; S_{e} = 0.174 \;\; DW = 2.14 \quad (5.9)$$

$$\Delta MUN^C = 0.117 - 0.080s_2 - 0.107s_3 - 0.128s_4 - 0.021MUN^C_{-1} + 0.168\Delta T^C$$
$$(0.026)\quad(0.037)\quad(0.039)\quad(0.008)\qquad\quad(0.034)$$
$$+0.073\Delta T^C_{-1} + 0.062\Delta D^C + 0.060\Delta\overline{MUN}$$
$$(0.029)\qquad\;(0.018)\qquad(0.024)$$
$$R^2 = 0.696\;\;S_e = 0.044\;\;DW = 1.40\quad(5.10)$$

$$\Delta r'_e = 0.070 - 0.152(r'_e)_{-1} + 0.200\bar{r}_{10}(L,15) + 5.313L^* - 3.860L^*_{-1}$$
$$(0.084)\qquad\quad(0.064)\qquad\qquad(1.870)\quad(1.949)$$
$$+0.084\Delta r_s + 0.053(\Delta r_s)_{-1}\quad R^2 = 0.591\;\;S_e = 0.090\;\;DW = 1.88\quad(5.11)$$
$$(0.033)\qquad(0.032)$$

$$\Delta C = 0.328 + 0.692s_2 + 0.797s_3 + 0.870s_4 - 0.112C_{-1} + 0.076Y$$
$$(0.095)\quad(0.081)\quad(0.125)\quad(0.075)\qquad(0.015)$$
$$-0.0010r_sY - 0.051\left[0.114\sum_{i=0}^{19}(.9)^iY_{t-i}\right] - 0.087\,(\Delta P/P)Y - 0.0021r_pY$$
$$(0.0004)\qquad(0.012)\qquad\qquad\qquad\qquad(0.064)\qquad\qquad\;(0.0012)$$
$$R^2 = 0.958\;\;S_e = 0.123\;\;DW = 1.83\quad(5.12)$$

$$\Delta D = -0.270 + 3.151s_2 + 4.040s_3 + 7.122s_4 - 0.127D_{-1} + 0.140Y$$
$$(0.644)\quad(0.617)\quad(1.003)\quad(0.081)\qquad(0.091)$$
$$-0.0066r_sY - 0.012r_pY$$
$$(0.0019)\qquad(0.010)$$
$$R^2 = 0.937\;\;S_e = 0.784\;\;DW = 1.55\quad(5.13)$$

$$\Delta T = 1.124 + 0.516s_2 - 0.017s_3 - 0.410s_4 - 0.077T_{-1} + 0.016r_pY$$
$$(0.481)\quad(0.425)\quad(0.478)\quad(0.055)\qquad(0.008)$$
$$-0.059\bar{r}_{10}(R,15)Y + 0.076Y_{-1}$$
$$(0.013)\qquad\qquad(0.032)$$
$$R^2 = 0.615\;\;S_e = 0.774\;\;DW = 1.36\quad(5.14)$$

$$\Delta CL = -2.398 - 0.281s_2 + 0.070s_3 - 0.985s_4 - 0.157CL_{-1} + 0.448\Delta H'$$
$$(0.258)\quad(0.274)\quad(0.402)\quad(0.043)\qquad(0.083)$$
$$-0.320(r'_e - r_s) + 0.163\Delta D^* + 0.081(Y - \Delta H')$$
$$(0.168)\qquad\qquad(0.044)\qquad(0.020)$$
$$R^2 = 0.735\;\;S_e = 0.434\;\;DW = 1.91\quad(5.15)$$

$$r_{10} - r_s = 3.756 - 0.484(\varDelta r_s)_{-1} - 2.906\varDelta S_1^* - 0.744\varDelta S_2^* - 6.206\bar{r}_{10}(R,10)$$
$$\phantom{r_{10} - r_s = 3.756} (0.124) \qquad (2.536) \quad (2.105) \qquad (1.344)$$
$$+ 3.770\bar{r}_{10}(R,5) \qquad\qquad R^2 = 0.610 \;\; S_e = 0.337 \;\; DW = 1.41 \quad (5.16)$$
$$(1.828)$$

$$r_3 - r_s = -1.54 - 2.248\bar{r}_3(R,10) + 2.872\bar{r}_3(R,5) - 0.139\varDelta r_s - 0.466(\varDelta r_s)_{-1}$$
$$ (0.407) \qquad\qquad (0.614) \qquad\quad (0.115) \qquad (0.095)$$
$$- 2.208\varDelta S_1^* + 1.055\varDelta S_2^* + 3.821 S_1^* + 1.487 S_2^*$$
$$(2.009) \qquad (1.571) \qquad (0.775) \quad (0.584)$$
$$R^2 = 0.627 \;\; S_e = 0.234 \;\; DW = 1.42 \quad (5.17)$$

$$I = -2.259 + 0.302 s_2 I_{-1} + 0.149 s_3 I_{-1} + 0.248 s_4 I_{-1} + 0.680 I_{-1}$$
$$ (0.013) \qquad\quad (0.009) \qquad\quad (0.009) \qquad\quad (0.045)$$
$$+ 1.405 K_{-1} + 0.053(Y - Y^*) + 0.027 Y - 0.0022 r_{10} Y + 0.147\varDelta CL$$
$$(0.617) \qquad (0.019) \qquad\qquad (0.010) \quad (0.0010) \qquad (0.040)$$
$$R^2 = 0.968 \;\; S_e = 0.153 \;\; DW = 1.70 \quad (5.18)$$

$$\varDelta H' = -4.184 + 1.229 s_2 + 0.359 s_3 + 2.128 s_4 - 0.070 H'_{-1} + 0.358\varDelta H'_{-1}$$
$$ (0.679) \quad (0.518) \quad (0.763) \quad (0.043) \qquad (0.113)$$
$$+ 0.115\varDelta U_{-1} + 0.097(Y - \varDelta H') - 0.128\varDelta(Y - \varDelta H') - 0.0068 r'_e \;\; (Y - \varDelta H')$$
$$(0.030) \qquad\quad (0.044) \qquad\qquad (0.056) \qquad\qquad (0.0033)$$
$$+ 0.283\varDelta CL \qquad\qquad R^2 = 0.788 \;\; S_e = 0.514 \;\; DW = 2.11 \quad (5.19)$$
$$(0.166)$$

$$C^{ND} = -3.452 + 2.122 s_2 + 3.087 s_3 + 7.515 s_4 + 0.202 Y^d + 0.333 C^{ND}_{-1}$$
$$\phantom{C^{ND} = -3.452} (1.340) \quad (0.604) \quad (0.763) \quad (0.100) \quad (0.145)$$
$$+ 0.326 C^{ND}_{-2} + 0.0043 W \qquad R^2 = 0.995 \;\; S_e = 0.421 \;\; DW = 1.82 \quad (5.20)$$
$$(0.110) \qquad (0.0025)$$

$$C^D = -12.101 + 1.756s_2 + 0.836s_3 + 2.272s_4 + 0.092Y^d + 0.354C^D_{-1}$$
$$ (0.307) \quad (0.242) \quad (0.318) \quad (0.019) \quad (0.121)$$
$$+ 0.128\Delta Y + 41.44(\Delta P)/P + 0.078(C+D)$$
$$ (0.059) \quad\quad (14.14) \quad\quad (0.026)$$

$$R^2 = 0.853 \quad S_e = 0.468 \quad DW = 1.97 \quad (5.21)$$

$$Y = C^{ND} + C^D + I + \Delta H' + G \tag{5.22}$$

$$Y^d = Y - Tx \tag{5.23}$$

$$CL^N + CL^C = CL \tag{5.24}$$

$$R^R = k_1 D^N + k_3 D^C + k_4(T^N + T^C) \tag{5.25}$$

$$D^{\dot{}} = \frac{Z - C - k_4(T^N + T^C)}{\left[\dfrac{k_1 D^N + k_3 D^C}{D^N + D^C}\right]} \tag{5.26}$$

$$R^R + E^N + E^C - B^N - B^C + C = Z \tag{5.27}$$

$$\frac{D^N}{D^C} = \gamma_1 \tag{5.28}$$

$$\frac{T^N}{T^C} = \gamma_2 \tag{5.29}$$

$$\frac{CL^N}{CL^C} = \gamma_3 \tag{5.30}$$

$$D^N + D^C = \gamma_4 D \tag{5.31}$$

$$T^N + T^C = \gamma_5 T. \tag{5.32}$$

As this summary reveals, only 21 of the 32 equations have actually been estimated. The remainder are identities, although, as we shall shortly see, these are of two distinct types. The endogenous variables determined by this system are as follows:

Y	– gross national product	S^C	– country short-term securities
C^{ND}	– nondurable consumption	O^N	– noncountry long-term securities
C^D	– durable consumption		
I	– fixed investment	O^C	– country long-term securities
$\Delta H'$	– inventory investment	MUN^N	– noncountry municipals
Y^d	– disposable income	MUN^C	– country municipals
D^N	– noncountry net demand deposits	r'_e	– commercial loan rate
		r_s	– bill rate
D^C	– country net demand deposits	r_3	– intermediate government rate
T^N	– noncountry time deposits	r_{10}	– long-term bond rate
T^C	– country time deposits	R^R	– required reserves
CL^N	– noncountry commercial loans	D^*	– potential demand deposits (member-bank)
CL^C	– country commercial loans		
E^N	– noncountry excess reserves	D	– demand deposit component of money supply
E^C	– country excess reserves		
B^N	– noncountry borrowing	C	– currency component of money supply
B^C	– country borrowing		
S^N	– noncountry short-term securities	T	– public's time deposits
		CL	– total commercial loans.

5.2.2. Some Technical Considerations

Before discussing the model in any detail, several technical comments are in order. These concern themselves with the problems of nonlinearities, of performing significance tests, of choosing exogenous variables for the first stage of our estimation procedure, and of choosing among various functional forms for some of our behavioral relationships.

5.2.2.1. *Nonlinearities.* It can be noted that our model contains numerous nonlinear elements. These nonlinearities pose problems both for the identification and estimation of the model and for the interpretation of the results. Standard identification conditions apply only to linear models. Fortunately, however, Fisher [44], has recently extended these conditions to certain types of nonlinear structural equations. Our model meets the requirements of Fisher's results, and making use of these extended conditions, it appears that each of our equations is appropriately identified.

The presence of nonlinearities also creates difficulties in estimation since two-stage least squares is not even well-defined in the nonlinear case. For nonlinear systems, the reduced form is no longer a simple linear function of the predetermined variables. In fact, the reduced form may not even have a representation in closed form. Hence, it is not clear how one goes about estimating the first stage.

One can, of course, use the predetermined variables in the standard linear way in the first stage, regarding this as a Taylor Series approximation to the true nonlinear reduced form. Even if we adopt this approach, there still remains one final detail before two-stage least squares becomes operational. It is necessary to specify the particular functional forms of the nonlinear constructs to be used as dependent variables in the first stage.

We have two alternatives:

(a) to use the nonlinear form (e.g., $\log y$) as a dependent variable. In this way we obtain directly a predicted value $(\widehat{\log y})$.

(b) to use the linear form (e.g., y) of the variable to obtain a predicted value $(\hat{y})$ and then by the appropriate transformation (of $\hat{y}$), obtain the required nonlinear function (e.g., $\log \hat{y}$).

Since it comes closer to meeting the rationale of two-stage least squares, procedure (a) promises to yield more satisfactory results. Moreover, sampling experiments, conducted in another context with two nonlinear models by the author and Richard Quandt, overwhelmingly supported the superiority of (a).[2] In view of this, procedure (a) was utilized throughout this study.

5.2.2.2. *Tests of Significance.* The interpretation of point estimates, or, more particularly, hypothesis testing with respect to individual coefficients or equations, is complicated by several factors. As noted earlier, even for linear models, little is known about the small sample properties of two-stage least squares. By introducing nonlinearities and lagged values of most of the dependent variables, we simply compound the problem. This means that the standard t-, F-, and Durbin-Watson tests are now doubly suspect.

What evidence there is, suggests that two-stage least squares tends to yield somewhat conservative t-values, i.e., tends to understate the

---

[2] See [52]. It is interesting to note that these experiments reveal that the approximative two-stage method described above yields parameter estimates which are distinctly superior to ordinary least squares and only slightly inferior to full-information maximum likelihood. It might also be mentioned that in these experiments ordinary least squares tended to do relatively worse than it had done elsewhere in experiments involving linear models.

significance of a particular coefficient.[3] This suggests, if anything, that we can afford to place greater emphasis on *a priori* specifications (such as the appropriate sign of a coefficient) and to be somewhat liberal with respect to the notion of significance.

5.2.2.3. *Selection of Exogenous Variables.* A third problem concerns the selection of the exogenous variables for the first stage. In the process of estimating the complete model, we naturally experimented with a variety of specifications for each equation. However, with two-stage least squares, these experiments run into certain difficulties.

Since in the first stage we regress each (function of an) endogenous variable on the exogenous variables,[4] structural estimates of any individual equation depend on the specification of the entire system. In particular, introducing a new exogenous variable into one equation technically requires re-estimation of all other equations. However, in practice when working with a large number of exogenous variables, the addition of but one more is unlikely to produce appreciable changes in any of the first-stage estimates or in the structural estimates.

Ordinarily, this problem did not arise since, when it was decided to modify an equation, the "new" variables involved had already appeared elsewhere in the system. There were a few exceptions to this, but because of the size of the system we did not re-estimate all the other equations during each phase of our experimentation with a given equation. Nevertheless, before presenting our final structural estimates, we re-estimated the entire model. In line with our argument, it turned out that the estimates changed very little.

5.2.2.4. *Alternative Functional Forms and Tests for Homoscedasticity.* In

---

[3] The evidence referred to consists of a comparison between the root mean square error of a parameter estimate and the mean (asymptotic) standard deviation of a coefficient. For consistent estimating methods, the latter is a consistent estimate of the former. However, it was found in [52] that for small samples the standard deviation measure tended to be much higher than the root mean square error. On the other hand, their ratio did appear to converge to unity as the sample size increased.

[4] It should be mentioned that we omitted the multiplicative seasonal dummy variables in the first stage, relying instead on the additive variables. We did this to avoid problems of multicollinearity. The selection of a subset of all the exogenous variables for inclusion in the first stage is also common practice when the number of exogenous variables exceeds the number of observations. Principal components can also be used to get around this difficulty.

our preliminary estimation of the various bank equations we utilized a functional form in which all variables entered linearly. A typical equation (with error term u_1) can be written as

$$\Delta A_t = b_0 + b_1 A_{t-1} + b_2 r_{1t} + b_3 r_{2t} + \ldots b_n X_t + u_1, \qquad \text{(i)}$$

where the change in holdings (ΔA_t) depends on the lagged stock (A_{t-1}), rates of return (r_{1t}, r_{2t}) and the constraint variables (X_t). In our structural estimation, we experimented with two additional functional forms. In particular, letting W represent the "wealth" (i.e., portfolio size measured somehow) of a bank class, the two forms we chose are as follows:

$$\frac{\Delta A_t}{W_t} = b_0 + b_1 \frac{A_{t-1}}{W_t} + b_2 r_{1t} + \ldots b_n \frac{X_t}{W_t} + u_2 \qquad \text{(ii)}$$

$$\Delta A_t = b_0 W_t + b_1 A_{t-1} + b_2 r_{1t} W_t + \ldots b_n X_t + u_3. \qquad \text{(iii)}$$

We made use of equations (ii) and (iii) to meet certain objections brought against form (i). Most importantly (ii) and (iii) are [as (i) is not] homogeneous of degree one in dollar magnitudes.[5] It has been suggested elsewhere that this is a reasonable assumption to impose on bank behavioral equations [29]. It has been similarly suggested that a wealth variable should be included in bank portfolio equations.[6]

We have chosen to measure bank "wealth" for each bank class as the sum of net demand and time deposits (i.e., $D^N + T^N$, $D^C + T^C$). Tables 5.1 to 5.5 below report the results of estimating various equations for the three functional forms. In these tables, "linear" corresponds to (i), "ratio" to (ii), and "multiplicative linear" to (iii). It should be noted that the multiplicative-linear results do not report a coefficient estimate for the level of the wealth variable. A coefficient was estimated but in every instance it proved but a fraction of its standard error. Hence, the equations were re-estimated with that variable omitted.[7]

---

[5] Thus, for example, a doubling of the banks' assets and liabilities will simply produce a doubling of the various flows.

[6] See [29]. We have intertwined the issues of dollar homogeneity and the use of a wealth variable. They can, of course, be viewed as separate problems. For example, in (iii) we could multiply all nondollar variables by A_{t-1} instead of W_t and still obtain a homogeneous form.

[7] The omission of W from (iii) still leaves the equation homogeneous of degree one in dollar values. However, the inclusion of an intercept term does not. See next footnote.

The lack of significance of the level of the "wealth" variable suggests that, in at least one sense, this type of variable may not be crucial to the specification of the bank equations. More generally, however, because of the abundance of alternative specifications, it is impossible formally to reject the broad hypothesis that a "wealth" variable is relevant for bank behavior. Similarly, neither can one formally test the dollar homogeneity assumption.[8]

As a result, only qualitative comparisons can be made. Comparisons of the results reported in table 5.1 to 5.5 reveal that, on the whole, there are only small differences between the three sets of estimates. The largest differences would appear to be obtained between the ratio estimates and the other two types.[9]

The differences between the ratio and the two linear forms arise, in part, because of underlying differences in the distribution of the error term. In particular, if (ii) is the correct specification of the equation and one estimates (iii), then the implicit assumption of the homoscedasticity of the error term would be violated. That is u_3 would be given by $u_2 W$.

It is important to establish which functional form is the appropriate one because the presence of heteroscedasticity will yield inefficient estimates.[10] In order to test for homoscedasticity, we rely on a recently-developed nonparametric test [53] which involves the following steps:

(a) Confining our attention to the linear form, let $\hat{u}_t$ be the tth residual corresponding to the tth value of the deflator, W_t. The set of residuals, $\{\hat{u}_t\}$, is ordered in the following manner. First order the value of the

---

[8] One possible way to test the homogeneity assumption is to include an intercept in (iii) or a term in $1/W$ in (ii) and to test the significance of its coefficient. When this was done for the $1/W$ variable, only for the two excess-reserve equations did the coefficient prove to be significantly different from 0 at the 5% level. The ratio results therefore suggest that one particular type of inhomogeneity can, on the whole, be rejected. The computer program utilized did not, unfortunately, produce standard errors for the intercepts. Hence, for (iii) testing proved infeasible.

[9] The form (dimensionality) of the dependent variable is different for the ratio estimates. Hence, strictly speaking, the R^2's and standard errors of estimate produced by this form are not comparable to the other two. The standard errors reported in the tables are adjusted figures. They were obtained by multiplying the raw standard errors by the mean of the deflator variable (N.B., $\overline{D^N + T^N} = 109.4$, $\overline{D^C + T^C} = 56.4$). To compare the coefficients of the seasonal and shift variables one should multiply the ratio estimates by these means (divided by 100) as well.

[10] We are, of course, reasoning by analogy with ordinary least squares. Virtually nothing is known about the effect of heteroscedasticity on nonlinear, two-stage least squares estimates.

deflator variable; i.e., renumber such that $W_t \leq W_{t'}$ if and only if $t < t'$. We then index the $\hat{u}_t$ so that they correspond to the W_t.[11]

(b) Count the number of *peaks* in the ordered residuals where we define a *peak* to be an instance where $|\hat{u}_{t'}| \geq |\hat{u}_t|$ for all $t < t'$.

If the residuals of the linear form are heteroscedastic such that the variance increases with W, the number of observed peaks will tend to be large. Under the null hypothesis, the probability of obtaining $0, 1, \ldots,$ $n-1$ peaks in a series of n residuals can be calculated explicitly. This has been done elsewhere [53]. Here, we need note that the probability of five or less peaks is 0.88 and the probability of six or less peaks is 0.95.

Tables 5.1 to 5.5 report, for each of the equations estimated, the relevant number of peaks.[12] At a significance level of 0.12, we need six peaks to reject the null hypothesis; at a level of 0.05, we need seven peaks. At the 0.12 level, we can reject the ratio form 4 times (for E^N, O^N, O^C, B^N) and the linear form once (for S^C). For the remaining equations no unambiguous choice is possible. It would seem, therefore, that only for country bank holdings of short-term securities is the ratio form preferable to the linear one. In view of this finding, we decided to choose the ratio equation for S^C for inclusion in the final model. It should be noted, however, that for convenience the equation as reported earlier (in the summary of the model) has been written in multiplicative-linear form.[13]

5.2.3. *Discussion of the Model*

Now, we turn to a discussion of the model. While our ultimate concern lies in examining implications and alternative specifications of the estimated equations, let us first briefly dispense with the various identities.

5.2.3.1. *Accounting Identities.* Equations (5.22)–(5.27) are straightforward accounting relationships. In (5.22) we simply add up the endogenous components of GNP, tack on an exogenous expenditure category, and equate the result to Y. Similarly (5.23) expresses the relationship between

---

[11] A similar procedure is carried out when testing the ratio form except that the ordering is carried out with $1/W_t$ rather than W_t.

[12] The number of peaks was substantially the same with the level of the deflator variable included in the multiplicative-linear form.

[13] The coefficients of the seasonals and the reserve-requirement variable were adjusted (at the mean of $D^C + T^C$) to be consistent with the linear form. It should also be noted that for the E^N, O^C, and O^N equations the form chosen was the multiplicative-linear one. This accounts for their similar appearance to the S^C equation.

TABLE 5.1

Excess reserves

Model form	Bank class	Intercept	s_2	s_3	s_4	E_{-1}	r_s	ΔD^*	ΔD^*_{-1}	d_1	R^2	S_e	DW	Peaks
Linear	City	0.127	0.056 (0.028)	−0.001 (0.023)	0.009 (0.029)	−1.070 (0.124)	−0.019 (0.010)	0.0067 (0.0038)	0.0098 (0.0035)	0.123 (0.019)	0.682	0.043	2.27	2
Ratio	City	0.110	0.057 (0.030)	0.002 (0.025)	0.007 (0.032)	−1.037 (0.126)	−0.00018 (0.00011)	0.0080 (0.0048)	0.0118 (0.0042)	0.151 (0.023)	0.657	0.050	2.22	6
Mult. linear	City	0.142	0.052 (0.027)	−0.004 (0.022)	0.004 (0.029)	−1.093 (0.122)	−0.00020 (0.00008)	0.0076 (0.0039)	0.0096 (0.0034)	0.114 (0.019)	0.700	0.041	2.34	4
Linear	Country	0.316	0.048 (0.023)	0.080 (0.018)	0.077 (0.025)	−0.595 (0.123)	−0.034 (0.011)	0.0041 (0.0033)	0.0048 (0.0028)	0.013 (0.012)	0.670	0.035	1.70	3
Ratio	Country	0.269	0.106 (0.051)	0.175 (0.041)	0.143 (0.056)	−0.301 (0.106)	−0.00055 (0.00026)	0.0039 (0.0042)	0.0032 (0.0035)	0.074 (0.040)	0.504	0.045	1.84	5
Mult. linear	Country	0.307	0.046 (0.024)	0.074 (0.019)	0.067 (0.025)	−0.595 (0.123)	−0.00047 (0.00016)	0.0059 (0.0033)	0.0056 (0.0028)	0.004 (0.014)	0.664	0.035	1.71	3

TABLE 5.2
Borrowings

(a) City equations

Model form	Intercept	s_2	s_3	s_4	B_{-1}^N	ΔCL^N	$(r_d - r_s)$	dp	ΔD^*	RR_2^N	$(r_d - r_s)^2$	R^2	S_e	DW	Peaks
Linear	0.049	0.081 (0.080)	0.077 (0.099)	0.187 (0.133)	−0.411 (0.088)	0.117 (0.035)	−0.153 (0.106)	0.311 (0.104)	−0.049 (0.016)	−11.43 (7.48)		0.705	0.133	2.34	4
Ratio	0.003	0.086 (0.075)	0.088 (0.095)	0.217 (0.127)	−0.405 (0.088)	0.115 (0.036)	−0.00127 (0.00105)	0.336 (0.099)	−0.056 (0.017)	−11.087 (7.40)		0.708	0.141	2.41	6
Mult. linear	0.002	0.123 (0.077)	0.126 (0.096)	0.273 (0.126)	−0.400 (0.088)	0.112 (0.030)	−0.00083 (0.00087)	0.301 (0.101)	−0.062 (0.014)	−10.02 (6.88)		0.708	0.133	2.37	3
Linear	0.045	0.079 (0.093)	0.076 (0.105)	0.186 (0.147)	−0.412 (0.108)	0.121 (0.041)	−0.175 (0.162)	0.305 (0.109)	−0.050 (0.019)	−11.70 (8.03)	0.045 (0.188)	0.696	0.136	2.44	4

(b) Country equations

Model form	Intercept	s_2	s_3	s_4	B_{-1}^C	ΔCL^C	$(r_d - r_s)$	dp	ΔD^*	ΔT^C	$(r_d - r_s)^2$	R^2	S_e	DW	Peaks
Linear	0.026	0.044 (0.013)	−0.011 (0.013)	0.034 (0.019)	−0.299 (0.060)	0.055 (0.020)	−0.040 (0.016)	0.061 (0.019)	−0.0066 (0.0024)	−0.022 (0.013)		0.722	0.024	2.27	3
Ratio	0.095	0.071 (0.023)	−0.038 (0.023)	0.020 (0.036)	−0.358 (0.071)	0.055 (0.022)	−0.0013 (0.0005)	0.137 (0.036)	−0.0047 (0.0027)	−0.042 (0.016)	0.00070 (0.00062)	0.726	0.025	2.41	2
Mult. linear	0.022	0.047 (0.015)	−0.004 (0.014)	0.043 (0.021)	−0.331 (0.072)	0.057 (0.022)	−0.0011 (0.0005)	0.056 (0.020)	−0.0088 (0.0028)	−0.023 (0.015)	0.00083 (0.00062)	0.683	0.026	2.39	3
Linear	0.031	0.043 (0.014)	−0.010 (0.014)	0.031 (0.020)	−0.331 (0.067)	0.056 (0.020)	−0.063 (0.026)	0.056 (0.019)	−0.0072 (0.0025)	−0.026 (0.013)	0.038 (0.032)	0.718	0.025	2.36	3

TABLE 5.3

Short-term securities

(a) City equations

Model form	Intercept	s_2	s_3	s_4	S_{-1}^N	$\Delta\bar{S}$	$\Delta\bar{O}$	ΔT^N	ΔCL^N	RR_2^N	ΔD^N	R^2	S_e	DW	Peaks
Linear	2.441	−1.656 (0.512)	−0.587 (0.512)	−1.742 (0.681)	−0.103 (0.034)	0.101 (0.049)	−0.330 (0.059)	0.830 (0.207)	−0.848 (0.217)	−160.0 (44.6)	0.672 (0.097)	0.881	0.740	2.20	4
Ratio	2.157	−1.521 (0.489)	−0.521 (0.484)	−1.618 (0.661)	−0.088 (0.031)	0.080 (0.055)	−0.326 (0.054)	0.482 (0.250)	−0.918 (0.201)	−153.5 (41.0)	0.719 (0.113)	0.883	0.760	2.26	5

(b) Country equations

	Intercept	s_2	s_3	s_4	S_{-1}^C	$\Delta\bar{S}$	$\Delta\bar{O}$	ΔT^C	ΔCL^C	RR_2^C	ΔD^C	ΔD^*	ΔD_{-1}^*	r_s or $[r_3(R, 15)]$	R^2	S_e	DW	Peaks
Linear	1.210	−0.442 (0.400)	−1.044 (0.580)	−1.325 (0.636)	−0.125 (0.044)	0.048 (0.044)	−0.146 (0.045)	1.373 (0.384)	−0.926 (0.716)	−77.13 (34.54)	0.925 (0.284)	0.147 (0.055)	0.109 (0.044)	0.300 (0.180)	0.796	0.500	2.29	8
Linear	−0.405	−0.447 (0.409)	−0.700 (0.507)	−0.808 (0.563)	−0.122 (0.045)	0.034 (0.046)	−0.157 (0.047)	2.013 (0.462)	−0.058 (0.559)	−92.59 (35.95)	0.842 (0.246)	0.128 (0.053)	0.128 (0.046)	1.381* (0.641)	0.786	0.513	2.32	8
Ratio	−0.588	−1.382 (0.703)	−2.138 (0.899)	−2.367 (1.002)	−0.121 (0.038)	0.011 (0.043)	−0.171 (0.043)	1.961 (0.469)	−0.644 (0.581)	−180.16 (65.28)	1.071 (0.229)	0.158 (0.054)	0.094 (0.041)	0.030* (0.011)	0.823	0.478	2.43	3

* This coefficient corresponds to $\bar{r}_3(R,15)$.

TABLE 5.4

Long-term securities

(a) City equations

Model form	Intercept	s_2	s_3	s_4	O^N_{-1}	$\Delta\bar{S}$	$\Delta\bar{O}$	r'_e	ΔCL^N	$\bar{r}_{10}(L,5)$	R^2	S_e	DW	Peaks
Linear	1.009	0.737 (0.234)	0.659 (0.336)	0.801 (0.379)	−0.035 (0.028)	−0.116 (0.043)	0.212 (0.039)	−0.269 (0.145)	−0.120 (0.134)	0.459 (0.584)	0.822	0.527	2.03	3
Ratio	1.154	0.692 (0.223)	0.754 (0.312)	0.904 (0.344)	−0.036 (0.030)	−0.146 (0.042)	0.191 (0.039)	−0.0030 (0.0016)	−0.206 (0.128)	0.0066 (0.0054)	0.815	0.552	2.00	8
Mult. linear	0.466	0.767 (0.236)	0.694 (0.337)	0.855 (0.376)	−0.036 (0.029)	−0.124 (0.044)	0.213 (0.040)	−0.0014 (0.0007)	−0.122 (0.134)	0.0056 (0.0051)	0.821	0.529	2.02	3

(b) Country equations

	Intercept	s_2	s_3	s_4	O^C_{-1}	$\Delta\bar{S}$	$\Delta\bar{O}$	r'_e	ΔCL^C	$r_{10}-r_s$	r_{10}	S^C_{-1}	R^2	S_e	DW	Peaks
Linear	0.893	0.352 (0.136)	0.255 (0.165)	0.349 (0.165)	−0.039 (0.025)	−0.069 (0.023)	0.146 (0.023)	−0.177 (0.080)					0.856	0.321	2.30	1
Linear	−0.279	0.301 (0.142)	0.360 (0.160)	0.460 (0.161)	−0.009 (0.023)	−0.091 (0.020)	0.120 (0.022)			0.161 (0.108)			0.851	0.327	2.25	1
Linear	−0.298	0.382 (0.039)	0.315 (0.174)	0.374 (0.167)	0.016 (0.056)	−0.072 (0.023)	0.140 (0.024)	−0.218 (0.088)				0.062 (0.056)	0.856	0.321	2.29	1
Mult. linear	0.159	0.476 (0.168)	0.334 (0.178)	0.554 (0.209)	−0.011 (0.032)	−0.091 (0.207)	0.141 (0.024)	−0.0079 (0.0049)	−0.421 (0.319)		0.0094 (0.0067)		0.838	0.341	2.27	2
Ratio	2.220	0.764 (0.295)	0.496 (0.324)	0.795 (0.351)	−0.044 (0.029)	−0.082 (0.024)	0.127 (0.024)	−0.0043 (0.0020)	−0.348 (0.304)				0.823	0.363	2.29	7

TABLE 5.5

Municipals

(a) City equations

Model form	Intercept	s_2	s_3	s_4	MUN^N_{-1}	ΔT^N	ΔT^N_{-1}	S^N_{-1}	$\Delta \overline{MUN}$	R^2	S_e	DW	Peaks
Linear	−0.282	−0.373 (0.074)	−0.078 (0.071)	−0.333 (0.072)	−0.019 (0.021)	0.192 (0.055)	0.105 (0.051)	0.024 (0.008)	0.132 (0.104)	0.732	0.174	2.14	4
Ratio	−0.449	−0.357 (0.064)	−0.063 (0.070)	−0.297 (0.063)	0.026 (0.043)	0.225 (0.056)	0.119 (0.054)	0.021 (0.007)	0.104 (0.100)	0.702	0.166	2.19	1

(b) Country equations

Model form	Intercept	s_2	s_3	s_4	MUN^C_{-1}	ΔT^C	ΔT^C_{-1}	ΔD^C	$\Delta \overline{MUN}$	r'_e	R^2	S_e	DW	Peaks
Linear	0.117	−0.080 (0.026)	−0.107 (0.037)	−0.128 (0.039)	−0.021 (0.008)	0.168 (0.034)	0.073 (0.029)	0.062 (0.018)	0.060 (0.024)		0.696	0.044	1.40	0
Ratio	0.287	−0.154 (0.050)	−0.219 (0.072)	−0.270 (0.076)	−0.025 (0.015)	0.146 (0.035)	0.067 (0.033)	0.070 (0.018)	0.056 (0.028)		0.548	0.046	1.29	5
Linear	0.276	−0.057 (0.024)	−0.059 (0.035)	−0.082 (0.036)	0.026 (0.015)	0.150 (0.030)	0.072 (0.025)	0.036 (0.017)	0.040 (0.024)	0.088 (0.026)	0.773	0.038	1.65	1

GNP and disposable income. For the time being, we lump the various reconciling items into a single exogenous variable.[14] Equation (5.24) is simply the commercial loan identity.

The relationship between required reserves, reserve requirements and the two types of deposits is expressed in (5.25), and the potential demand-deposit variable is defined in (5.26).[15] Finally, (5.27) represents the open-market identity. The substantive element in this identity is that we treat Z—the sum of unborrowed reserves and currency—as an exogenous (but policy controlled) variable. A case can also be made for treating Z endogenously and we return to this briefly later.

5.2.3.2. *Definitional Identities.* The remaining five identities are of a different type. In particular, equations (5.28)–(5.32) are definitional relationships which "explain" the distribution of various items between country and city banks and between member and nonmember banks. The five γ's in these equations should not be regarded as constants but rather as exogenous variables. Since the demand functions for commercial loans, demand deposits, and time deposits are estimated at an aggregate level, this device is necessary to make endogenous the various bank class-deposit and loan flows. In order to give an intuitive feel for the nature of the γ's we briefly discuss these equations and describe the historical patterns of the γ's.

Equations (5.28) and (5.29) concern themselves with the bank-class distribution of net demand deposits and time deposits.[16] As equation (5.25)—the required reserve identity—reveals, it is these deposits against

---

[14] More explicitly Y^d equals Y less taxes less depreciation allowances less undistributed corporate profits less social insurance contributions less inventory valuation adjustments plus transfers. A good case can be made for treating part of these as endogenous. See below, p. 185.

[15] It should be noted that the definition of D^* omits k_2, the reserve requirement on demand deposits at reserve city banks. We did take into account differences between k_1 and k_2 in computing D^*. However, as the distinction between k_1 and k_2 is no longer relevant it is simpler to omit the latter variable from (5.26) and from our impact multiplier calculations below.

[16] In interpreting these equations it is of considerable importance to keep in mind the following definitions:

  (i) Net demand deposits (D^N, D^C) – gross member-bank demand deposits less member-bank cash items in the process of collection less demand balances due member banks by domestic commercial banks.

  (ii) Demand deposits adjusted (D, total member and nonmember) – gross demand deposits at all commercial banks less those due to domestic commercial banks and

which member banks must hold reserves. From 1950 to 1962, D^N/D^C has been generally declining although it has done so at an extremely irregular rate. D^N/D^C was about 2.1 in the early part of the period and declined to about 1.7 toward the end of the period. The quarter-to-quarter variations in the ratio were occasionally as large as 0.1 (approximately one-fourth of the range). T^N/T^C, on the other hand, exhibited a slight upward trend going from about 0.97 in the third quarter of 1950 to 1.17 in 1962, but the movements in T^N/T^C were equally irregular. Like D^N/D^C, CL^N/CL^C has irregularly declined, going from over 4.5 in the early part of the period to slightly under 2.0 by the end of the period. Some thought was given to the possibility of providing an endogenous explanation for D^N/D^C and T^N/T^C but some simple-minded attempts at a specification revealed that this was beyond the scope of this study.[17]

The remaining two γ's have fluctuated over a relatively narrow range with no apparent trend: γ_4 was contained in the range 0.91 to 0.96 while γ_5 ranged from 0.800 to 0.826. It should be noted that unlike previous γ's, those corresponding to $(D^N + D^C)/D$ and $(T^N + T^C)/T$ reflect not only pure distributional considerations but also reconcile some definitional differences.[18]

---

the U.S. Government less cash items in the process of collection less Federal Reserve float plus foreign demand balances at Federal Reserve Banks.

(iii) Time deposits adjusted (T, total member and nonmember) – time deposits at all commercial banks other than those due to domestic commercial banks and the U.S. Government.

[17] CAWTHORNE [18], has cited a number of hypotheses which purport to explain both the secular and cyclical behavior of deposit distribution. Some of the long-run influences on deposit distribution include industrial relocation, migration of population (growth of suburbs), relative rates of growth of business corporations and banks, and the fact that New York and Chicago banks had limited locations and could hardly be expected to grow as rapidly as banks in other areas. On the cyclical side, it can be argued that high interest rates encourage aggressive cash management. If one assumes that this behavior is confined to large business and wealthy individuals who are customers of large banks, then the share of deposits at large banks may decline with high interest rates. The difficulties in translating these various arguments into a statistical explanation of deposit distribution are manifold. For one thing, considerations of suburbanization and aggressive cash management do not nicely translate themselves into the particular bank classification we are using. It would seem, therefore, that the exogeneity assumption, in the context of this model, is the only reasonable alternative.

[18] D and T are all-bank measures so γ_4 and γ_5 reflect, on the one hand, member-nonmember distributions. However, in addition, these γ's reflect the definitional differences cited in footnote 16 above.

5.2.3.3. *The Bank Equations.* We examine now equations (5.1)–(5.11), the eleven estimated bank equations. We discuss in turn the categories of excess reserves, borrowings, the various types of security holdings, and the supply of commercial loans.

Excess Reserves. The most obvious feature of the results for excess reserves [(5.1) and (5.2)] is that the final equations include precisely the same variables in both country and city sectors. In particular, for both sectors the major determinants of excess-reserve holdings appear to be interest-rate considerations and the change in the availability of reserves (as measured by the potential-deposit variable, D^*). Attempts to include deposit or loan flow variables in the two equations met with singular lack of success. For these variables, all estimated coefficients were a fraction of their standard errors and often incorrectly-signed.

Comparing the equations somewhat more closely, we see that in the country-bank equations seasonal variables are considerably more important, with the pre-Accord shift variable considerably less important. The speed of adjustment is roughly unity for the city sector and only 0.6 for the country sector. In addition, the response to a dollar change in D^* is about twice as large for the city sector.[19]

Finally, we may compute the interest elasticity of excess-reserve holdings with respect to the Treasury bill rate. The short-run and long-run elasticities calculated at the relevant means are:[20]

	Short-run	Long-run
Country	—0.152	—0.253
City	—0.376	—0.345

As these estimates reveal, the city-bank sector is more responsive to interest considerations in the management of their excess reserves.

---

[19] The long-run response to D^* flows are comparable. However, as the flows are constantly changing, the notion of a long-run response becomes somewhat uninteresting.

[20] The short-run elasticity was calculated by $[\partial(\Delta E)/\partial r_s] \cdot (\bar{r}_s/\bar{E})$. That is, the relevant mean used was the mean of the stock of excess reserves. One cannot very well use the mean of the flow variable—it might even be zero. One could, of course, utilize something like the mean absolute change. The long-run elasticities are obtained by setting the flows equal to zero, solving for the steady-state E, and differentiating as above.

Borrowing. On the whole, as for the previous group of equations, the same set of explanatory variables proved of importance for both the city and country classes. More particularly, reserve flows, loan flows and cost considerations all emerged as important determinants of member-bank borrowing.

There are, however, considerable sectoral differences in the magnitudes of some of these influences. For example, in response to an expansion of D^* by \$1 billion, we estimate that city banks will repay borrowings to the extent of \$49 million and country banks to the extent of only \$7 million. This ratio of 7:1 is to be contrasted with a ratio of the mean volume of borrowings, $(\overline{B^N}/\overline{B^C})$, of about 3:1. Hence, it would appear open-market operations are more successful in influencing the level of city-bank borrowings. Sectoral differences also exist with respect to an inflow of loan demand. City banks increase their borrowings by \$12 for every \$100 of new loan demand while country banks increase theirs by less than \$6.

In addition to these differences, time deposit flows were found to be important only for the country sector, while a reserve-requirement variable appears in the city sector only.

Finally, we calculate interest elasticities with respect to the bill and discount rates:[21]

		Short-run	Long-run
r_s	country	0.785	2.625
	city	0.877	2.134
r_d	country	−0.875	−2.926
	city	−0.979	−2.382

As these elasticities reveal, in the short-run the city sector is slightly more responsive. Surprisingly, this situation is reversed in the long-run.

One curious feature of the interest sensitivity of member-bank borrowing is revealed by the two equations in table 5.2 which include terms in $(r_d - r_s)^2$. It will be recalled that Polakoff has argued that member-bank reluctance to borrow implies that $\partial B/\partial (r_s - r_d)$ (the partial derivative of borrowing with respect to the least-cost spread) will become less positive (or perhaps even negative) as the spread increases [96]. For this to happen

---

[21] The elasticities with respect to the two interest rates differ only because the two rates have different sample means.

the coefficient of the squared differential must be negative. As table 5.2 reveals both country and city coefficents are positive, although statistically insignificant.[22] This suggests that once one allows for reserve availability and loan-induced borrowing the apparent unwillingness to expand borrowings at high spreads seems to vanish.[23]

Short-term Securities. The short-term security equations perform quite well, both in terms of explanatory power, and in the extent to which the results agree with our *a priori* notions. For the city banks, the supply, loan-flow, the deposit-flow, and reserve-requirement variables all perform as expected. Moreover, the coefficients tell a remarkably consistent story. In particular, an inflow of demand deposits of $1 produces, in the absence of new loan demand, an increase of short-term security holdings of $.67. A corresponding inflow of $1 of time deposits increases S^N by $.83. The difference between these two effects, i.e., $.16, roughly corresponds to the differential in required reserves on the two types of deposits.

The coefficient on ΔCL^N is similarly consistent with the deposit coefficients. A bank granting a loan simultaneously creates a deposit of the same amount. However, in order for the bank to meet the reserve requirement, it must transfer funds from some other asset into required reserves. Since city banks have a typically small volume of excess reserves we would expect most of these funds to come from short-term securities. This is, in fact, what equation (5.5) tells us. In particular, a $1 expansion in both loans and demand deposits produces a decline in S^N of $.176 (i.e., 0.848–0.672). This figure compares quite favorably with the reserve requirement on demand deposits. Similarly-sensible results are obtained by assuming that an inflow of time deposits is invested in commercial loans.

In addition to these variables, both the reserve requirement variable

---

[22] The reader will observe that, following Polakoff, we have changed the sign on the least-cost spread. The positive coefficient on $(r_d — r_s)^2$ naturally leads to a conclusion opposed to Polakoff's. For example, from the linear equation we have

$$\frac{\partial(\Delta B^C)}{\partial(r_s - r_d)} = 0.063 + 0.076(r_s - r_d) \ .$$

Hence the derivative steadily increases for increases in $(r_s — r_d)$. The derivative actually becomes negative if r_d exceeds r_s by more than 0.82. This differential existed for several quarters in our sample.

[23] We might also note that the elasticities with respect to r_s and r_d calculated from the equations including $(r_d — r_s)^2$ were quite comparable to the ones reported above.

and the relative supply variables also prove of considerable importance in explaining bank security transactions. The reserve-requirement coefficient, naturally enough, implies that an increase in required reserves will be felt to a considerable extent in city-bank holdings of short-term securities. The coefficient on $\Delta \bar{O}$ (i.e., the change in the public's holdings of government securities with maturity in excess of five years), implies that roughly 33 percent of the long-term security changes will result in an increase of S^N.

The one class of variable which exhibited little or no influence on ΔS^N was interest rates. The loan-rate variable was consistently negative but yielded a statistically insignificant coefficient. The bill rate, the three-year rate and the expectation variables proved similarly inconsequential. It would appear that the buffer-stock nature of short-term security holdings dominate interest-cost considerations.

Turning now to the country-bank sector, we find that the determinants of short-term security holdings include the variables which proved to be of importance in the city sector, as well as some additional ones. In particular, ΔCL^C, ΔD^C, ΔT^C, and RR_2^C all obtain appropriately-signed coefficients. As table 5.3 reveals, the deposit and loan variables exhibit roughly the same internal consistency described above. For country-banks, of course, excess reserves play a much larger role in providing for required-reserve needs.

In addition to these variables, as anticipated both ΔD^* and ΔD^*_{-1} yield positive coefficients. Finally, both the bill rate and the three-year rate [introduced via $\bar{r}_3(R,15)$] produce statistically-significant positive coefficients. It will be recalled that the short-term category is 0–5 years, so that either of these rates may be regarded as an "own" yield. The ratio equation in table 5.3 implies an interest elasticity of 0.108 with respect to r_3 in the short-run. The corresponding long-run estimate is 0.892.

Long-term Securities. Besides (5.7) and (5.8), table 5.4 reports various equations explaining bank holdings of long-term securities. As their absence from the table reveals, neither actual nor potential deposit flows nor reserve-requirement variables proved of any consequence in explaining ΔO^N and ΔO^C. In fact, aside from the relative supply variables the only important variables were interest rates and loan flows. For both classes of bank, the loan rate yielded consistently negative (and usually significant coefficients) and various forms of the long-term bond rate uniformly yielded positive coefficients. The city-bank equations imply short-run interest elasticities with respect to the loan and bond rates of -0.08 and 0.24 [(from 5.7)]. The corresponding country elasticities are -0.29 and 0.26.[24]

Table 5.4 also contains an attempt at including the lagged stock of short-term securities in the country bank equation. It obtained a positive coefficient but its introduction succeeded in making the coefficient of O^C_{-1} positive. This sort of occurrence was rather typical of attempts to utilize lagged ("cross") stocks at various points in the model.

We also experimented with including two expectational variables in the same equation. A sample result is

$$\Delta O^N = 1.035 + 0.673 s_2 + 0.478 s_3 + 0.560 s_4 - 0.037 O^N_{-1} - 0.100 \Delta \bar{S}$$
$$ (0.228) \quad (0.278) \quad (0.287) \quad (0.028) \quad\quad (0.040)$$
$$+ 0.216 \Delta \bar{O} + 0.717 \bar{r}_{10}(R,15) - 0.537 \bar{r}_{10}(R,10) - 0.300 r'_e$$
$$(0.039) \quad\quad (1.66) \quad\quad\quad\quad (2.29) \quad\quad\quad\quad (0.150)$$
$$R^2 = 0.821 \quad S_e = 0.529 \quad DW = 2.02.$$

Thus, while the expectational variables produce the anticipated sign pattern, neither proves of any importance to the explanatory power of the equation.

On the whole, therefore, the major determinants of long-term security holdings would appear to be the total supply of these securities in the hands of the public, the yields on these securities, and the yield obtainable from a close substitute (i.e., loans).

Municipal Securities. The most important determinants of holdings of municipal securities by city banks are current and lagged time deposit flows and the lagged stock of short-term securities.[25] Neither actual or potential demand deposit flows, loan flows, or interest rates aided in explaining ΔMUN^N. We also experimented with a municipal supply variable ($\Delta \overline{MUN}$) in the equation.[26] As (5.9) shows, it yielded a positive and reasonably-sized coefficient.

---

[24] The several equations in table 5.4 imply interest elasticities which vary over a fairly wide range. This indicates a high degree of sensitivity of these estimates to the specification of the equation. In addition, the small coefficients on the lagged stocks of long-term securities imply long-run elasticities many times the short-run ones.

[25] This was one of the few instances in which a lagged stock of a different asset did not seem to create difficulties for several other variables in the equation.

[26] For a discussion of the problems which this type of variable, see above, p. 62.

For the country-bank sector a demand-deposit flow variable as well as the time-deposit flows and municipal-supply variable proved important. With respect to the municipal supply variable, the sum of the coefficients of $\Delta\overline{MUN}$ in the city and country equations is about 0.2. This is not too different from the 25% share of municipals held by member-banks in 1962. Table 5.5 also reports an attempt at including an interest rate variable in the country equation. In particular, the loan rate produced a significant negative coefficient. While this is, of course, the appropriate sign, the inclusion of this variable causes the coefficient of MUN^C_{-1} to switch from -0.021 to $+0.026$.

Supply of Commercial Loans. It will be recalled that there are two un-settled issues concerning the specification of the loan-supply function:

(a) Should the dependent variable be the (change in the) short-term loan rate r'_e or the weighted-average rate, r''_e?

(b) Are lagged values of the loan-deposit ratio, L^*, also important determinants of the loan rate?

As both rates can be explained in a satisfactory manner, we must choose between them in terms of their relative performance in the rest of the model. In the course of structural estimation it was found that r'_e tended to produce slightly better results.[27] Consequently, we utilize this rate throughout the model.

Table 5.6 sheds some light on the second issue. When L^*_{-1}[28] is in-troduced along with L^* the former obtains a negative coefficient and the latter a positive one. The coefficients in (5.11) can be rearranged as follows:

$$5.313L^* - 3.860L^*_{-1} = 1.453L^* + 3.860\Delta L^* .$$

In other words, the equation implies a positive response of the loan rate to both the level of the loan-deposit ratio and a larger response to changes in that level. This finding seems quite reasonable.

As for the remainder of the equation, both changes in the bill rate, lagged changes of that rate, and the expectations variable all perform as anticipated. By this we mean that increases in the bill rate and expected increases in the bond rate lead to increases in the loan rate. However, the

---

[27] The notion of "better results" is a somewhat subjective matter. It includes a tendency for r'_e to give more significant interest rate coefficients (researchers' biases enter the game as well!) and to interact less with other variables.

[28] L^*_{-1} introduced by itself obtains a positive and insignificant coefficient in the r'_e equation and a positive and significant coefficient in the r''_e equation.

TABLE 5.6

Supply of commercial loans

Dependent variable	Intercept	s_2	s_3	s_4	$(r_e)_{-1}$	$\bar{r}_{10}$ (L,15)	Δr_s	$(\Delta r_s)_{-1}$	L^*	L^*_{-1}	R^2	S_e	DW
$\Delta r'_e$	0.062				−0.285 (0.083)	0.220 (0.067)	0.069 (0.035)	0.069 (0.031)	2.967 (0.986)		0.562	0.093	1.55
$\Delta r'_e$	0.070				−0.152 (0.084)	0.200 (0.064)	0.084 (0.033)	0.053 (0.032)	5.313 (0.870)	−3.860 (1.949)	0.591	0.090	1.75
$\Delta r''$	0.181	0.083 (0.032)	0.026 (0.034)	0.015 (0.030)	−0.180 (0.052)	0.322 (0.049)	0.107 (0.031)	0.057 (0.025)	1.500 (0.584)		0.810	0.061	2.30

speed of adjustment is quite low and the response therefore is distributed over a large number of quarters.

Bank Equations: A Summary. As a group, the bank equations appear to explain bank portfolio management quite well. The equations both provide numerous entries for the operation of monetary policy and contain as well a number of interesting implications regarding the effectiveness of policy. We return to these problems shortly.

As to the country-city distinction, the striking thing about the equations is the extent to which the same variables prove important for both sectors. For example, excess reserve holdings for both sectors are largely determined by the opportunity costs involved and the availability of reserves. Similarly, for both sectors borrowing from the Fed is influenced by the interest-cost differential, $r_d - r_s$, the availability of reserves, commercial loan demand, and the excess-profits tax which prevailed in the early part of the sample period.

Despite this overall similarity of form, there are numerous differences between the two sectors. There are instances of certain variables which are relevant for only one sector. In addition, there are many variables common to both sectors which yield parameter estimates with extremely different implications. Examples of both these types of sectoral differences were cited in the foregoing discussion.

Finally, it might also be noted that differing seasonal patterns emerge for the several equations both within a bank class and across bank classes. One feature of this overall pattern is the simultaneous marked increase in borrowings and excess reserves in the second quarter.[29] This points up that our sectoral classification, while a step in the right direction, is still aggregating banks in different circumstances.

5.2.3.3. *Demand for Money.* As the reader will recall, our model includes separate equations for currency and demand deposits. Tables 5.7 and 5.8 report various alternative specifications of these two relationships and for an aggregate money-demand equation as well.

Currency holdings were found to depend positively on GNP and

---

[29] For country banks the second quarter results in the largest seasonal increase in borrowings. This may reflect increased loans to the agricultural sector and the fact that the Fed has long regarded agricultural demands as an appropriate basis for member-bank borrowing.

negatively on the bill rate, the time-deposit yield, a price variable and a weighted GNP variable. A net worth variable was also experimented with, but it yielded an incorrectly signed (negative) and statistically significant coefficient.[30] As for the variables included in the final currency equation, (5.12), only the price and weighted GNP variables were not discussed in our preliminary specification. However, both have been previously mentioned in the money-demand literature. The percentage rate-of-change of prices,[31] since it has the dimensions of an interest rate, is entered in multiplicatively with Y. It obtains an expected negative coefficient. The weighted GNP variable is one that has been previously utilized by de Leeuw.[32] The weights approximate Friedman's "permanent income" weights and the variable can be interpreted as a measure of normal or expected income. Its negative coefficient may seem puzzling but if we denote the weighted GNP variable by Y^p we can rewrite the two income coefficients in (5.12) as follows:

$$0.076Y - 0.051Y^p = 0.076(Y - Y^p) + 0.025Y^p.$$

The variable $(Y - Y^p)$ represents unexpected or transitory income and hence (5.12) implies a positive response to both expected and unexpected income. This is precisely what an inventory approach to the demand for money would suggest.

Demand deposit holdings also depend positively on GNP, and negatively on the time-deposit yield and the bill rate. Introducing net worth into this relationship yields an appropriately positive (and significant) coefficient which reduces, but does not overwhelm, the income variable. However, the multicollinearity difficulties noted earlier make this result difficult to interpret. As table 5.7 reveals, attempts to include the price and weighted GNP variables in the demand-deposit equation met with little success. The former obtained a positive coefficient and the latter caused the coefficient of D_{-1} to become positive.

It is interesting to compare an aggregate money equation with the two component equations. As table 5.8 shows, aggregate money holdings respond to essentially the same variables which collectively influence the

---

[30] Multicollinearity difficulties — witness the marked change in the speed of adjustment in table 5.7 — make it difficult to ascribe any particular significance to this result. Similar comments would seem to apply to all the specifications including W in the two tables above.

[31] This variable is used in [72].

[32] [29].

TABLE 5.7

Demand for money and money components (linear)

Dep. var.	Inter-cept	s_2	s_3	s_4	$\left(\frac{\Delta P}{P}\right)Y$	$0.114\sum_{i=0}^{19}(0.9)^i Y_{t-i}$	C_{-1}	D_{-1}	Y	$r_s Y$	$r_p Y$	W	R^2	S_e	DW
ΔC	0.328	0.692 (0.095)	0.797 (0.081)	0.870 (0.125)	-0.087 (0.064)	-0.051 (0.012)	-0.112 (0.075)		0.076 (0.015)	-0.0010 (0.0004)	-0.0021 (0.0012)		0.958	0.123	1.83
ΔC	2.646	0.696 (0.102)	0.748 (0.088)	0.982 (0.151)			-0.217 (0.054)		0.052 (0.015)	-0.0036 (0.0037)	-0.0026 (0.0015)	-0.0015 (0.0006)	0.939	0.147	1.13
ΔD	-0.270	3.151 (0.644)	4.040 (0.617)	7.122 (1.003)				-0.127 (0.081)	0.140 (0.091)	-0.0066 (0.0019)	-0.012 (0.010)		0.937	0.784	1.55
ΔD	-8.254	3.583 (0.712)	4.580 (0.732)	7.409 (1.022)	0.262 (0.322)	-0.027 (0.023)		0.002 (0.127)	0.173 (0.096)	-0.009 (0.003)	-0.005 (0.012)		0.937	0.787	1.61
ΔD	6.540	2.654 (0.578)	3.361 (0.570)	6.835 (0.880)				-0.297 (0.085)	0.129 (0.080)	-0.0065 (0.0017)	-0.028 (0.010)	0.012 (0.003)	0.952	0.684	1.81

Dep. var.	Inter-cept	s_2	s_3	s_4	M_{-1}	M_{-2}	Y	$r_s Y$	$r_p Y$	W	R^2	S_e	DW
ΔM	2.996	3.875 (0.629)	4.763 (0.602)	8.202 (0.936)	-0.151 (0.065)		0.173 (0.083)	-0.0065 (0.0019)	-0.015 (0.010)		0.948	0.837	1.56
ΔM	7.372	5.493 (1.316)	5.251 (0.795)	8.895 (0.937)	-0.054 (0.143)	-0.197 (0.124)	0.159 (0.077)	-0.0064 (0.0018)	-0.026 (0.009)	0.009 (0.003)	0.958	0.753	2.26

TABLE 5.8

Demand for money and money components (logarithmic)

Dep. var.	Inter-cept	s_2	s_3	s_4	$\ln M_{-1}$	$\ln M_{-2}$	$\ln D_{-1}$	$\ln C_{-1}$	$\ln Y$	$\ln r_s$	$\ln r_p$	$\ln W$	R^2	S_e	DW
$\ln C$	0.072	0.027	0.029	0.041				0.815	0.117	−0.001	−0.034		0.988	0.005	1.14
		(0.003)	(0.003)	(0.004)				(0.048)	(0.034)	(0.002)	(0.012)				
$\ln D$	−0.189	0.029	0.036	0.072			0.793		−0.004	−0.011	−0.047	0.163	0.993	0.006	1.54
		(0.004)	(0.004)	(0.005)			(0.056)		(0.046)	(0.003)	(0.017)	(0.043)			
$\ln D$	0.126	0.032	0.040	0.072			0.915		0.055	−0.013	−0.010		0.991	0.007	1.36
		(0.004)	(0.004)	(0.006)			(0.052)		(0.050)	(0.004)	(0.017)				
$\ln M$	0.179	0.058	0.051	0.076	1.264	−0.372			0.068	−0.0089	−0.012		0.993	0.005	2.12
		(0.010)	(0.006)	(0.006)	(0.134)	(0.125)			(0.037)	(0.0028)	(0.012)				

two components. For all three equations, the various long-run income and interest elasticities are summarized below.

		Y	r_s	r_p
Currency	linear	0.64	−0.07	−0.14
	logarithmic	0.63	−0.00	−0.18
Demand deposits	linear	0.80	−0.11	−0.18
	logarithmic	0.65	−0.15	−0.12
Money	linear	0.73	−0.07	−0.08
	logarithmic	0.63	−0.08	−0.11

As these estimates reveal the income elasticity of currency is lower than the elasticity of demand deposits with the elasticity of total money inbetween. The logarithmic income elasticities are uniformly lower than the linear ones, while the interest-rate elasticities show a reverse tendency. This finding and the somewhat more erratic behavior of the logarithmic specification led us to the choice of the linear form of the equations for the final model.[33]

5.2.3.4. *Demand for Time Deposits.* Table 5.9 reports estimates for both linear and logarithmic specifications of the public's demand for time deposits. These holdings respond positively to income and the yield on time deposits and negatively to the long-term bond rate. Neither the bill rate nor net worth proved of importance in this equation.

As in the preliminary results, income works better in lagged form. Long-run elasticities are as follows:

	Y	r_p	$\bar{r}_{10}(R,15)$
Linear	0.65	0.37	−1.62
Logarithmic	0.44	0.62	−0.79

While based on quite different data, the elasticities with respect to Y and r_p are similar to those reported by Feige.[34]

---

[33] The higher R^2's for the logarithmic version reflect the use of a stock variable as a dependent variable in that specification.

[34] See [42]. The estimates are for the specification using lagged income. Table 5.9 also reports a curious result for the case of including both Y and Y_{-1} in the same equation. The coefficient of Y is negative and statistically significant while Y_{-1} yields a positive and significant coefficient.

TABLE 5.9

Demand for time deposits

(a) Linear

Intercept	s_2	s_3	s_4	T_{-1}	$r_{\mathrm{p}}Y$	$\bar{v}_{10}(\mathbf{R},15)Y$	Y	Y_{-1}	R^2	S_e	DW
3.860	−0.353 (0.348)	−0.665 (0.343)	−1.324 (0.451)	−0.051 (0.065)	0.019 (0.009)	−0.048 (0.017)	0.023 (0.053)		0.566	0.822	1.55
1.124	0.516 (0.481)	−0.017 (0.425)	−0.410 (0.478)	−0.077 (0.055)	0.016 (0.008)	−0.059 (0.013)		0.076 (0.032)	0.615	0.774	1.36
2.905	1.758 (0.703)	0.793 (0.531)	1.431 (0.916)	−0.017 (0.058)	0.017 (0.008)	−0.038 (0.015)	−0.172 (0.074)	0.165 (0.049)	0.662	0.725	1.34

(b) Logarithmic

Intercept	s_2	s_3	s_4	$\ln T_{-1}$	$\ln r_{\mathrm{p}}$	$\ln \bar{v}_{10}(\mathbf{R},15)$	$\ln Y$	$\ln Y_{-1}$	R^2	S_e	DW
0.428	−0.004 (0.005)	−0.009 (0.005)	−0.021 (0.007)	0.861 (0.052)	0.106 (0.031)	−0.113 (0.032)	0.023 (0.066)		0.998	0.012	1.23
0.270	0.002 (0.006)	−0.005 (0.006)	−0.015 (0.006)	0.854 (0.043)	0.091 (0.032)	−0.116 (0.028)		0.064 (0.049)	0.998	0.012	1.21
0.375	0.023 (0.013)	0.009 (0.009)	0.014 (0.017)	0.921 (0.057)	0.080 (0.031)	−0.085 (0.033)	−0.241 (0.136)	0.223 (0.102)	0.998	0.012	1.23

5.2.3.5. *Demand for Commercial Loans.* Table 5.10 sets out several alternative specifications of the demand for commercial loans. Although our pilot investigation of this function produced rather unsatisfactory results, equation (5.15) would seem to be a quite reasonable characterization of loan demand. More explicitly, loan demand is seen to be a function of inventory investment, sales, the relative cost of loans, and the potential-deposit variable. The strong role for inventory investment is in accord with our earlier discussion. The cost variable implies that the demand for loans depends negatively on its own price and positively on the price of alternative sources of finance.[35] The potential deposit variable, which we are using as our indirect measure of open-market operations, yields a positive coefficient. This can be interpreted as reflecting an availability effect. That is, D^* captures some of the nonprice elements of the set of loan terms. Hence, when monetary policy is tight (small positive or perhaps negative D^*) and nonprice rationing may be taking place, loan demand will be lower than when there is an easy credit policy.

It is also interesting to note (second and third quations in table 5.10) the effect of adding a measure of unfilled orders to our loan function. Both U_{-1} and ΔU_{-1} yield negative coefficients. It was suggested earlier that unfilled orders may serve as a measure of tightness in the market for goods. Given the interdependence of the financial and goods sectors, like D^*, this variable may also serve as a measure of credit availability. Unfilled orders, however, may reflect tightness in the market for trade credit which is an alternative source of funds.

For comparability with our earlier results, table 5.10 also reports results using dividend and business income variables. It will be recalled that *DIV* produced a large positive coefficient in our preliminary results. It continues to do so in one of our structural estimates. In the presence of ΔD^*, however, it produces a small positive and insignificant coefficient.

Finally it might be noted that business income, F, produces a positive coefficient. This may reflect its use as a proxy for sales or may support Budzeika's argument for a positive association between loan demand and internal funds.[36]

---

[35] The positive coefficient on r_s may reflect one or both of two effects. For one, it may reflect the cost of finance out of stocks of liquid assets. However, it may also reflect the cost of finance by commercial paper. In fact, using the differential of the loan rate over the commercial paper rate yields a result similar to the one reported above.

[36] See above, p. 84.

TABLE 5.10

Demand for commercial loans

Inter-cept	s_2	s_3	s_4	CL_{-1}	$\Delta H'$	$(r'_e - r_s)$	ΔD^*	$(Y - \Delta H')$	U_{-1}	ΔU_{-1}	DIV	F	R^2	S_e	DW
-2.398	-0.281 (0.258)	0.070 (0.274)	-0.985 (0.403)	-0.157 (0.043)	0.488 (0.083)	-0.320 (0.168)	0.163 (0.044)	0.081 (0.020)					0.735	0.434	1.91
-0.415	-0.156 (0.247)	0.022 (0.258)	-0.767 (0.389)	-0.137 (0.041)	0.374 (0.091)	-0.533 (0.180)	0.145 (0.042)	0.070 (0.019)	-0.018 (0.007)				0.766	0.408	1.94
-2.276	-0.055 (0.305)	0.287 (0.316)	-0.886 (0.405)	-0.143 (0.044)	0.633 (0.135)	-0.308 (0.166)	0.158 (0.044)	0.074 (0.020)		-0.046 (0.034)			0.701	0.475	1.70
0.092	0.022 (0.254)	0.216 (0.282)	-0.134 (0.361)	-0.132 (0.035)	0.298 (0.101)	-0.441 (0.186)	0.150 (0.048)					0.262 (0.059)	0.702	0.474	2.03
-0.693	0.469 (0.192)	0.527 (0.240)	0.757 (0.192)	-0.157 (0.035)	0.165 (0.113)	-0.409 (0.183)					1.287 (0.596)	0.134 (0.079)	0.707	0.456	2.51

5.2.3.6. *Term-structure Equations.* In our preliminary investigations, as dependent variables we experimented with each of three rate differentials. As the listing of the final model reveals, we need only two term-structure relationships to ensure that we have a complete system. The elimination of the $r_{10} - r_3$ differential was made on empirical grounds. The two included differentials are $r_{10} - r_s$ and $r_3 - r_s$.[37]

Equation (5.16) explains $r_{10} - r_s$ as a function of the lagged change in the bill rate, two of our expectational variables, and changes in the proportion of government debt of 0–1 year and 1–5 years maturity. The expectational variables yield coefficients with the anticipated sign. The adjustment behavior is consistent with the expectation that when rates are high relative to a long (short)-term average, capital gains (losses) are expected. The negative signs for ΔS_1^* and ΔS_2^* indicate that increases in either of the two proportions lead to a narrowing of $r_{10} - r_s$.

In addition to ΔS_1^* and ΔS_2^* we attempted to use the levels of the proportions as well. Two such equations are

$$r_{10} - r_s = 0.095 - 0.464(\Delta r_s)_{-1} - 4.582\Delta S_1^* - 1.822\Delta S_2^* - 1.087\bar{r}_{10}(L,15)$$
$$\quad (0.126) \qquad (2.575) \qquad (2.242) \qquad (0.293)$$
$$\quad + 2.299 S_1^* + 1.20 S_2^* + 0.22\Delta Y$$
$$\quad (1.092) \quad (0.974) \quad (0.012) \qquad R^2 = 0.545 \; S_e = 0.364 \; DW = 1.39$$

and

$$r_{10} - r_s = 1.67 - 0.550(\Delta r_s)_{-1} - 3.331\Delta S_1^* - 0.775\Delta S_2^* - 7.918\bar{r}_{10}(R,10)$$
$$\quad (0.130) \qquad (2.746) \qquad (2.185) \qquad (1.612)$$
$$\quad + 6.776\bar{r}_{10}(R,5) + 1.711 S_1^* + 0.722 S_2^* - 0.159\Delta r_s$$
$$\quad (2.519) \qquad (1.055) \quad (0.829) \quad (0.155)$$
$$\qquad\qquad R^2 = 0.632 \; S_e = 0.327 \; DW = 1.22$$

As these equations reveal, the levels tend to produce positive coefficients. However, the net effect of the levels and changes in these levels remains negative in both instances. We also experimented with the actual dollar changes in these two debt categories (i.e., $\bar{S}_1$, $\bar{S}_2$). These variables did not perform nearly as well as the proportion variables.

---

[37] The three differentials are, of course, linearly dependent. Hence, even if three interest-rate equations were needed to complete the model, these three differentials could not all be used as dependent variables. It seems sensible to make the choice as to which one to eliminate on empirical grounds.

The second included differential, $r_3 - r_s$, was explained [see (5.17)] in much the same fashion as $r_{10} - r_s$. In particular, the sign pattern of coefficients of the bill-rate and expectational variables are completely parallel. However, there were noticeable differences with respect to the supply variables. In particular, the levels of both proportions proved highly significant in explaining $r_3 - r_s$.

As a matter of fact, $r_3 - r_s$ was the differential we had preliminarily eliminated. However, on the basis of including the level variables this equation now performs better than the one for $r_{10} - r_3$. Coefficients of S_1^*, S_2^* and ΔS_2^* are all positive. While ΔS_1^* yields a negative coefficient, it is smaller than the S_1^* coefficient. As noted earlier, we expect increases of debt in the 1–5 year category to increase the differential and this is what the equation implies. The effect of increases in the 0–1 year class on the differential are ambiguous *a priori*.

For completeness we record a typical estimate using $r_{10} - r_3$ as a dependent variable. We have

$$r_{10} - r_3 = 1.077 - 0.943\bar{r}_{10}(L,15) - 1.350\Delta S_1^* - 2.298\Delta S_2^* + 0.019\Delta D^*$$
$$\qquad (0.189) \qquad\qquad (1.095) \qquad (1.456) \qquad (0.012)$$
$$+ 0.014(\Delta D^*)_{-1} - 1.297 S_1^* - 0.309 S_2^*$$
$$(0.013) \qquad\quad (0.662) \quad (0.619)$$
$$R^2 = 0.591 \quad S_e = 0.238 \quad DW = 0.48$$

All variables yield anticipated signs but the extremely low Durbin-Watson statistic and the somewhat lower R^2 make this equation less satisfactory than (5.16) or (5.17).[38]

5.2.3.7. *Investment and Consumption Functions.* Before discussing each of the functions, two general explanations are in order. In our preliminary examination of investment and consumption functions we estimated all relationships, both in nominal and real terms. We began our structural estimation with the intention of duplicating this parallel estimation. However, our initial attempts at structural estimation (largely for fixed and inventory investment) in both current and real forms quickly revealed

---

[38] In an earlier chapter we reported an attempt at estimating a term-structure equation involving the municipal rate which proved only marginally satisfactory. Structural estimation yielded equally marginal equations. Since the municipal rate did not enter the final equations of the model, we do not report these attempts.

the superiority of the deflated version.[39] As a consequence, we concentrate upon relationships of the latter type.

A second problem relates to our specification of the seasonal variables. In our preliminary work, we utilized multiplicative seasonal variables for fixed investment but not for the other relationships. In the course of our structural estimation, we experimented with a similar specification for the rest of the income components. It was found, however, that the multiplicative specification was superior only for fixed investment. Hence, our final model incorporates this asymmetrical specification.

Fixed Investment. Table 5.11 reports alternative specifications for a fixed-investment demand function. The best specification would appear to include capacity, GNP, deviations of GNP from its previous peak, the bond rate (multiplicatively) and the flow of commercial loans. It should be noted, however, that the choice between a linear and a multiplicative form of the interest rate is not terribly critical.[40] Equation (5.18) implies a long-run interest elasticity of about -0.6 while the linear version implies one of about -0.5.

We also experimented with putting unfilled orders in the equation. As indicated in earlier discussions, unfilled orders can serve, in the same sense as a capacity variable, as a measure of the need for new productive facilities. The variable, U_{-1}, does indeed yield a positive coefficient. However, its introduction causes the coefficient of capacity to become quite insignificant. Finally, table 5.11 reports one other way in which a capacity variable can be satisfactorily introduced, i.e., as $(Y/K - Y_{-1})$.

Inventory Investment. Table 5.12 reports the alternative specifications tried for an inventory function. In our preliminary estimates, we employed two measures of inventory investment. In the structural estimation it became clear that the $\Delta H'$ measure yielded more satisfactory financial effects. Hence, the final model makes this our dependent variable.

Inventory holdings appear to be determined by sales, changes in sales, unfilled orders, the loan rate, and the commercial-funds variable. As the table shows, both actual sales measures (SA, ΔSA) and "final" sales

---

[39] Financial variables seem to be especially improved when deflation is carried out. However, income and sales variables also behaved better in the deflated case.

[40] The relevant t-values are 2.2 and 1.5 for the multiplicative and linear form respectively. The effect of omitting ΔCL is to reduce slightly the coefficient of the interest rate.

TABLE 5.11

Fixed investment

Interest rate form	Seasonal form	Inter-cept	s_2	s_3	s_4	I_{-1}	K_{-1}	$(Y-Y^*)$	Y	$r_{10}Y$	ΔCL	U_{-1}	R^2	S_e	DW
Mult.	Mult.	−2.259	0.302 (0.013)	0.149 (0.009)	0.248 (0.009)	0.680 (0.045)	1.405 (0.617)	0.053 (0.019)	0.027 (0.010)	−0.0022 (0.0010)	0.147 (0.040)		0.968	0.153	1.70
Linear	Mult.	−1.668	0.303 (0.014)	0.149 (0.009)	0.248 (0.009)	0.687 (0.045)	1.424 (0.626)	0.053 (0.020)	0.020 (0.007)	−0.161 (0.108)	0.143 (0.040)		0.967	0.155	1.66
Mult.	Linear	−3.494	2.201 (0.112)	1.179 (0.083)	1.896 (0.083)	0.850 (0.057)	1.359 (0.730)	0.062 (0.023)	0.027 (0.012)	−0.0020 (0.0012)	0.146 (0.047)		0.954	0.181	2.09
Mult.	Mult.	−2.026	0.300 (0.013)	0.152 (0.009)	0.248 (0.009)	0.617 (0.054)	0.220 (0.845)	0.040 (0.020)	0.037 (0.011)	−0.0024 (0.0010)	0.237 (0.059)	0.008 (0.004)	0.969	0.149	1.86
Mult.	Mult.	−1.031	0.300 (0.012)	0.147 (0.008)	0.248 (0.008)	0.692 (0.046)	0.021* (0.004)	0.037** (0.023)	0.028 (0.009)	−0.0012 (0.0010)	0.147 (0.035)		0.973	0.139	1.90

*This variable is $(Y/K - Y_{-1})$
**This variable is ΔY

TABLE 5.12

Inventory investment

Notes	Intercept	s_2	s_3	s_4	H'_{-1}	$\Delta H'_{-1}$	ΔU_{-1}	$(Y-\Delta H')$	$\Delta(Y-\Delta H')$	r'_e	ΔCL	K	U_{-1}	R^2	S_e	DW
	1.307	1.190 (0.708)	0.404 (0.535)	2.424 (0.776)	−0.103 (0.041)	0.429 (0.103)	0.124 (0.031)	0.026 (0.012)	−0.133 (0.055)					0.765	0.543	2.00
	−1.437	1.234 (0.729)	0.364 (0.555)	2.154 (0.816)	−0.060 (0.048)	0.345 (0.121)	0.116 (0.032)	0.062 (0.031)	−0.129 (0.060)	−0.643 (0.455)	0.276 (0.178)			0.783	0.520	2.07
Interest rate is $r_e(Y-\Delta H')$	−4.184	1.229 (0.679)	0.359 (0.518)	2.128 (0.763)	−0.070 (0.043)	0.358 (0.113)	0.115 (0.030)	0.097 (0.044)	−0.128 (0.056)	−0.0068 (0.0033)	0.283 (0.166)			0.788	0.514	2.11
	−5.872	0.954 (0.605)	0.173 (0.459)	2.000 (0.669)	−0.102 (0.035)	0.256 (0.010)	0.103 (0.027)	0.040 (0.011)	−0.126 (0.046)			7.034 (1.949)		0.830	0.461	2.07
	1.150	1.260 (0.674)	0.403 (0.508)	2.212 (0.743)	−0.219 (0.065)	0.414 (0.098)	0.102 (0.031)	0.067 (0.021)	−0.150 (0.052)				0.029 (0.013)	0.787	0.516	1.98
Uses $SA, \Delta SA$ instead of $(Y-\Delta H'), \Delta(Y-\Delta H')$	−3.139	−0.229 (0.48)	−0.591 (0.351)	0.951 (0.452)	−0.036 (0.044)	0.182 (0.110)	0.120 (0.030)	0.085 (0.027)	−0.030 (0.043)	−0.398 (0.215)	0.220 (0.168)			0.802	0.498	2.31
uses ΔH instead of $\Delta H'$	−6.563	−4.273 (1.590)	−2.800 (1.002)	−4.760 (1.653)	−0.185 (0.053)	0.263 (0.111)	0.152 (0.039)	0.146 (0.042)	−0.0003 (0.096)					0.826	0.703	2.55

measures $[(Y-\Delta H'), \Delta(Y-\Delta H')]$ yield satisfactory results. Since we wished to minimize the number of variables in the model we used the $(Y-\Delta H')$ form in the final model.

The loan rate has the same quantitative effect in either the linear or multiplicative form. It is, however, somewhat more significant in the latter form. The loan-funds variable yields the anticipated (positive) coefficient. Its introduction slightly increases the coefficient on r_e'.

If introduced without the financial variables, both capacity and the level of unfilled orders are significant and positive. In the presence of the former, neither retains significance. In addition, as in the case of fixed investment, when K and U_{-1} are introduced simultaneously, neither variable obtains any quantitative importance.

In summary, then, it would appear that ΔCL and interest rates are important determinants for both fixed and inventory investment.

Consumption Functions. Table 5.13 reports consumption functions for nondurable, durable, and total consumption. Nondurable expenditures are simply a function of disposable income, net worth, and consumption lagged one and two quarters. As the table shows, introduction of W serves to diminish the propensity to consume out of disposable income.

Durable consumption is made a function of Y^d, C^D_{-1}, ΔY, $(C+D)$ and $\Delta P/P$. A positive response is obtained both with respect to money and price increases. The former may either be a liquid asset effect or a proxy for wealth. The latter, since we have estimated in real terms, may reflect a response to extrapolated (i.e., expected) price changes. A two-quarter lag was also tried for durable consumption but it yielded an insignificant coefficient. Similarly, money plus time deposits was tried as a liquid-asset variable. However, it proved less satisfactory than the narrower definition.

A relationship for total consumption found only Y^d, $\Delta P/P$ and C^T_{-1} to be of any consequence. Net worth, liquid-asset variables or higher-order lags both separately and together added little to the equation. Finally. it is curious to note that the R^2 for nondurable consumption is higher than that for total consumption.

5.3. The Complete Model: an Overview

Having dissected the model equation-by-equation, let us next look at the model in its entirety. We do so as follows. First, we examine briefly the predictive performance of the model. Then, we compare structural and

TABLE 5.13

Consumption expenditures

Dependent variable	Intercept	s_2	s_3	s_4	Y^d	C_{-1}	C_{-2}	W	ΔY	$\Delta P/P$	$(C+D)$	R^2	S_e	DW
C^{ND}	−5.690	5.518 (0.759)	4.016 (0.563)	9.074 (0.600)	0.303 (0.094)	0.644 (0.113)						0.994	0.460	2.55
C^{ND}	−4.438	2.086 (1.368)	3.071 (0.617)	7.486 (0.779)	0.290 (0.088)	0.338 (0.148)	0.329 (0.112)					0.995	0.430	1.82
C^{ND}	−3.452	2.122 (1.340)	3.087 (0.604)	7.515 (0.763)	0.202 (0.100)	0.333 (0.145)	0.326 (0.110)	0.0043 (0.0025)				0.995	0.421	1.82
C^D	−7.296	2.001 (0.322)	1.061 (0.249)	2.638 (0.319)	0.056 (0.017)	0.527 (0.115)			0.173 (0.062)		0.048 (0.026)	0.825	0.510	2.33
C^D	−12.101	1.756 (0.307)	0.836 (0.242)	2.272 (0.318)	0.092 (0.019)	0.354 (0.121)			0.128 (0.059)	41.44 (14.14)	0.078 (0.026)	0.853	0.468	1.97
C^T	−5.851	4.446 (1.222)	2.859 (0.875)	9.549 (0.966)	0.731 (0.131)	0.235 (0.138)				48.10 (21.25)		0.987	0.795	1.77

ordinary least-squares estimates. Finally, we conclude this section with an analysis of the policy implications of our model.

5.3.1. *Prediction*

Table 5.14 juxtaposes actual and predicted values for the third and fourth quarters of 1962.[41] It also contains the standard errors of estimate of the

TABLE 5.14

Predictions

Variable	1962-Third quarter		1962-Fourth quarter		Standard error of estimate
	Actual	Predicted	Actual	Predicted	
E^N	0.017	0.079	0.130	0.101	0.041
E^C	0.438	0.475	0.442	0.482	0.035
B^N	0.050	0.190	0.256	0.272	0.133
B^C	0.030	0.015	0.048	0.064	0.024
S^N	21.49	21.34	22.19	24.14	0.740
S^C	19.14	19.35	19.99	20.81	0.823
O^N	4.72	5.02	5.20	4.86	0.529
O^C	5.56	5.67	5.23	5.54	0.341
MUN^N	11.60	11.65	12.08	11.95	0.174
MUN^C	8.53	8.51	8.69	8.67	0.044
C^{ND}	76.0	77.2	83.6	85.1	0.421
C^D	10.7	12.4	15.2	15.0	0.468
I	9.62	9.45	10.18	10.37	0.153
H'	56.80	56.79	57.21	57.10	0.514
C	30.1	30.1	31.2	31.3	0.123
D	114.6	114.5	121.3	119.3	0.784
T	94.0	94.9	97.1	97.8	0.714
CL	45.90	45.89	47.97	47.44	0.434
r'_e	5.21	5.23	5.28	5.22	0.090
$r_{10} - r_s$	1.16	1.30	1.00	1.28	0.337
$r_3 - r_s$	0.78	1.08	0.57	1.07	0.234

[41] The nonlinearity of the model precluded obtaining an analytic solution for the reduced form or even a precise numerical solution. Hence, predictions were made in an approximative way. In particular, actual values of both endogenous and exogenous variables were substituted on the right-hand side of each equation and predictions were made equation-by-equation. This method has been termed partial forecasting analysis. This procedure has the defect of suppressing the simultaneity in making predictions. However, it does cast light on the adequacy of the individual equations. See GOLD-BERGER, [51], p. 49.

various equations. This table reveals that the model does a reasonable job of prediction.[42]

The largest absolute prediction errors occur for city-bank short-term securities (fourth quarter), nondurable consumption (both quarters), durable consumption (third quarter), demand deposits (fourth quarter) and the $r_3 - r_s$ differential (fourth quarter). These six instances are the only ones in which the absolute prediction error exceeds the corresponding standard error of estimate by more than 50%. In fact, over two-thirds of these absolute errors are less than one standard error. In terms of percentages (i.e., the absolute prediction error as a percent of the actual value), 10 of the 42 prediction errors exceed 10%. These large percentage errors occur for C^D, E^N, B^N, B^C, and the two interest-rate differentials. However, on the positive side, 24 of the 42 errors are 2% or less.

Inevitably, for what such explanations are worth, maverick predictions can be explained on an *ad hoc* basis. For instance, the prediction error for S^N may be the result of the growth of the certificate of deposit (*CD*) market. We indicated earlier that the advent of *CD*'s provided banks with an alternative to holding short-term securities for liquidity. In particular, banks in need of funds on short notice can, by raising the rate they offer on *CD*'s attract short-term funds. Thus, they can afford to shift funds from short-term securities to other (presumably more attractive) earning assets.

5.3.2. *A Comparison of Structural and Ordinary Least-squares Estimates*
Ordinary least-squares (*OLS*) estimates produced in earlier chapters were in the nature of pilot investigations. They served to guide preliminary work, providing valuable information about differing specifications of the various equations. In the structural estimation, we used this information to obtain a first approximation to a complete model. However, in the course of structural estimation, we introduced variables which had been rejected in the *OLS* estimations. In addition, we experimented with the introduction of wholly new variables and, in fact, the final model includes a number of these (e.g., a municipal-bonds supply variable and the levels of the debt proportions). As a result of these modifications a completely

---

[42] It will be recalled that the equations for C^{ND}, C^D, $\Delta H'$ and I were estimated in real terms. Predictions were made, however, in money terms. This was done by multiplying through the various equations by the value of the implicit price deflator for the relevant quarter. For the most part, this changed only the intercept and seasonal coefficients.

systematic comparison (such as is done in sampling experiments) of *OLS* and structural estimates is not possible.[43] However, an examination of the two types of estimates in equations with no new variables reveals (a) that there are differences between the two sets of estimates and (b) these differences are virtually all in the direction of making the final equations agree more closely with our *a priori* notions. To support these assertions, we briefly list some of these differences.

The banking equations provide numerous instances of variables which obtain an appropriately-signed (and significant) coefficient only for the structural estimates. The short-term security equations provide a particularly good example of this. In the city equation, the demand-deposit variable (ΔD^N) yielded an insignificant coefficient of about 0.2 when estimated by *OLS*. It yields a quite significant coefficient of 0.67 in the structural estimation. Similarly, ΔCL^N increases both in absolute size and in significance when estimated by structural methods.

For country bank holdings of short-term securities, the changes are even more striking. With *OLS* estimation, ΔD^C and ΔCL^C both produced signs counter to our expectations. This is happily reversed in the final estimates. Furthermore, the reserve-requirement variable, which appeared to be unimportant in the preliminary estimates, becomes quite important in the final ones.

In addition to the short-term security equations, other bank equations yield similar contrasts. For example, only with structural estimation does the country borrowing equation produce a significant coefficient for ΔCL^C.

The financial-asset equations also reveal some important differences between *OLS* and structural estimates. For the latter, the income elasticities of currency and demand deposits are larger and more in accord with both theory and estimates found by other researchers.

With respect to the inventory equation, structural estimation increases the importance and statistical significance of both financial variables. For the loan rate, at least, this is the textbook version of what should happen when simultaneous-equations techniques are used. It might be noted, however, that the final equation for fixed investment differs very little from the *OLS* estimate (compare equation (4.6) and (5.18)).

---

[43] After obtaining the final model one could, of course, re-estimate all the equations by *OLS*. As detailed estimate comparisons were not a major interest of our study, this was not done. The available information suffices for our purposes.

As even this brief listing shows, important differences exist between a large fraction of our *OLS* and structural estimates.[44] In summary, then, our experience strongly supports the case for structural estimation.

5.3.3. *Monetary Policy: Some Impact Multipliers*

The equations estimated above (or, more explicitly, their individual structural parameters) allow us to test various economic hypotheses. We have already denumerated some of the more important of these hypotheses. Here we wish to focus, in somewhat more detail, on two particular aspects: (1) the linkages between financial and nonfinancial variables; (2) the linkages between policy-controlled variables and both the real and financial sectors.

With regard to the first set of linkages, let us begin by reviewing our results. Fixed investment responds to changes in the long-term bond rate and to the availability of commercial loans. Similarly, inventory investment also responds to loan-market considerations. Finally, durable consumption is, in part, influenced by a liquid-asset variable.[45] These findings are interesting, partly for their own sake, but more importantly because they establish channels through which monetary policy may influence the real sector.

This brings us to the second set of linkages. The standard list of policy instruments includes reserve-requirement changes, discount policy, open-market operations, and debt-management techniques. The model presented above includes in one way or another quantitative measures for each of these instruments.

Clearly, the statuatory percentage reserve requirements (k_1, k_3 and k_4 above) represent the first instrument. Moreover, the discount rate serves to measure discount policy, although (as we emphasized earlier) r_d is but one dimension of discount policy.

On the other hand, the variable directly reflecting open-market operations is the Fed's holdings of U.S. Government securities. We have

---

[44] In addition to the type of differences cited above, there are other differences which are more difficult to evaluate. For example, with structural estimation, the speed of adjustment increases for country bank excess reserves and consumer durable expenditures. It is difficult to know on *a priori* grounds whether this is a reasonable result or not.

[45] Nondurable consumption is, of course, influenced by the net-worth variable which is also of a financial nature. However, since we have left *W* exogenous, there exists no way, in the context of this model, to vary it for policy purposes.

chosen to represent open-market operations by Z, the sum of unborrowed reserves and currency. There are several sources of discrepancy between these two measures, the most important being gold movements and the Federal Reserve float. On the assumption that the Fed can offset gold movements, de Leeuw has compared changes in Z with changes in the Fed's holdings of securities plus gold. The correspondence between the two measures is quite good. The discrepancies appear minor enough to warrant the simplification of treating Z as a policy variable.[46]

Finally, debt-management operations are reflected in the supply of debt variables for various maturities $(\overline{S}_1, \overline{S}_2, \overline{O})$.

The presence of these various policy instruments in the model allows us to examine the second set of linkages. The chain of events implicit in the model is the textbook one: policy actions influence financial variables (e.g., the bond rate, the loan rate, the money supply, and the availability of commercial loans), with these latter variables affecting investment and consumption directly.

5.3.3.1. *The Reduced Form.* In its structural form, the model is appropriate for tracing out this second set of linkages. It is not, however, suitable for assessing the quantitative effects of different policy actions. For this purpose, we need the reduced form, expressing all the endogenous variables as explicit functions of exogenous variables only. Hence, we now turn to a calculation of the reduced form of our model.

Let us consider a system of structural relations in a set of endogenous variables y and a set of exogenous variables z which we write

$$F(y,z) = 0$$

where F is a matrix of functional operators. Taking total differentials we have,

$$dF = \left(\frac{\partial F}{\partial y}\right)dy + \left(\frac{\partial F}{\partial z}\right)dz = 0$$

---

[46] See DE LEEUW [29, Appendix]. It might also be noted that "currency" included in the definition of Z is currency in the hands of the public. Hence, another adjustment item is vault cash. In view of the change in the treatment of vault cash occurring during our sample period, it would have been better to include this as an endogenous variable as well. See FRIEDMAN [47].

or

$$dy = -\left(\frac{\partial F}{\partial y}\right)^{-1}\left(\frac{\partial F}{\partial z}\right)dz = \Pi dz \; .$$

For a linear structural system, the matrix Π will be a constant matrix. In the nonlinear case, however, Π will depend on the values of both the endogenous and exogenous variables. However, when the partial derivatives $(\partial F/\partial y)$ and $(\partial F/\partial z)$ are evaluated at a set of points (y_0, z_0) we will obtain a constant Π matrix. This provides a linearized version of the reduced form.[47] In the calculations that follow, we have evaluated all the relevant derivatives at the values for the second quarter of 1962.[48]

The typical element of Π, i.e., π_{ij} represents the change in y_i induced by a unit change in z_j with all other predetermined variables held constant. In other words, $\pi_{ij} = \partial y_i / \partial z_j$. The π_{ij}'s are hence akin to the typical "multiplier" concept and are, in fact, termed *impact multipliers*. Tables 5.15–5.19 present estimates of impact multipliers under various alternative hypotheses. Before discussing these results, several matters of interpretation need to be stressed.

First, it must be noted that the impact multipliers provide information about the response, in the same quarter, of a change in the value of an exogenous variable. Because there are numerous lags present in the model, these responses may differ considerably from the long-run response. Second, the magnitude of the coefficients does not measure the relative (historical) importance of the predetermined variables in influencing the endogenous variables. This depends on the relative variation of the predetermined variables as well as on the actual multipliers. Of course, for policy variables, the relative variation is under control. Third, since the multipliers are partial derivatives, they assume all other predetermined variables are held constant. In some instances, it may make more sense to consider combinations of changes in predetermined variables rather than individual changes. An example of this is discussed below where we examine open-market operations. With these qualifications in mind, we turn directly to some impact multipliers.

Table 5.15 contains the first set of impact multipliers we shall examine. As is clear from its dimensionality, the table does not contain the entire

---

[47] In the linear case one obtains $y = \Pi z$ rather than $dy = \Pi dz$. However, the former also implies $\Delta y = \Pi \Delta z$. It is to this version that the nonlinear reduced form corresponds. See GOLDBERGER [51], chapter 3.

[48] Goldberger linearizes at the sample means. It seems more appropriate for current evaluation of policy to use the values latest in time. For a typical linearization see [51].

TABLE 5.15

Impact multipliers

	k_1	k_3	k_4	$\bar{S}_1$	$\bar{S}_2$	$\bar{O}$	Z	r_d	G	Tx
	−1.094	−0.594	−1.183	0.0048	−0.0026	−0.0048	1.506	−0.203	1.646	−0.484
ᵗD	−0.221	−0.120	−0.239	0.0010	−0.0005	−0.0010	0.304	−0.041	0.333	−0.300
	−0.327	−0.174	−0.351	0.0010	−0.0006	−0.0010	0.442	−0.075	0.369	−0.200
	−0.308	−0.167	−0.333	0.0019	−0.0011	−0.0019	0.424	−0.058	0.091	−0.027
	−0.238	−0.132	−0.260	0.0008	−0.0005	−0.0008	0.335	−0.029	−0.145	0.043
	−1.094	−0.594	−1.183	0.0048	−0.0026	−0.0048	1.506	−0.203	1.646	−1.484
	−0.540	−0.273	−0.567	−0.0003	0.0002	0.0003	0.692	−0.195	−0.001	0.000
	−0.314	−0.159	−0.330	−0.0002	0.0001	0.0002	0.403	−0.114	−0.001	0.000
	−0.488	−0.244	−0.510	0.0044	−0.0025	−0.0044	0.619	−0.188	−0.096	0.028
	−0.418	−0.209	−0.437	0.0038	−0.0021	−0.0038	0.530	−0.161	−0.082	0.024
ₙ	−0.297	−0.193	−0.349	0.0005	−0.0003	−0.0005	0.491	0.095	0.019	−0.006
ₒ	−0.104	−0.067	−0.121	0.0002	−0.0001	−0.0002	0.171	0.033	0.007	−0.002
	−0.041	−0.023	−0.045	−0.0001	0.0000	0.0001	0.059	−0.003	−0.008	0.002
	−0.034	−0.017	−0.036	−0.0000	0.0000	0.0000	0.043	−0.013	−0.006	0.002
	0.174	0.134	0.222	0.0004	−0.0002	−0.0004	−0.341	−0.116	0.053	−0.015
	0.058	0.031	0.062	−0.0000	0.0000	0.0000	−0.078	−0.025	0.012	−0.004
	−1.405	−0.173	−1.018	0.1036	0.0996	−0.3326	0.438	−0.331	−0.086	0.025
	−1.045	−1.323	−1.800	0.0191	0.0117	−0.1846	1.446	−0.180	−0.159	0.047
	0.049	0.030	0.056	−0.1242	−0.1239	0.2132	−0.077	−0.009	−0.001	0.000
	0.331	0.174	0.353	−0.0941	−0.0893	0.1441	−0.442	0.086	0.048	−0.014
UN^N	−0.094	−0.047	−0.098	0.0009	−0.0005	−0.0009	0.119	−0.036	−0.018	0.005
UN^C	−0.090	−0.045	−0.094	0.0006	−0.0004	−0.0006	0.114	−0.034	−0.014	0.004
	0.184	0.088	0.189	−0.0010	0.0005	0.0010	−0.225	0.087	0.038	−0.011
	0.890	0.445	0.930	0.0010	−0.0006	−0.0010	−1.129	0.341	0.165	−0.048
	0.928	0.465	0.970	0.0023	0.0079	−0.0120	−1.178	0.355	0.172	−0.051
	0.547	0.274	0.572	−0.0049	0.0027	0.0049	−0.695	0.210	0.101	−0.030
	0.505	0.307	0.575	0.0003	−0.0002	−0.0003	0.220	−0.063	−0.009	0.003
	−2.932	−1.820	−3.366	−0.0040	0.0020	0.0040	4.618	0.532	−0.529	0.156
	−0.908	−0.459	−0.953	−0.0005	0.0003	0.0005	1.163	−0.328	−0.002	0.001
	−0.198	−0.102	−0.209	0.0002	−0.0001	−0.0002	0.259	−0.061	0.087	−0.026
	−1.097	−0.549	−1.146	0.0099	−0.0055	−0.0099	1.392	−0.422	−0.216	0.064
	−0.437	−0.284	−0.513	0.0007	−0.0004	−0.0007	0.722	0.140	0.028	−0.008

reduced form. The complete reduced form (Π-matrix) was calculated. However, because our primary interest is in the impact of changes in policy-controlled variables, we have presented only what we might call the policy submatrix. A typical element of table 5.15, say,

$$\frac{\partial Y}{\partial k_1} = -1.094$$

indicates that a one percentage point change in the reserve requirement on city-bank demand deposits causes an opposite change in GNP of $1.094 billion (*at quarterly rates*).[49]

Let us turn now to a systematic evaluation of the implications of table 5.15. We concentrate first on reserve-requirement changes and open-market operations and discuss the multipliers in terms of increasing the tightness of monetary policy.[50]

5.3.3.2. *Reserve-requirement Changes and Open-market Operations.* A more stringent monetary policy would be associated with an increase in reserve requirements or an open-market sale of securities (i.e., a reduction in Z). We would expect these types of actions to lead to one or more of the following:

    (i)   a decrease in GNP and its several components
    (ii) an increase in interest rates
    (iii) a decrease in the money supply and in time deposits
    (iv) a decrease in bank holdings of various assets
    (v) an increase in bank borrowing from the Fed.

With one minor exception, this is precisely the story told by table 5.15. GNP and all its components have negative entries corresponding to the reserve-requirement variables and positive entries for Z. All deposit variables, currency, and all but one of the bank asset variables produce the same sign pattern.[51] In addition, bank borrowing [52] and the several interest rates yield the expected (opposite) sign pattern.

---

[49] For purposes of presenting the multipliers we have changed the units on the reserve-requirements (the k's) to percentages. It should also be emphasized that all changes in the policy variables are to be construed as starting from the second quarter values for 1962. In fact, the multipliers are valid only in the neighborhood of the point at which the reduced form was linearized.

[50] Due to the linearization, the quantitative effects of an increase or a decrease in an exogenous variable are symmetric. As we shall see shortly, in some instances this is an unreasonable assumption.

[51] Bank-holdings of long-term securities appear to increase with a tightening of monetary policy. Technically, this comes about largely because in the structural equations for O^N and O^C there is a negative dependence on $(D^N + T^N)$ and $(D^C + T^C)$ respectively.

[52] The fact that increased reserve requirements cause reduced excess reserves and increased borrowing, reflects the dependence of the latter variables on D^* (which in turn depends on the k's). It is interesting to note that $\partial B^N/\partial k_1$ and $\partial B^N/\partial k_4$ are positive despite the negative role found for RR_2^N in the equation for B^N.

Table 5.16 below presents the effects, on a selected subset of the endogenous variables, of the following three policy actions:

(A) an increase of one percentage point in the demand deposit reserve-requirements (k_1, k_3),

(B) \$1 billion open-market sale conducted in bills,

(C) an across-the-board increase in reserve requirements of one percentage point.

TABLE 5.16

	Policy A	Policy B	Policy C
Y	-1.688	-1.501	-2.871
r_e'	0.272	0.224	0.461
r_s	1.335	1.130	2.265
r_{10}	0.821	0.690	1.393
D	-1.367	-1.164	-2.320
C	-0.300	-0.259	-0.509
T	-1.646	-1.382	-2.792
CL	-0.721	-0.721	-1.234
$(B^N + B^C)$	0.397	0.419	0.681
$(S^N + S^C)$	-3.946	-1.761	-6.764

It should be noted that the specification of an open-market action must include the type of security in which the operation is conducted. Open-market operations necessarily alter one or more of $\bar{S}_1$, $\bar{S}_2$, or $\bar{O}$ (government securities in the hands of the public). These changes, as table 5.15 reveals, also have an impact on the endogenous variables. Hence, in order to obtain the response to policy B one must combine the decrease in Z of \$1 billion with the increase in $\bar{S}_1$ of the same amount. For example, the increase in r_e' of 0.224 results from adding $\partial r_e'/\partial \bar{S}_1$ and $\partial r_e'/\partial Z$ (i.e., $0.224 = 0.225 - 0.001$).[53]

Table 5.16 reveals a number of interesting features. For one, policies A and B, in terms of their impact on income, interest rates and money, yield substantial and quite comparable effects.[54] For both policies, for

---

[53] Except for the effect on bank government security holdings, table 5.15 implies it is of only secondary consequence in what maturity open-market operations are conducted.

[54] Depending upon precisely which variable we select as the basis for comparison, it would appear that for income, interest rates, and money, a one percentage point increase in k_1 and k_3 is equivalent to open-market operations of between \$1.1 and \$1.2 billion.

example, GNP (in current dollars) declines by more than $1.5 billion —or more than $6 billion at annual rates. These restrictive policies produce a rise in the loan rate of roughly 0.25, in the bill rate of 1.2, and in the bond rate of 0.75. This pattern is consistent with the observed stickiness of the loan rate and the greater volatility of short-term government rates. With respect to the money supply, these policies result in a reduction of between $1.4 and $1.7 billion.[55] In view of these findings, it would seem that open-market operations and reserve-requirement changes have strong impacts on both financial and nonfinancial variables.

It might also be noted that changes in the time-deposit reserve requirement (k_4) appear to have a strong impact on the several endogenous variables examined in table 5.16. In fact, policy C yields almost twice the effect of policy A. Since a relatively low value (4%) of k_4 currently prevails, however, this does not leave much room for further decreases. Hence, for expansionary purposes at least, only limited use can be made of this instrument.[56]

Despite their broad similarity, open-market operations and reserve-requirement changes do have different impacts on the composition of bank portfolios. In particular, reserve-requirement changes appear to involve a shift away from U.S. securities. For example, from table 5.16 we see that policy A produces a roughly $2 billion greater decline in bank holdings of short-term securities. Part of this is reflected in the greater decline in commercial loans occasioned by open-market sales. However, the bulk of the difference is reflected in miscellaneous asset items which we have netted out.[57]

The differential shift away from U.S. securities with policy A was also

---

[55] It might be wondered, in view of the change in currency caused by policy A, if that policy is leaving Z unchanged. From (5.27) above, we have $Z = R^R + E^N + E^C - B^N - B^C + C$. From table 5.15 we have $\Delta Z = \Delta R^R + \Delta E^N + \Delta E^C - \Delta B^N - \Delta B^C + \Delta C = 0.812 - 0.064 - 0.051 - 0.308 - 0.089 - 0.300 = 0$.

[56] With one exception, all reserve-requirement changes since February 1951 have decreased one or more of the k's. This may partially be explained in terms of the implications of reserve-requirement changes for bank portfolio composition and hence, for bank profits. In fact, k_4 was reduced from 5% to 4% in the fourth quarter of 1962. It might be interesting, in the context of the above model, to examine this change in detail.

[57] The reader will recall that the "other loans" category and the bank balance-sheet identity were both eliminated from the model. It is clear from this identity, however, that the residual nature of the "other loan" category must account for the security imbalance.

found by de Leeuw in his simulation study.[58] That study and some limited evidence from the Okun study cited earlier, provide us with some roughly comparable estimates of monetary multipliers. De Leeuw has reported the response to various policy actions of r_s, r_{10}, $(B^N + B^C)$, $(C + D)$ and T. Okun, on the other hand, just provides estimates with respect to the two interest rates.[59] Okun's estimates for policies A and B are as follows.[60]

	Policy A	Policy B
r_s	0.42–0.44	0.19–0.41
	(1.34)	(1.13)
r_{10}	0.09–0.13	0.06–0.08
	(0.82)	(0.69)

There is a considerable number of differences between Okun's and our methods (especially structural estimation and allowance for lags). In view of this, we simply note without explanation that our impact multipliers are uniformly higher than those obtained by Okun.

In that it utilizes a complete model of the financial sector, the de Leeuw study is more like our own. De Leeuw evaluates a reserve-requirement increase of 1/2 percent and an open-market sale of $500 million. With respect to these two policies, his findings are:[61]

	r_s	r_{10}	$(C+D)$	$(B^N + B^C)$	T
Reserve-requirement	0.8	0.4	−0.7	0.2	−0.9
increase	(0.7)	(0.4)	(−0.8)	(0.2)	(−0.8)
Open-market sale	0.9	0.4	−0.7	0.2	−0.9
	(0.6)	(0.4)	(−0.7)	(0.2)	(−0.7)

[58] This differential shift has been anticipated on theoretical grounds as well. However, the arguments (and implicit assumptions) pointing toward this conclusion have met with considerable criticism. The above finding suggests that a less restrictive set of assumptions may also produce the same results. See [125] and the references contained therein.

[59] Okun does not use a reduced form approach. He estimates a single equation and makes a rough allowance for the simultaneous impact of policy on member-bank borrowing and currency holding by the public.

[60] The range of values reflect the several alternative specifications presented by Okun. See table 4.5, [91, p. 361]. The values for the present study are in parentheses.

[61] [125]. Again we place our corresponding (rounded) estimates in parentheses below

As the above estimates reveal, de Leeuw's findings and ours are virtually identical. It should be mentioned, however, that de Leeuw's simulation results yielded longer-run interest-rate responses which were considerably reduced from the initial impacts. De Leeuw explained this result in terms of the relatively slow speeds of adjustment he found for currency and demand deposits.[62] As (5.12) and (5.13) have comparably slow speeds of adjustment, some of the longer-run results for the present model may be also quite different from the impact results. Before turning to an examination of several other policy instruments, we conclude this section with a brief discussion of the relationship between open-market operations and member-bank borrowing.

5.3.3.3. *Member-bank Borrowing.* A general impression given by the Fed is that administration of the discount window is a well-integrated component of overall credit policy which acts in the *same* direction as open-market operations. Thus, there is a tendency on the part of some Federal Reserve officials to view increased member-bank borrowing as a force intensifying credit restraint. This view is based on the belief that member banks, in keeping with their tradition against borrowing, will limit credit when they themselves are forced to borrow from the Fed. Hence, it is sometimes argued, the larger the volume of borrowings brought about by open-market sales, the more restrictive will be the operation of monetary policy.[63]

---

de Leeuw's. His estimates were read from a bar graph. It should be mentioned that de Leeuw allows for asymmetrical responses to increases and decreases. For example, he finds a bill-rate response of -1.5 percentage points to an increase in Z of \$500 million.

[62] Consider a simple model with an exogenous supply of money, single interest rate r, and a stock-adjustment demand for money of the form

$$\Delta M_t = a - b M_{t-1} - c r_t .$$

Then we can write

$$r_t = a/c - (1/c)[\Delta M_t + b M_{t-1}] .$$

A change in M causes an initial change in r of $-\Delta M/C$ and a permanent change equal to $-b\Delta M/C$. Hence, if b is small, a quite large initial reaction is to be expected. See [125].

[63] For a discussion of this and related points see [119] and [121]. This attitude toward the role of the discount mechanism during a period of credit restraint is reflected in the practice of using the level of free reserves as an indication of the tightness in the money market. That this view is not accepted totally, even by the authorities, is indicated by the Fed's attempt to limit borrowing.

The kernel of truth in this argument is that for a given total volume of member-bank reserves, the larger the share generated by borrowings, the more restrictive will be the lending policy of member banks. However, the view cited above ignores the fact that borrowing can increase the volume of member-bank reserves. As table 5.15 reveals, a decrease in Z (open-market sales) will lead to an increase in borrowing. This partially offsets the effect of the open-market operations. This does not mean that the authorities cannot attain a given target of total reserves. However, it does indicate that a larger volume of open-market operations will be required to achieve a given target. Hence, our results imply not only that borrowing makes monetary policy less effective, but also provides quantitative estimates of the reduced effectiveness. It would seem advisable to utilize estimates of this type of predictable portfolio readjustment in the operation of monetary policy.[64]

In view of the escape-valve nature of borrowing it may be wondered why the discount window should not be abolished.[65] In view of its selective nature, it seems desirable to retain it on a number of grounds. For example, while the Fed could supply by open-market operations the *volume* of reserves needed to replace an unforeseen loss of reserves, there is no assurance that the reserves created by open-market purchases will be distributed among member banks in proportion to the reserve losses which they are intended to replace. In addition, the existence of the discount window means that borrowing can appropriately act as a way of cushioning the uneven impact of such general credit instruments as open-market sales and increases in reserve requirements.

5.3.3.4. *Discount-rate Changes.* First, we note that on the whole, the responses to changing the discount rate are quite small. A one-point rise in r_d only raises r_s by 0.34 and r_{10} by 0.21.[66] These estimates are larger

---

[64] As a general proposition Fed officials seem willing to accept the predictable nature of borrowing. For example, Ralph Young has noted: "A Federal Reserve decision to limit the volume of member banks' reserves is, in a sense, a decision to put member banks as a group under pressure to borrow reserve funds. A higher level of member-bank borrowings, representing increasing frequency, amount, and duration of discountings by a growing number of banks, is a normal and expected reaction to a restrictive monetary policy." [124, p. 34]. Hence, it would seem a short step to the use of quantitative estimates and the abandonment of the borrowing-stringency argument cited above.

[65] Friedman has, in fact, made this proposal. See his testimony in [46, p. 636].

[66] The small response of the bill rate may partially reflect the fact that our member-bank borrowing equations have no built-in nonnegativity constraints.

than Okun's which for r_s ranged from 0.04 to 0.14 and for r_{10} from 0.01 to 0.03. Our estimates are considerably smaller than de Leeuw's impact estimates, but seem to be more like his estimates after two or three periods.

With respect to other endogenous variables, the responses to changes in r_d are also somewhat small. In response to a one-point increase in r_d, both the money supply and time deposits decline by about \$400 million and GNP declines by about \$200 million. It is curious to note that increasing r_d appears to increase commercial loans. Examining table 5.15 reveals the reason. Increasing r_d increases r_s which decreases the demand for currency. With Z fixed, the decline in the demand for currency produces an increase in D^* (\$.5 billion) which then increases CL. In terms of the banks' portfolios, the decline in short-term securities (roughly \$.5 billion) facilitates this expansion of loans. It would seem, therefore, that (by themselves) changes in the discount rate are somewhat unreliable as a policy instrument.[67]

5.3.3.5. *Debt Management.* Debt-management techniques involve shifting the composition of a Federal debt, treated as fixed in size. In our model, this is accomplished by changing $\bar{S}_1$, $\bar{S}_2$, and $\bar{O}$ so that the sum of the changes is zero. The quite small multipliers in table 5.15 indicate, however, that shifting the composition of the Federal debt appears to affect little other than the composition of bank-security holdings. In particular, the composition of the debt appears to have minimal significance for the term-structure of interest rates. Table 5.17 reports Okun's and our estimates for two sample debt operations. It is clear that neither set of estimates attributes much importance to the quantitative impact of debt management operations on interest rates.

TABLE 5.17

		r_s	r_{10}	r_3
$\Delta\bar{S}_2 = -1, \Delta\bar{O} = +1$	Our estimate	−0.0004	0.002	−0.020
	Okun's estimate	−0.024	0.020	
$\Delta\bar{S}_1 = -1, \Delta\bar{O} = +1$	Our estimate	−0.002	0.010	−0.014
	Okun's estimate	−0.024	0.010	

---

[67] With respect to discount-rate changes, we have ignored any possible impact on expectations. Many writers have indicated an uneasiness connected with the stability of the "announcement" effects attendant to a change in r_d. See [46, p. 449] and [106].

5.3.3.6. *Fiscal Policy.* In addition to monetary policy, the presence of the G and Tx variables allows us to make some statements about the impact of some rudimentary fiscal policies. In particular, the multiplier effect of a $1 billion increase in government spending (G) on Y is to increase it by $1.65 billion.[68] This is distributed over the components of GNP as follows: $C^{ND} = \$.33$; $C^D = \$.37$, $I = \$.09$; $H' = -\$.15$.[69]

In addition, a $1 billion increase in G increases the rates on U.S. Government securities from 0.10 to 0.17 percentage points. It also increases commercial loans and decreases time deposits. The latter decreases because the bond rate and GNP rise.[70] Due to increased r_s, there is a decrease in excess reserves and an increase in borrowing. Finally, we may note that the balanced-budget multiplier (obtained from a simultaneous increase in G and Tx) is 1.16, considerably smaller than the simple expenditure multiplier, $\partial Y / \partial G$.

One important qualification to these fiscal multipliers should be noted. We have heretofore treated Tx as a predetermined variable. Thus, an increase in G can not cause taxes to change. However, with our current tax structure, the increase in Y caused by an increase in G is likely to increase tax revenues. Put another way, the system possesses a certain amount of built-in flexibility. This flexibility stems from the fact that as GNP increases, corporate profits and personal income taxes rise more than proportionately. Similarly on the expenditure side, subsidies and government transfer payments decrease more than proportionately. Hence, disposable income does not increase (or decrease) as much as GNP. Put another way,

$$\mathrm{d}Y^d = \alpha \mathrm{d}Y$$

where $0 < \alpha < 1$. In order to allow for tax leakages we chose several values

---

[68] Since there are small responses to changes in $\bar{S}_1$, $\bar{S}_2$, and $\bar{O}$, if the expenditure is financed by increasing the debt (as the figure in the text assumes), it makes little difference which maturity is used. If the expenditure is financed by increasing Z, there will be a further expansionary effect. The case of finance by increased taxes is considered below.

[69] The decline in H' comes about largely because the coefficient of the *change* in final sales exceeds — in absolute value — the coefficient of the *level* of final sales. This property of the inventory equation holds for many of the specifications reported by LOVELL in [73].

[70] The specification in equation (5.14) makes time deposits, for the most part, respond to GNP with a lag of one quarter. Given the multiplicative interest-rate specification, there is actually a slight negative effect on T of changing current Y.

of α,[71] replaced the total differential of equation (5.23), i.e.,

$$dY^d = dY - dTx$$

by the above expression and recalculated the impact multipliers. For $\alpha = 0.3$, table 5.18 gives some selected impact multipliers. As these estimates show, the government expenditure multiplier, $\partial Y / \partial G$, is considerably reduced, going from 1.65 to 1.23. As is expected, the bulk of this change is reflected in the reduction of the impact on consumption (e.g., the impact on C^{ND} goes from 0.333 to 0.075).

In addition to reduction of the government-expenditure multipliers, allowance for tax leakage also changes some of the monetary multipliers. In particular, it somewhat reduces the impact of reserve-requirement changes and open-market operations on GNP.[72] As expected, in terms of the income components, most of the change is accounted for by the reduced responsiveness of durable and nondurable consumption. Even allowing for these reductions, however, monetary policies continue to have a strong impact on income and interest rates.

5.3.3.7. *Unborrowed Reserves as a Policy Variable.* One final point concerning the impact multipliers should be noted. We have chosen the sum of unborrowed reserves *plus* currency to be a policy variable rather than the reserve variable alone. The former, of course, corresponds more closely to the Fed's holdings of U.S. securities. Given this correspondence, it would seem to be a more sensible choice for a policy variable. Nevertheless, some writers have chosen to utilize the reserve variable as a policy variable.[73]

Use of unborrowed reserves (R^u) as a policy variable gets one into certain difficulties. If R^u is policy-controlled and if an increase in R^u causes no change in excess reserves demanded, then that increase could support the same deposit expansion irrespective of any induced increase in currency holdings. That is, the assumption of a given *ex post* increase in reserves means that, in order to yield the desired increase in reserves, the authorities must offset any cash drain. The cash drain will be reflected in a change in Z of the same amount. Hence, with R^u exogenously controlled, the impact of a change in any of our policy instruments is composed of

---

[71] For a discussion of built-in flexibility, see ACKLEY [1], pp. 299–303 and DUESENBERRY, ECKSTEIN and FROMM [33].

[72] Table 5.18 just reports the results for k_1. The results for k_3 and k_4 were similar.

[73] See, for example, [126].

TABLE 5.18

Y	C^{ND}	C^D	I	H'	Y^d	r_s	D	C	T
-0.817	-0.050	-0.212	-0.293	-0.262	-0.245	0.917	-0.908	-0.183	-1.133
1.125	0.068	0.284	0.403	0.369	0.337	-1.167	1.163	0.239	1.442
1.230	0.075	0.196	0.067	-0.109	0.369	0.128	-0.001	0.065	-0.161

TABLE 5.19

k_1	k_3	k_4	$\bar{S}_1$	$\bar{S}_2$	$\bar{O}$	R^u	r_d	G	Tx
-0.267	-0.138	-0.283	0.0002	-0.0001	-0.0002	0.350	-0.083	0.118	-0.035
-1.219	-0.619	-1.281	-0.0002	0.0001	0.0002	1.570	-0.424	0.135	-0.040
-4.165	-2.456	-4.672	-0.0029	0.0016	0.0029	6.232	0.150	0.015	-0.004
1.191	0.601	1.249	0.0007	-0.0004	-0.0007	-1.524	0.434	0.032	-0.009

two effects: (1) the direct effect (as reported in table 5.15) of the instrument on the endogenous variable; and (2) the indirect impact of the change in Z (induced by the currency drain).

In order to estimate this indirect effect, we recalculated the impact multipliers under the assumption that R^u is predetermined. This was done by suppressing the currency term in (5.26) and (5.27) and replacing Z by R^u. Table 5.19 reports a sample of the results for the predetermined tax case.

From tables 5.19 and 5.15 it is now easy to see the two effects cited above. For example, from 5.19 we see that the impact of a one-percentage point reduction in k_1 increases C by 0.267 and decreases r_s by 1.191. This latter estimate can also be obtained from 5.15 in the following way:

(1) direct effect of reduction in k_1 is to decrease r_s by 0.890
(2) indirect effect of increased Z of 0.267 decreases r_s by (0.267) (1.129) or 0.301.

The sum of these two is clearly 1.191 as expected.

Similarly, an increase of one unit in R^u causes an increase in C of 0.350. Thus, a one-unit change in R^u is equivalent to a 1.350 unit change in Z. This is, of course, again borne out since, for example,

$$\frac{\partial r_s/\partial R^u}{\partial r_s/\partial Z} = \frac{-1.524}{-1.129} = 1.350 \, .$$

Thus, using the "currency row" of 5.19, one can construct the analog of table 5.15 where R^u is a policy variable.

These sample comparisons reveal that it is quite important to carefully specify which variable is being treated as exogenous. Furthermore, in terms of the decision-making procedures of the monetary authorities, Z would appear to be the more natural choice.

5.4. Some Miscellaneous Issues

Having concluded our overall examination of the model, it remains only to clean up several loose ends. In particular, we deal briefly with each of the following issues: (1) the objectives of the monetary authorities; (2) an aggregate money-supply relationship; and (3) an aggregate free-reserve relationship.

5.4.1. *Monetary Police Objectives*

The very term monetary *policy* implies that some variable or variables are being manipulated to achieve a set of objectives. This element of volition raises questions of the nature of the authorities' objectives. More particularly, to what variables and with what timing does policy respond? These questions are not easily answered and are, for the most part, beyond the scope of this study. However, we can indicate the nature of the problem and a possible direction for future solution.

If policy responses are reactions to the current behavior of certain economic objectives, then policy variables should be treated as endogenous. Failure to do so would simply be an element of misspecification. In other words, if policy response is automatic, we should specify behavioral relations for the monetary authorities. In this context, it should be noted that D^* is already an endogenous variable in our model: it is a function of currency and time deposits as well as of exogenous variables. Hence, a behavioral relationship for the monetary authorities would allow us to make Z endogenous as well.

It is, of course, possible that the authorities react with sufficient lags so that policy variables are related only to predetermined variables. In this instance, consistency of estimation would not require one to specify policy behavioral relations. Even in this case, however, anyone interested in the dynamic behavior of policy actions would have need for detailed policy relations.

Two attempts at estimating behavioral relations of the monetary authorities have been made, one by Reuber [98] (for Canada) and one by Dewald and Johnson [65] (for the United States). In both approaches, one chooses a policy instrument and regresses it on measures of presumed policy objectives. Thus, for example, one might regress the money supply on measures of unemployment, economic growth, balance of payments, and price behavior. The resulting equation—which they term a reaction function—can be used to decode the implicit tradeoffs made by the monetary authorities.

This approach seems elegant in its simplicity. As its proponents are aware, however, there are certain methodological problems which complicate the interpretation of any estimated reaction function. For one, it is difficult to be sure one has chosen either the right policy variable or the right objectives. More seriously, however, the functions we estimate entangle several aspects of the problem. In particular, the following three facets would seem to be intertwined:

(1) tradeoff possibilities objectively present in the economy (between such goals as high level employment and greater economic growth);

(2) these tradeoffs as they are perceived by the monetary authorities;

(3) the preferences of the monetary authorities.

Disentangling these various aspects would seem to be a necessary prerequisite to proper interpretation of a reaction function. While progress has been made toward the resolution of these problems [98], it seems fair to say that, in the current state of the art, difficulties still exist. In view of this, we did not include any reaction functions in our final model. However, we did estimate several functions and we briefly present our results.[74]

With D^* as a dependent variable and UN representing the unemployment rate we obtained the following (typical) results:

$$D^* = 37.24 + 2.31s_2 + 1.79s_3 + 4.68s_4 + 0.62D^*_{-1} - 16.14\ 1/U$$
$$\qquad\quad (0.76)\quad (0.79)\quad (0.78)\quad (0.09)\qquad (5.17)$$

$$-26.58\Delta Y/Y \qquad\qquad\qquad R^2 = 0.81\ \ S_e = 1.76\ \ DW = 2.22 \quad \text{(i)}$$
$$\ \ (16.78)$$

$$D^* = 37.37 + 2.45s_2 + 2.01s_3 + 4.90s_4 + 0.66D^*_{-1} - 12.19\ 1/U$$
$$\qquad\quad (0.76)\quad (0.79)\quad (0.78)\quad (0.09)\qquad (5.51)$$

$$-0.22(Y - Y^*) - 4.76\bar{r}_{10}(R, 15)$$
$$\ \ (0.14)\qquad\qquad (3.27)$$
$$\qquad\qquad\qquad\qquad R^2 = 0.81\ \ S_e = 1.75\ \ DW = 2.35 \quad \text{(ii)}$$

---

[74] The estimates reported were obtained by two-stage least-squares. Both studies cited above estimate the reaction functions by ordinary least squares. As income influences policy and policy affects income, structural estimation would seem preferable.

$$\ln D^* = 2.03 + 0.020 s_2 + 0.018 s_3 + 0.047 s_4 + 0.46 \ln D^*_{-1} + 0.025 \ \ln U$$
$$ (0.008) \quad (0.008) \quad (0.008) \quad (0.10) (0.014)$$

$$-0.11 \ \ln \bar{r}_{10}(R,15) + 0.07 \ln Y$$
$$ (0.04) (0.03) R^2 = 0.83 \ \ S_e = 0.017 \ \ DW = 2.10 \quad \text{(iii)}$$

Equation (i) says an increase in unemployment or a decrease in the rate of growth of GNP causes the monetary authorities to increase D^*. Equation (ii) expresses the growth consideration in another way. This equation says if GNP is below previous peak GNP then the monetary authorities will expand D^*. Equation (ii) also includes a long-term interest-rate variable with the idea that lower interest rates encourage investment and growth. A low value of $\bar{r}_{10}(R,15)$ indicates that interest rates are expected to rise. From (ii), this will cause an increase in D^* which may mitigate the rise. Equation (iii) is a logarithmic form of a reaction function. The unemployment and interest variables behave as before, but the level of GNP receives a positive coefficient. It should be noted that this is the sign obtained by the GNP variable used by Dewald and Johnson to approximate the growth objective. It would seem that a growth rate variable, however, should yield a negative sign. The difficulty may be that the level of Y does not adequately capture the notion of growth.[75]

We also experimented with Z as a dependent variable but we did not obtain satisfactory results. Similarly, we included price and balance-of-payments variables in (i)-(iii) above, but they typically produced insignificant (and occasionally incorrectly-signed) coefficients. On the whole, therefore, attempts to specify reaction functions met with only limited success. This would appear, however, to be a promising direction for future research.

5.4.2. A Money-supply Equation

An aggregate variable "money" does not enter into our final specification of the model. On the demand side, we have replaced money by its two component demands, namely currency and demand deposits. On the supply side, the situation is somewhat more involved. In particular,

---

[75] The positive coefficient on Y may also reflect the lack of identification of a behavior relationship for the monetary authorities. This may be especially true for the function cited in [65] which uses the stock of money as a dependent variable and hence partially resembles a demand function for money.

construction of the money-supply equation implicit in our model involves combining the following: (a) bank portfolio equations for excess reserves and borrowings; (b) the required-reserve identity; (c) the Federal Reserve open-market identity; and (d) several of the distributional relationships. In view of the recent appearance of consolidated money-supply relationships (e.g., Teigen [110]), some interest attaches to the derivation of our implicit money-supply equation. Combination of these four types of realtionships will allow us to calculate (and compare with other estimates of) various elasticities of the money supply relationship.

In particular, the following six relationships hold:

(i) $\quad R^R = k_1 D^N + k_3 D^C + k_4 T^N + k_4 T^C$

(ii) $\quad R^R + E^N + E^C - B^N - B^C + C = Z$

(iii) $D^N + D^C = \gamma_4 D$

(iv) $T^N + T^C = \gamma_5 T$

(v) $\quad D^N / D^C = \gamma_1$

(vi) $T^N / T^C = \gamma_2$

These can be manipulated to yield

(vii)
$$D = \frac{Z - E^N - E^C + B^N + B^C - C - k_4 \gamma_5 T}{\dfrac{k_1 \gamma_4 \gamma_1 + k_3 \gamma_4}{(1 + \gamma_1)}}.$$

The values of the γ's for the second quarter of 1962 are $\gamma_1 = 1.718$; $\gamma_2 = 1.167$; $\gamma_4 = 0.941$; $\gamma_5 = 0.826$. Making the relevant substitutions into $M = C + D$ yields

(viii)
$$M = \frac{Z - E^N - E^C + B^N + B^C - 0.86C - 0.041 T}{0.140}.$$

As (viii) reveals, the interest-responsiveness of the money supply stems from the responsiveness of excess-reserves, borrowings, currency, and time deposits. From (viii) and the various estimated relationships for these variables we can calculate the following interest elasticities:

	Bill rate	Discount rate
Short-run	0.042	−0.029
Long-run	0.222	−0.076

Money-supply interest elasticities have been reported in the literature by both Teigen and de Leeuw. Teigen's (long-run) estimates are 0.195 and -0.170 for the prime commercial paper rate and the discount respectively.[76] De Leeuw's (long-run) estimates are 0.245 and -0.348 for the bill and discount rates, respectively.[77] Thus, it appears that our bill-rate elasticity estimate is quite comparable to other published estimates. However, the elasticity with respect to the discount rate is seen to be somewhat lower than other estimates.[78]

5.4.3. *An Aggregate Free-reserve Equation*

We have earlier made reference to Meigs' detailed study of bank holdings of free reserves. In that study, Meigs utilizes an aggregate equation to explain free reserves. In view of this precedent, it seems worthwhile to examine briefly how an aggregate equation compares with the four component equations. With this in mind we estimated (by two-stage least-squares) several equations using ΔR^F as a dependent variable. A typical result is as follows:

$$\Delta R^F = -0.010 - 0.441R_{-1}^F - 0.041s_2 - 0.045s_3 - 0.020s_4 + 0.314(r_d - r_s)$$
$$\qquad (0.083) \qquad (0.106) \quad (0.127) \quad (0.190) \quad (0.151)$$

$$+0.047\Delta D^* - 0.478dp + 0.213d_1 - 0.093\Delta CL$$
$$(0.023) \qquad (0.151) \qquad (0.081) \quad (0.030)$$

$$R^2 = 0.677 \quad S_e = 0.179 \quad DW = 2.62 \quad \text{(i)}$$

There are several differences between the implications of (i) and of the four component equations, (5.1)–(5.4), above. Compared with the component equations, (i) yields a smaller response to changes in D^* and loan demand and a larger response to interest-rate changes. In addition, ΔD_{-1}^* proved to be insignificant in the aggregate equation although it was of importance in the individual equations for excess reserves. The unimportance of ΔD_{-1}^* in (i) may reflect the undesirable effects of aggregation on estimates of the time pattern of the partial adjustment

---

[76] Teigen used the rate on 4–6 month commercial paper instead of the bill rate in both his demand and supply functions. See [110].

[77] As de Leeuw did not estimate a single supply equation, his estimates were derived in a manner similar to the one used above. See [29].

[78] It should be emphasized that these various elasticities are all partial estimates. To determine the effect of a discount rate change (say), one must resort to the multiplier analysis performed above.

mechanism. In this regard, equations (5.1)–(5.4) reveal a considerable degree of diversity with respect to both the country-city distinction and the excess reserve-borrowing separation. It is to be expected that an aggregate equation cannot satisfactorily account for this diversity.

Finally, it was found that the four component equations did a better job of predicting free reserves than the aggregate equation. For our two post-sample prediction periods we found the following:

	Actual Free Reserves	Predicted by (5.1)–(5.4)	Predicted by (i)
1962–III	0.375	0.349	0.238
1962–IV	0.268	0.247	0.212

CHAPTER 6

CONCLUDING REMARKS

6.1. Summary

The important characteristics of the model developed above can be conveniently summarized as follows:

Bank Behavior. We have investigated commercial-bank behavior because it provides an interesting example of the problem of asset choice and is an important link between monetary policy and income generation. We have found that bank portfolio management appears to lend itself quite nicely to explanation by a stock-adjustment model. Interest rates, the supply of various securities, and (constraint) flows of reserves, of deposits, and of commercial-loan demand are among the more important determinants of bank asset choices. With respect to the latter flow it, should be noted that, in the absence of an inflow of deposits, short-term securities provide the primary source of funds to meet customer loan demand. However, the evidence suggests that banks will also borrow from the Fed or sell longer-term securities to secure loan funds.

Our findings also indicate that significant differences emerge when we disaggregate both by asset and by class of bank. In terms of asset disaggregation, important differences are revealed by both the separation of free reserves into its proximate components and the use of a short- and long-term security category. As to the second breakdown, the equations for the two bank classes often yield instances of (1) a variable being relevant for one class but not another and (2) a variable whose quantitative significance is quite different for the two classes.

As indicated above, however, our interest in the banking sector goes deeper than a desire to explain bank behavior for its own sake. More particularly, we are concerned with that sector because in our interdependent economy, commercial banks play an important role in the determination of national income. They do so directly, for example, by setting the loan rate. This influences inventory investment and the demand for commercial loans. They also do so indirectly: their decisions with respect to excess and borrowed reserves enter in an important way into the determination of the money supply and thus interest rates. Finally, as the presence of potential-deposit and reserve-requirement variables in the bank equations attest, the banks play an integral role in the transmission of monetary policy.

Demand for Financial Assets. The model provides separate explanations for the public's demand for currency, demand deposits, and time deposits. All three of these relationships are of the stock-adjustment variety with various interest rates and GNP as major explanatory variables. We disaggregated money demand into currency and demand deposits for several reasons. For one, limited prior evidence suggested that the income elasticity of currency was lower than the corresponding elasticity for demand deposits. The easiest way to examine this hypothesis—which is supported by our study—was to disaggregate. Second, as we have seen, the effect of monetary policy actions depends, in part, on the marginal currency to unborrowed-reserve ratio. Rather than pick this number out of a hat, it seemed more desirable (and reliable) to provide an endogenous explanation of the demand for currency. In this way, the extent of the currency "drain" could be made to vary with income and interest rates, thus providing a more realistic assessment of monetary policy.

The demand for the remaining financial asset, commercial loans, was found to depend in part on the volume of inventory investment, the price of loans, and the potential-deposit variable. The significance of the latter supports the hypothesis that both nonprice and price aspects of loan terms are relevant for loan demand.

Investment and Consumption. Our primary interest in the specification of consumption and investment functions was to provide linkages to financial variables. For consumption, we estimated separate equations for durables and nondurables. It was found that somewhat different variables proved important for the two categories. In particular, currency plus demand deposits—which can be viewed as either a liquid asset variable or a wealth proxy—was relevant only for consumer durables. For fixed and inventory investment, we found significant (multiplicative) roles for the bond and loan rates respectively. In addition, the availability of commercial loans was a determinant in both investment equations.

Monetary Policy. We calculated the reduced form of the model by linearizing at values for the second quarter of 1962. The impact multipliers corresponding to reserve-requirement changes and open-market operations were virtually all in accord with prior expectations as to sign. In addition, the quantitative effects of these policies on income, money, and interest rates were quite significant. This would suggest that monetary policy is capable of playing a more important role in stabilization than has heretofore been generally assumed.[1] The impact multipliers indirectly point up another reason for estimating bank portfolio equations. In particular, it appears that changes in reserve requirements and open-market operations have different impacts on the composition of bank portfolios. Thus, if the monetary authorities have reasons for preferring one type of bank portfolio to another (e.g., due to considerations of bank profits), these bank equations provide a basis for implementing the authorities' preferences.

Finally, we note that changes in the composition of the Federal debt and in the discount rate both appear (at least in terms of initial impact) to be weak policy instruments. The former supports Okun's finding that the maturity in which open-market operations are conducted is relatively inconsequential.

6.2. Suggestions for Future Research

Following the broad lines set forth in the above study, there are two directions in which further research might proceed. The calculation of the reduced form and the examination of the impact of various policies are but a first step in the evaluation of the effectiveness of monetary policy. In order to assess monetary policy more generally, we should have information as to its impact over a number of quarters. Hence, the first suggestion for future research involves the gathering of this longer-run evidence. Unfortunately, the impact multipliers calculated above are only valid in the neighborhood of the point at which the linearization was performed.[2] For this reason, one cannot simply simulate the model by use of constant multipliers.[3] Rather, one must either perform the linearization on an iteration-by-iteration basis, or, what is even better, one must be able to solve numerically the nonlinear system as it stands. While neither

---

[1] Advocacy of more vigorous use of monetary policy for stabilization purposes should ultimately rest on longer-run evidence of the dynamics of the economy. See the next section.

[2] This suggests that it might pay to examine the variations in the impact multipliers induced by changing the point of linearization.

of these tasks is trivial, modern computing equipment certainly makes them feasible.

The second direction fur future research involves refinement of the model set forth above. For one, the wage-price nexus might be introduced. This would bring in supply considerations and make the price level endogenous. Second, we could examine the behavior of other financial institutions and the implications of this behavior for monetary policy. Finally, use of the model for the post-sample period would entail some changes in the treatment of time deposits as a constraint.[4]

---

[3] Similarly, one cannot evaluate the "equilibrium" multipliers by the analog of the device which sets all lagged values of variables equal to the same value.

[4] The growth of the certificate-of-deposit has induced changes in bank asset portfolios, in their deposit structure, and their cost structure. Careful attention should be devoted to this instrument's impact on each of these.

DATA APPENDIX

Bank Assets and Liabilities

General Comments. Except for total reserves, excess reserves, and borrowings, all data were taken from member bank *Call Reports* and hence, were measured as of the call dates. The former were taken from the *Federal Reserve Bulletin* and are for the last month of the quarter. All bank data are in billions of dollars and are seasonally unadjusted. The noncountry (city) data were obtained by summing reserve-city and central-reserve-city data. The variables utilized were as follows:

Total reserves (R): This series does not appear explicitly in the model but is used in the calculation of unborrowed reserves and hence of D^* and Z.

Excess reserves (E^N, E^C)

Member-bank borrowing from the Federal Reserve (B^N, B^C)

Short-term securities (S^N, S^C): Obtained by summing bills, certificates of indebtedness, notes, and bonds with less than five years to maturity.

Long-term securities (O^N, O^C): Corresponds to bonds with more than five years to maturity.

Municipals (MUN^N, MUN^C): State and local government securities.

Commercial and industrial loans (CL^N, CL^C): Beginning with the third quarter of 1959 certain loans to financial institutions were separated out of the commercial-loan category. These items were reintroduced to make the series homogeneous over time.

Net demand deposits (D^N, D^C)

Time deposits (T^N, T^C)

Interest Rates

General Comments. All interest-rate variables were measured in percentages. That is, an interest rate of two percent is written 2.00. Unless otherwise indicated the data are from the *Federal Reserve Bulletin.*

Bank loan Rate (r_e'): The data are an average of bank rates on short-term business loans as reported in nineteen large cities. The rate is for loans which range in size from one hundred to two hundred thousand dollars. It is reported for March, June, September, and December, and is based on new loans and renewals for the first fifteen days of the month.

Weighted-average yield on private securities (r_e''): An average of the rates on bank loans, state and local government securities, residential mortgages, nonresidential mortgages, and corporate bonds. See [29, Appendix] for a precise description of its construction.

Treasury bill rate (r_s): Data are market yields on three-month bills for the last month of the quarter.

Discount rate (r_d): Rate set by the Federal Reserve Bank of New York prevailing on the last day of the quarter.

Intermediate security yield (r_3): Yield on 3–5 year issues of U.S. Government securities.

Yield on long-term U.S. government bonds (r_{10}): The series includes bonds as follows: beginning April, 1953, fully taxable marketable bonds due or callable in ten years or more; from April, 1952 through March, 1953, fully taxable marketable bonds due or first callable after twelve years; prior thereto, bonds due or callable after fifteen years. Data are for the last month of the quarter. It should be noted that beginning with April, 1953, figures were computed on the basis of closing bid quotations on the over-the-counter market, while prior to that they were computed on the basis of the mean of the closing bid and asked quotations.

Yield on commercial bank time deposits (r_p): Annual series as reported in Annual Reports of the Federal Deposit Insurance Corporation. The quarterly interpolation used to create the series used is described in [29].

Yield on municipal bonds (r_m): Standard and Poor's average of yields to maturity of fifteen high-grade domestic municipal bonds.

Security Supply Variables

General Comments. The data are in billions of dollars and, unless otherwise indicated, are taken from the *Federal Reserve Bulletin*.

Privately-owned marketable U.S. securities ($\bar{S}_1$, $\bar{S}_2$, $\bar{O}$): The data are based on the Treasury Survey of Ownership giving the ownership of marketable securities by maturity and type of holder. The data used exclude securities held by U.S. Government agencies and trust funds. $\bar{S}_1$ is the stock of securities maturing within one year, $\bar{S}_2$ securities maturing from one to five years, and $\bar{O}$ maturing in over five years. The data are for the last month of the quarter and are seasonally unadjusted. Beginning with the September, 1953, issue of the *Federal Reserve Bulletin*, the basis for classifying bonds with optional call dates was altered from a first call to a final maturity date. Finally, it should be noted that $\bar{S} = \bar{S}_1 + \bar{S}_2$, and that

$$S_1^* = \bar{S}_1/(\bar{S}_1 + \bar{S}_2 + \bar{O}) \text{ and } S_2^* = \bar{S}_2/(\bar{S}_1 + \bar{S}_2 + \bar{O}).$$

Municipal securities ($\Delta \overline{MUN}$): The net change in obligations of state and local governments. The data are seasonally adjusted and expressed as quarterly rates. The source is *Flow of Funds Accounts*, 1945–1962.

Financial Assets

General Comments. All financial assets are in billions of seasonally unadjusted dollars and, unless indicated, are from the June, 1964 issue of the *Federal Reserve Bulletin*.

Currency (C): Currency outside the Treasury, the Federal Reserve System, and the vaults of all commercial banks. Data are for the last half-month of the quarter.

Demand deposits (D): Demand deposits at all commercial banks, other than those due to domestic commercial banks and the U.S. Government, plus foreign demand balances at Federal Reserve Banks, less cash items in the process of collection and the Federal Reserve float. Data are for the last half-month of the quarter.
(N.B.: $M = C + D$).

Time deposits (T): Time deposits at all commercial banks other than those due to domestic commercial banks and the U.S. Government. Data are for the last half-month of the quarter.

Net worth of household sector (W): Constructed from Goldsmith's data by Albert Ando. See [15].

Volume of commercial loans (CL): Series supplied by Board of Governors, Federal Reserve. It does not exactly correspond to the sum of CL^N and CL^C. In calculating impact multipliers, adjustment was made for this slight discrepancy.

Reserve Requirement Variables

General Comments. The requirements are measured as fractions between 0 and 1. When a requirement is changed during a quarter, the figure used is a weighted-average requirement where the weights are the fractions of the quarter each requirement prevailed. The data are from the *Federal Reserve Bulletin*.

Central reserve city demand deposit requirement (k_1)

Reserve city demand deposit requirement (k_2): As of July, 1962 the distinction between reserve city and central-reserve city was terminated. The two requirements (k_1 and k_2) were actually the same from December 1960 on.

Country bank demand deposit requirement (k_3)

Time deposit requirement (k_4): Throughout the sample period the requirement has been the same for all bank classes.

National Income Variables

General Comments. All dollar variables are in billions of dollars and are expressed as quarterly rates. Unless indicated, the variables are seasonally unadjusted. The data were taken from *U.S. Income and Output* and various issues of the *Survey of Current Business*.

Gross National Product (Y).

Disposable income (Y^d): Series only available seasonally adjusted.

Durable consumption expenditures (C^D).

Nondurable consumption expenditures (C^{ND}): Defined as total consumption (C^T) less durable consumption.

Fixed investment (I): Expenditures on plant and equipment.

Inventory investment (ΔH).

Manufacturers' inventory investment $(\Delta H')$.

Autonomous expenditures (G): Computed as $(Y - C^{ND} - C^D - I - \Delta H')$.

Corporate dividends (DIV): Seasonally adjusted.

Business income after taxes (F): Undistributed corporate profits and capital consumption allowances, seasonally adjusted.

Implicit GNP price deflator (P).

Miscellaneous Variables

Capacity utilization (K): Expressed as a fraction between 0 and 1. The series was constructed by de Leeuw and appears in [30].

Manufacturers' unfilled orders (U): Seasonally unadjusted in billions of dollars. The data are for the last month of the quarter and were taken from *U.S. Business Statistics* and the *Survey of Current Business*.

Manufacturers' sales (SA): Same comments as for unfilled orders.

Unemployment rate (UN): Expressed as a percent, the data are for the last month of the quarter. They are taken from various issues of the *Survey of Current Business*.

BIBLIOGRAPHY

1. ACKLEY, G., *Macroeconomic Theory*, New York, The Macmillan Company, 1961.
2. ALHADEFF, DAVID A., *Monopoly and Competition in Banking*, Berkeley, University of California Press, 1954.
3. ALMON, SHIRLEY, The Distributed Lag between Capital Appropriations and Expenditures, *Econometrica*, January, 1965, pp. 178–196.
4. AMERICAN BANKERS ASSOCIATION, *The Commercial Banking Industry*, Englewood Cliffs, N. J., Prentice-Hall, Inc., 1962.
5. ANDO, ALBERT, *A Contribution to the Theory of Economic Fluctuations and Growth*, Unpublished doctoral dissertation, Carnegie Institute of Technology, 1959.
6. –, An Empirical Model of the U.S. Economic Growth: An Exploratory Study in Applied Capital Theory, in [90], pp. 327–380.
7. – and FRANCO MODIGLIANI, The 'Life Cycle' Hypothesis of Saving, *American Economic Review*, March 1963, pp. 55–85.
8. ANDERSON, W. H. L., *Corporate Finance and Fixed Investment*, Division of Research, Harvard Graduate School of Business Administration, 1964.
9. BAILEY, M. J., *National Income and the Price Level*, New York, McGraw-Hill, 1962.
10. *Banking and Monetary Studies*, edited by Deane Carson, for the Comptroller of the Currency, U.S. Treasury, Richard D. Irwin, 1963.
11. BLACK, ROBERT P., The Impact of Member Reserves upon the Money Supply, *Southern Economic Journal*, January, 1963, pp. 199–210.
12. BLOCH, E., The Treasury's Deposit Balances and the Banking System, in [38], pp. 19–24.
13. Board of Governors of the Federal Reserve System, *The Federal Funds Market*, Washington D.C., 1959.
14. –, *The Federal Reserve System: Purposes and Functions*, fourth edition, Washington, D.C., 1961.
15. BROWN, E. CARY, ROBERT M. SOLOW, ALBERT K. ANDO and JOHN H. KAREKEN, Lags in Fiscal and Monetary Policy, in [22], pp. 1–164.
16. BUDZEIKA, G., Commercial Banks as Suppliers of Capital Funds to Business, in [38], pp. 67–71.
17. CAGAN, PHILLIP, The Demand for Currency Relative to the Total Money Supply, *Journal of Political Economy*, August, 1958, pp. 303–328.
18. CAWTHORNE, D. R., Long-run and Short-run Influences on Deposit Distribution, in [36], pp. 55–64.

19. CHILDS, GERALD L., *Linear Decision Rules for Explaining Finished Goods, Inventories and Unfilled Orders*, unpublished doctoral dissertation, Massachusetts Institute of Technology, August, 1963.

20. COHEN, KALMAN J., and DONALD R. HODGMAN, A Macroeconometric Model of the Commercial Banking Sector, paper presented at Econometric Society Meetings, December, 1962.

21. Commission on Money and Credit, *Impacts of Monetary Policy*, Englewood Cliffs, N. J., Prentice-Hall, 1963.

22. Commission on Money and Credit, *Stabilization Policies*, Englewood Cliffs, N. J., Prentice-Hall, 1963.

23. CONARD, J. W., *Introduction to the Theory of Interest*, Berkeley, University of California Press, 1959.

24. CULBERTSON, JOHN M., The Term Structure of Interest Rates, *Quarterly Journal of Economics*, November, 1957, pp. 485–517.

25. CURRIE, L., *The Supply and Control of Money in the United States*, Cambridge, Mass., Harvard University Press, 1934.

26. DARLING, P. G., and MICHAEL C. LOVELL, Factors Influencing Investment in Inventories, in *The Brookings Quarterly Econometric Model of the United States*, Chicago, Rand McNally & Co., 1965.

27. DARLING, P. G., Manufacturers' Inventory Investment, 1947–58, *American Economic Review*, December, 1959, pp. 950–963.

28. DAVIS, RICHARD G., and JACK M. GUTTENTAG, Are Compensating Balance Requirements Irrational? *Journal of Finance*, March, 1962, pp. 121–127.

29. DE LEEUW, FRANK, A Model of Financial Behavior, in *The Brookings Quarterly Econometric Model of the United States*, Chicago, Rand McNally & Co., 1965.

30. –, Testimony in hearings before the Subcommittee on Economic Statistics of the Joint Economic Committee, published as *Measures of Productive Capacity*, Washington, U.S. Government Printing Office, 1962, pp. 121–137.

31. –, The Demand for Capital Goods by Manufacturers: A Study of Quarterly Time Series, *Econometrica*, July, 1962, pp. 407–424.

32. DUESENBERRY, JAMES S., *Business Cycles and Economic Growth*, New York, McGraw-Hill, 1958.

33. –, O. ECKSTEIN and G. FROMM, A Simulation of the United States Economy in Recession, *Econometrica*, October, 1960, pp. 749–810.

34. EISEMANN, DORIS M., Manufacturers' Inventory Cycles and Monetary Policy, *Journal of the American Statistical Association*, September, 1958, pp. 680–689.

35. EISNER, R., and R. STROTZ, Determinants of Business Investment, in [21], pp. 60–338.

36. Federal Reserve Bank of Kansas City, *Essays on Commerical Banking*, 1962.

37. –, Reserve Adjustment of City Banks, *Monthly Review*, February, 1958.

38. Federal Reserve Bank of New York, *Essays in Money and Credit*, 1964.

39. –, Borrowing from the Fed, *Monthly Review*, September, 1959, pp. 138–142.

40. Federal Reserve Bank of St. Louis, Currency and Demand Deposits, *Review*, March 1965, pp. 3–6.

41. *Federal Reserve Bulletin*, 1947–1965.

42. FEIGE, E. L., *The Demand for Liquid Assets: A Temporal Cross-Section Analysis*, Englewood Cliffs, N. J., Prentice-Hall, 1964.

43. FIELDHOUSE, R. C., Certificates of Deposit, in [38], pp. 42–46.
44. FISHER, FRANKLIN M., Identifiability Criteria in Nonlinear Systems, *Econometrica*, October 1961, pp. 574–598 and Identifiability Criteria in Nonlinear Systems: A Further Note, *Econometrica*, January, 1965, pp. 197–205.
45. FISHER, IRVING, *The Theory of Interest*, New York, Kelley and Millman, Inc., 1954.
46. FRIEDMAN, MILTON, Testimony given in Joint Economic Committee, Hearings: Employment, Growth and Price Levels, part 4, Washington, D.C., U.S. Government Printing Office, 1959.
47. –, Vault Cash and Free Reserves, *Journal of Political Economy*, April, 1961, pp. 181–2.
48. GEHRELS, FRANZ and SUZANNE WIGGINS, Interest Rates and Fixed Investment, *American Economic Review*, March, 1957, pp. 79–93.
49. GLAUBER, R. R. and J. R. MEYER, *Investment Decisions, Economic Forecasting and Public Policy*, Cambridge, Mass., Harvard University Press, 1964.
50. GOLDBERGER, A. S., *Econometric Theory*, New York, John Wiley & Sons, 1964.
51. –, *Impact Multipliers and Dynamic Properties of the Klein-Goldberger Model*, North-Holland, 1959.
52. GOLDFELD, S. M. and R. E. QUANDT, Nonlinear Simultaneous Equations: Estimation and Prediction, paper presented to the World Congress of the Econometric Society, Rome, September, 1965.
53. –, Some Tests for Homoscedasticity, *Journal of the American Statistical Association*, June, 1965, pp. 539–547.
54. GOLDFELD S. M., The Financial Sector: Some Further Results, paper prepared for Brookings econometric model.
55. GRAMLEY, L. E., Commercial Bank Investments in Recession and Expansion, in [36], pp. 65–76.
56. –, Interest Rates and Credit Availability at Commercial Banks, in [36], pp. 77–86.
57. GRILICHES, ZVI, Capital Stock in Investment Functions: Some Problems of Concept and Measurement, in *Measurement in Economics*, Stanford University, 1963, pp. 115–137.
58. HAAVELMO, TRYGVE, *A Study in the Theory of Investment*, Chicago, University of Chicago Press, 1960.
59. HAMMER, F. S., *The Demand for Physical Capital: Application of a Wealth Model*, Englewood Cliffs, N. J., Prentice-Hall, 1964.
60. HART, ALBERT J. and PETER B. KENEN, *Money, Debt, and Economic Activity* (3rd ed.), Englewood Cliffs, N. J., Prentice-Hall, 1961.
61. HAWTREY, R. G., *Capital and Employment*, New York, Longmans, Green and Co., 1952.
62. HICKS, J. R., *Value and Capital* (2nd. ed.), London, Oxford at the Clarendon Press, 1946.
63. HODGMAN, D. R., The Deposit Relationship and Commercial Bank Investment Behavior, *Review of Economics and Statistics*, August, 1961, pp. 257–268.
64. JOHNSON, H. G., Monetary Theory and Policy, *American Economic Review*, June, 1962, pp. 335–384.
65. – and W. DEWALD, An Objective Analysis of the Objectives of American Monetary Policy, 1952–61, in [10], pp. 171–189.

66. KALDOR, NICHOLAS and JAMES A. MIRRLEES, A New Model of Economic Growth, *Review of Economic Studies*, June, 1962, pp. 174–193.

67. KANE, E. J. and B. G. MALKIEL, Bank Portfolio Allocation, Deposit Variability, and the Availability Doctrine, *Quarterly Journal of Economics*, February, 1965, pp. 113–134.

68. KLEIN, L. R., A Postwar Quarterly Model: Description and Applications, in [90], pp. 11–58.

69. KUZNETS, P. W., Financial Determinants of Manufacturing Inventory Behavior, *Yale Economic Essays*, Vol. 4, no. 2, 1964, pp. 331–369.

70. LATANE, HENRY A., Cash Balances and the Interest Rate — A Pragmatic Approach, *Review of Economics and Statistics*, September, 1954, pp. 456–460.

71. LINDBECK, ASSAR, *The "New" Theory of Credit Control in the United States*, Stockholm Economic Studies, Pamphlet Series 1, Stockholm, Almquist and Wiksell, 1959.

72. LIU, T. C., An Exploratory Quarterly Econometric Model of Effective Demand in the Postwar U.S. Economy, *Econometrica*, July, 1963, pp. 301–348.

73. LOVELL, M. C., Determinants of Inventory Investment, in [90], pp. 177–232, and comment by Ruth Mack, pp. 224–231.

74. –, Manufacturers' Inventories, Sales Expectations and the Acceleration Principle, *Econometrica*, July, 1961, pp. 276–97.

75. –, Seasonal Adjustment of Economic Time Series and Multiple Regression Analysis, *Journal of the American Statistical Association*, December, 1963, pp. 993–1010.

76. LUCKETT, DUDLEY G., Compensatory Cyclical Bank Asset Adjustments, *Journal of Finance*, March, 1962, pp. 53–63.

77. LUTZ, FRIEDRICH A., The Structure of Interest Rates, *Quarterly Journal of Economics*, November, 1940, pp. 36–63.

78. LYON, ROGER A., *Investment Portfolio Management in the Commercial Bank*, New Brunswick, N. J., Rutgers University Press, 1960.

79. McGOULDRICK, PAUL F., The Impact of Credit Cost and Availability on Inventory Investment, in *Inventory Fluctuations and Economic Stabilization*, Part II, Washington, D.C., U.S. Government Printing Office, 1961, pp. 91–120.

80. McKINNEY, GEORGE W., Jr., *The Federal Reserve Discount Window*, New Brunswick, N. J., Rutgers University Press, 1960.

81. MALKIEL, B. G., Expectations, Bond Prices and the Term Structure of Interest Rates, *Quarterly Journal of Economics*, May, 1962, pp. 197–218.

82. – and E. J. KANE, United States Tax Law and the Locked-in Effect, *National Tax Journal*, December, 1963, pp. 389–396.

83. MEIGS, A. JAMES, *Free Reserves and the Money Supply*, Chicago, University of Chicago Press, 1962.

84. MEISELMAN, DAVID, *The Term Structure of Interest Rates*, Englewood Cliffs, N. J., Prentice-Hall, 1962.

85. MELTZER, A. H., Monetary Policy and the Trade Credit Practices of Business Firms, in [22], pp. 471–498.

86. MEYER, JOHN R., and EDWIN KUH, Investment, Liquidity and Monetary Policy, in [21], pp. 339–474.

87. MODIGLIANI, FRANCO and MERTON H. MILLER, The Cost of Capital, Corporation

Finance and the Theory of Investment, *American Economic Review*, June, 1958, pp. 261–297.

88. MODIGLIANI, FRANCO, The Monetary Mechanism and its Interaction with Real Phenomena: A Review of Recent Developments, *Review of Economics and Statistics*, a supplement to the February 1963 issue.

89. –, Comment on Capacity, Capacity Utilization and the Acceleration Principle, in Conference on Research in Income and Wealth, volume 19, *Problems of Capital Formation*, Princeton, N. J., Princeton University Press, 1957.

90. National Bureau of Economic Research, *Models of Income Determination*, volume 28, Studies in Income and Wealth, Princeton, N. J., Princeton University Press, 1964.

91. OKUN, ARTHUR M., Monetary Policy, Debt Management and Interest Rates: A Quantitative Approach, in [22], pp. 331–380.

92. ORR, D. and W. J. MELLON, Stochastic Reserve Losses and Expansion of Bank Credit, *American Economic Review*, September, 1961, pp. 614–623.

93. *Oxford Studies in the Price Mechanism*, edited by T. Wilson and P.W.S. Andrews, Oxford, Clarendon Press, 1951.

94. PATINKIN, DON, *Money, Interest and Prices*, Evanston, Illinois, Row, Peterson, and Company, 1956.

95. PIERCE, J. L., The Monetary Mechanism: Some Partial Relationships, Cowles Foundation Discussion Paper No. 168, New Haven, April, 1964.

96. POLAKOFF, MURRAY E., Reluctance Elasticity, Least Cost and Member-Bank Borrowing: A Suggested Integration, *Journal of Finance*, March, 1960, pp. 1–18.

97. PORTER, RICHARD C., A Model of Bank Portfolio Selection, *Yale Economic Essays*, vol. 1, no. 2, pp. 323–359.

98. REUBER, G. L., The Objectives of Canadian Monetary Policy, 1949–61, *Journal of Political Economy*, April, 1964, pp. 109–132.

99. ROBINSON, JOAN, The Production Function and the Theory of Capital, *Review of Economic Studies*, 1953–54, pp. 81–106.

100. ROBINSON, ROLAND S., *The Management of Bank Funds*, New York, McGraw-Hill, 1951.

101. –, *Postwar Market for State and Local Government Securities*, Princeton, Princeton University Press, 1960.

102. SAMUELSON, PAUL A., Parable and Realism in Capital Theory: The Surrogate Production Function, *Review of Economic Studies*, June, 1962, pp. 193–207.

103. SCOTT, R. H., Liquidity and the Term Structure of Interest Rates, *Quarterly Journal of Economics*, February, 1965, pp. 135–145.

104. SHAPIRO, HAROLD, *The Canadian Monetary Sector: An Econometric Analysis*, Dissertation submitted to Department of Economics, Princeton University, 1964.

105. SILVERBERG, STANLEY C., Compensatory Cyclical Bank Asset Adjustments: Comment, *Journal of Finance*, December, 1962, pp. 651–655.

106. SMITH, WARREN L., The Discount Rate as a Credit-Control Weapon, *Journal of Political Economy*, April, 1958, pp. 171–77.

107. SOLOW, ROBERT M., Substitutions and Fixed Proportions in the Theory of Capital, *Review of Economic Studies*, June, 1962, pp. 207–219.

108. STANBACK, THOMAS, Jr., *Postwar Cycles and Manufacturers' Inventories*, NewYork, National Bureau of Economic Research, 1962.

109. SUITS, D., The Determinants of Consumer Expenditure: A Review of Present Knowledge, in [21], pp. 1–59.
110. TEIGEN, RONALD L., Demand and Supply Functions for Money in the United States: Some Structural Estimates, *Econometrica*, October, 1964, pp. 476–509.
111. TINBERGEN, JAN, *Business Cycles in the United States, 1919–32*, Geneva, League of Nations, 1939.
112. TOBIN, JAMES, Commercial Banks as Creators of Money, in [10], pp. 408–419.
113. –, The Interest Elasticity of Transactions Demand for Cash, *Review of Economics and Statistics*, August, 1956, pp. 241–247.
114. –, unpublished monetary manuscript, New Haven, 1959 (mimeographed).
115. TURNER, ROBERT C., *Member-Bank Borrowing*, Columbus, Ohio State University, 1938.
116. United States Congress, Joint Economic Committee, *Staff Report on Employment, Growth, and Price Levels*, Washington, D.C., U.S. Government Printing Office, 1959.
117. U.S. Department of Commerce, *Survey of Current Business*, various issues.
118. U.S. Department of Commerce, *U.S. Income and Output*, U.S. Government Printing Office, 1958.
119. WALKER, C. E., Discount Policy in the Light of Recent Experience, *Journal of Finance*, May, 1957, pp. 223–237.
120. WHITE, WILLIAM H., The Changing Criteria in Investment Planning, in *Variability of Private Investment in Plant and Equipment*, Part II, Washington, D.C., U.S. Government Printing Office, 1962, pp. 1–25.
121. WHITTLESEY, CHARLES R., Credit Policy at the Discount Window, *Quarterly Journal of Economics*, May, 1959, pp. 207–216.
122. WILLIS, PARKER B., *The Federal Funds Market: Its Origin and Development*, Boston, The Federal Reserve Bank of Boston, 1964.
123. WOOD, JOHN H., The Expectations Hypothesis, the Yield Curve, and Monetary Policy, *Quarterly Journal of Economics*, August, 1964, pp. 457–470.
124. YOUNG, RALPH A., Tools and Processes of Monetary Policy, *United States Monetary Policy*, Neil H. Jacoby, editor, New York, The American Assembly, 1958.
125. DE LEEUW, FRANK, Financial Markets in Business Cycles: A Simulation Study, *American Economic Review*, May, 1964, pp. 309–323.
126. TEIGEN, R. L., A Structural Approach to the Impact of Monetary Policy, *Journal of Finance*, May 1964, pp. 284–308.

INDEX